Early Twentieth Century LIGHTING

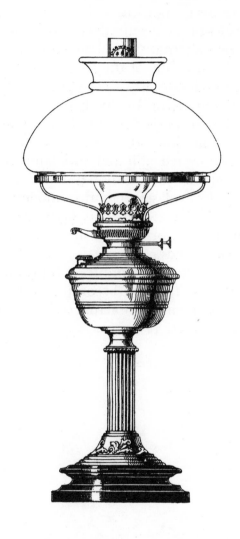

by SHERWOODS Ltd.
of Birmingham

Schiffer Publishing Ltd

West Chester, Pennsylvania

Editor's Note

Innovations in lighting design were rampant in the early decades of the twentieth century when electricity opened a new alternative, and therefore opportunity, to home finishing. One of the largest manufacturers of new lighting devices was the English firm Sherwoods Ltd. in Birmingham. In this book are displayed and specifically described all forms of illumination devices then available for sale. Oil burning as well as electrically powered table and floor lamps, chandeliers, sconces, and lanterns are shown in vast numbers. The styles range from classical to ultra-modern with all the revival styles in between. It is fascinating to see the variations in size, ornament, materials, and use—all made by Sherwoods.

Today, as authentic examples of lights from the early years of this century are becoming scarce, this book remains a testament to the actual styles produced. It has become a valuable resource.

Published by Schiffer Publishing, Ltd.
1469 Morstein Road
West Chester, Pennsylania 19380
Please write for a free catalog
This book may be purchased from the publisher.
Please include $2.00 postage.
Try your bookstore first.

Code 5th Edition.

"THREE TREE"
TRADE MARK.

Telephone Nos.
Mid. 361 & 362.

Telegrams :
"Sherwoods, Birmingham."

Sherwoods Limited,

MANUFACTURERS

. . OF . .

LAMPS, BURNERS, LANTERNS,

CANDLE LAMPS

. . AND .

ELECTRIC LIGHT FITTINGS.

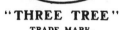

Works and Offices :
44, 46, 48 & 50, Granville Street,

Showrooms, Stores and Warehouse :
37, Granville Street,

Birmingham,

ENGLAND.

Catalogue No. D123.

All Previous Issues are Cancelled.

"ELEPHANT"
TRADE MARK,

"LION"
TRADE MARK

Contents

SHERWOODS LAMPS.

Wicks.

All Wicks supplied by us are ENGLISH MADE, purified by chemical process, and specially prepared to suit our Burners, and we recommend all our customers to use our wicks to obtain the best results, and which we guarantee to give a larger and whiter flame than any other wick.

Specially Prepared Wicks for SUN Circular Burners.

BOXED IN DOZENS CUT TO LENGTH.

12''' Sun.
Per doz. **2/6** doz.
Per gro. **2/3** ,,

16''' Sun.
Per doz. **3/-** doz.
Per gro. **2/9** ,,

20''' Sun
and Belge Wick.
Per doz. **4/-** doz.
Per gro. **3/6** ,,

30''' Sun.
Per doz. **6/-** doz.
Per gro. **5/6** ,,

Superior Quality Duplex Wick.

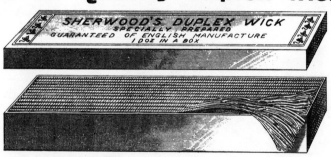

SHERWOOD'S DUPLEX WICK
SPECIALLY PREPARED
GUARANTEED OF ENGLISH MANUFACTURE
1 DOZ IN A BOX

$1\frac{1}{16}''$ Duplex Wicks, boxed in dozens, 10" lengths, **1/-** doz.

1" Wicks, boxed in dozens, 10" lengths, **1/-** doz.

Specially Prepared Chemical RED Wick,

for KRANZOW, WANZER, & PUCCA Mechanical Lamps.

1/3 doz.   1 gross lots **1/-** doz.

Boxed in dozens

ROUND WICKS.

Night Light Wick, in Gross Packets, 5" long, **1/9** gro.

Benzo Wick, in Gross Packets, 7" long, **2/6** gro.
¼-lb. hanks, 12 yards, **1/6** per hank.
Not less than 14 lbs. supplied.

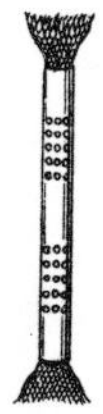

Spirit Wick for 18 & 19 Stoves, **6/-** gro.
Perforated Brass Tubes with Wick complete. **4/-** doz.

FLAT WICKS.
Best A1 Scarlet Quality.
In Gross Packets.

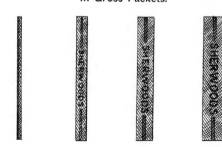

¼"	⅜"	½"	⅝"	¾"	⅞"	1"	1⅛"	1¼"	1½"
2/-	2/6	3/-	4/6	6/-	7/-	8/-	8/-	8/-	8/6 per gro.

6" lengths,   8" lengths.

COSMOS WICK in Rolls of 12 yards.

6'''	10'''	14'''
2/6	4/-	5/6 per roll.

In Gross Packets.

7" long.	8" long.	9" long.
6/-	10/-	18/- per gross.

FLAT WICKS in Rolls of 12 yards.
DUPLEX.

⅝"	¾"	⅞"	1"	$1\frac{1}{16}''$	1⅛"	1¼"	1½"
1/6	1/9	2/-	2/6	2/6	2/6	3/6	4/6 per roll.

SHERWOODS LAMPS.

Chimneys.

GEM
1⅝ in. fitting,
15/- gross.
Per original case,
6 gross,
12/- gross.

BIJOU
1¾ in. fitting.
3/6 doz

BIJOU DUPLEX
5/- doz.

Best Fireproof Crystal
Quality.

EUREKA
For ⅝ in. Burner,
2½ in. fitting,
5/- doz.
For ⅞ in. Burner,
3 in. fitting,
6/- doz.

COSMOS
6''' 1¼ in. fitting,
3/- doz.
10''' 1½ in. fitting,
3/6 doz.

Best Fireproof Crystal
quality.

STRAIGHT SLIP
For ⅞ in. Burner,
1¼ in. fitting,
4/6 doz.
For 1 in. Burner,
2 1/16 in. fitting,
5/- doz.

Best Crystal Fireproof
quality.

BULGE
For ⅞ in. Burner,
1¼ in. fitting,
4/6 doz.
For 1 in. Burner,
2 1/16 in. fitting,
5/- doz.

Best Crystal Fireproof
quality.

TIGER
(for 74B 1½" wick Burner)
2⅝ in. fitting,
12/- doz.

Best Fireproof Crystal
quality.

HURRICANE
(for Defiance Lantern).
6½" × 3⅜" × 2¾"
5/- doz.

Superior Crystal Quality.
Packed 2 gross per case.

ECLIPSE
(for Syntax Lamps)
3 in. fitting,
10/- doz.

Superior Crystal Quality.
Packed 12 doz. per case.

BAT
(for " Dreadnought " and
" Squall " Lanterns)
6½" × 3⅜" × 2¾"
5/- doz.

Superior Crystal Quality.
Packed 2 gross per case.

PARAGON
(For 121B 1½ in. Wick Burner)
2⅜ in. fitting,
8/- doz.

Superior Crystal Quality.
Packed 2 gross per case.

  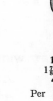 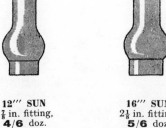  

DUPLEX
2½ in. fitting,
5/6 doz.

Per original case,
2 gross,
4/6 doz.

Best Fireproof Crystal
Quality.

BELGE
2½ in. fitting,
8/- doz.
Per original case,
2 gross,
6/- doz.

Best Fireproof Crystal
Quality.

12''' SUN
1⅞ in. fitting,
4/6 doz.

Per original case,
2 gross,
3/6 doz.

Best Fireproof Crystal
Quality.

16''' SUN
2⅛ in. fitting,
5/6 doz.

Per original case,
2 gross,
4/6 doz.

Best Fireproof Crystal
Quality.

20''' SUN
2½ in. fitting,
8/- doz.

Per original case,
2 gross.
6/- doz.

Best Fireproof Crystal
Quality.

30''' SUN
3⅜ in. fitting,
12/- doz.

Per original case,
1 gross,
10/- doz.

Best Fireproof Crystal
Quality.

Shades

THE MAGIC N'T. L'T. GLOBE.

Best Ribbed Opal Quality.

Loose price per dozen.	Case price per dozen.	Case quantity per gross.
2/-	**1/6**	**10**

Suitable for lamps fitted with **104B** Nt. Lt. Burners.

VESTA SHAPE SHADES.

Best Opal Quality.

	Loose price, per dozen.	Case price, per dozen.	Case quantity, per dozen.
7¼ in.	**9/-**	**7/6**	**12**
9¼ in.	**15/-**	**13/6**	**6**

THE ELVELIT N'T. L'T. GLOBE.

Best Ribbed Opal Quality.

Loose price, per dozen.	Case price, per dozen.	Case quantity, per gross.
3/-	**2/6**	**6**

Suitable for lamps fitted with **93B** Gem Burners.

JUGEND SHAPE SHADES.

Best Opal Quality.

	Loose price per dozen.	Case price, per dozen.	Case quantity, per dozen.
7¼ in.	**11/-**	**9/-**	**12**
9¼ in.	**18/-**	**16/-**	**6**

UNBREAKABLE SPUN WHITE METAL SHADE.

7¼ in.	...	**5/-** each.
9¼ in.	...	**6/-** each.
10 in.	...	**7/-** each.

JUGEND SHAPE SHADES.

Best Green Cased Opal Quality.

	Loose price, per dozen.	Case price, per dozen.	Case quantity, per dozen.
7¼ in.	**30/-**	**27/-**	**12**
9¼ in.	**42/-**	**36/-**	**6**

DOME SHAPE SHADES.

Best Albatrine Quality.

	Loose price, per dozen.	Case price, per dozen.	Case quantity, per dozen.
11 in.	**23/-**	**19/-**	**6**
12 in.	**24/-**	**20/-**	**6**
14 in.	**48/-**	**36/-**	**3**
16 in.	**90/-**	**60/-**	**2**

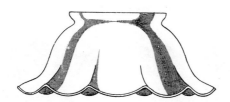

CRIMPED SHAPE SHADES.

Best Albatrine Quality.

With assorted fancy coloured edges.

	Loose price per dozen.	Case price, per dozen.	Case quantity, per dozen.
14 × 7 in.	**42/-**	**36/-**	**3**
16 × 8 in.	**60/-**	**54/-**	**3**

TAPER SHAPE SHADES.

Best Albatrine Quality.

	Loose price, per dozen	Case price, per dozen.	Case quantity, per dozen.
14 in.	**48/-**	**36/-**	**3**

SHERWOODS LAMPS.

Globes

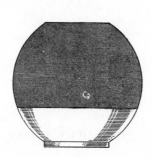

F

6½ × 3 in.

Best Crystal Monography Globe,

16/- dozen.

Assorted Patterns.
Special price 12 dozen original case quantity.
14/- dozen.

G

7½ × 4 in.

Best Quality ¾ in. Frosted Globe,

20/- dozen.

H

7½ × 4 in.

Best Crystal Monography Globes,

19/- dozen.

Assorted Patterns.
Special price 8 dozen, original case quantity.
16/- dozen.

I **J** **K** **L**

Best Quality Crystal Etched Globes, Flushed, Assorted Patterns, 4 in. Fitting, Rose, Green and Blue,

42/- dozen.

SUPERIOR ENGLISH-MAKE GLOBES.

M **N** **O**

Superior English Make Bijou Globes, 3 in. Fitting, Assorted Patterns, Flint and Ruby Britched and Ruby Opalescent.

36/- dozen.

P **Q** **R** **S**

Superior English Make Duplex Globes, 4 in. Fitting, Assorted Patterns, Flint and Ruby Britched and Ruby Opalescent,

54/- dozen.

Silk Shades.

D 25

Best China Material, Fancy Shade,
with Pompoms and Lace,

12 in.   15 in.   18 in.
13/- each.   **15/-** each.   **18/-** each.

D 26

Goffered Plain Linen Shade,
Assorted Colours,
Gimped with Bead Fringe.
9 in.   -   **60/-** doz.
Special price 6 doz. lots,
54/- doz.

D 27

Best Florentine Silk Shade,
with Chiffon Rouches and Lace Flounces.

12 in.   15 in.   18 in.
24/- each.   **30/-** each.   **36/-** each.

D 28

EMPIRE.

Best China Material Shade,
with Fancy Gimp and Bead Fringe,

15 in.   18 in.   21 in.
15/- each.   **18/-** each.   **21/-** each.

D 29

THAMES.

Best Box Pleated Ruche Silk Shade,
with Scalloped Flounce and Bead Fringe.

15 in.   18 in.   21 in.
30/- each.   **36/-** each.   **42/-** each.

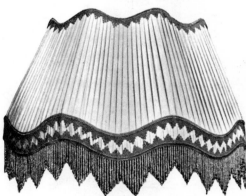

D 30

DOMINION.

Best China Material and Fancy Shade,
with Fancy Gimp and Vandyke Bead Fringe.

15 in.   18 in.   21 in.
20/- each.   **24/-** each.   **28/-** each.

SHERWOODS LAMPS.

Brass Tube Sockets.

D 31

In and outside Brass tube socket rolled over edge.
30/- gross.
1 in. dia. × ¾ in. long.

D 32

In and outside Brass tube socket, single grooved.
36/- gross.
1 in. dia. × ⅞ in. long.

D 33

In and outside Brass tube socket, single grooved.
48/- gross.
1¼ in. dia. × 1⅛ in. long.

D 34

In and outside Brass tube socket single grooved.
60/- gross.
1½ in. dia. × 1¼ in. long.

THE " GENIE " REFLEX.
Patent No. 261416.
Ruby Reflex rear Light.

BRASS INCREASING SOCKETS.

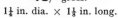

BRASS REDUCING SOCKETS.

D 35
⅝ in. thread to ⅞ in thread.
30/- gross.

D 36
Nickel Plated with Double Straps.
D 36, 2 in. ... **15**/- doz.
D 37, 2¼ in. ... **20**/- „
D 38, 2½ in. ... **24**/- „

D 39
⅞ in. thread to ⅝ in. thread.
30/- gross.

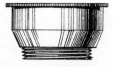

D 40
⅞ in. thread to 10 ‴ Cosmos thread.
33/- gross.

D 42
14 ‴ Cosmos or Duplex to ⅞ in. thread.
36/- gross.

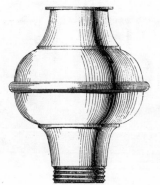

D 43
⅞ in. thread to 14 ‴ Cosmos or Duplex.
36/- gross.

D 41
Polished Brass connecting Pillar to Increase Height of Lamps.
9/- doz.
Screwed to suit No. **10** Sockets and leaf pieces.

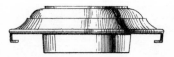

D 44
Bayonet, Duplex, to Screw, Duplex.
6/- doz.

Under Mounts.

D 45
Medium Quality.
No. **7** - **10/-** gross.
No. **10** - **12/-** ,,

D 46
Strong Quality.
No. **7/8**G - **15/-** gross.
No. **10/8**G - **15/-** ,,

D 47
Extra Strong Quality.
Cut Threads.
No. **10/15**G - **36/-** gross.

D 48
Heavy Cast Quality.
Cut Threads.
No. **7** - **5/-** dozen.
No. **10** - **5/-** ,,

D 49
Ditto, Extra Deep.
No. **7** and **10** - **6/-** dozen.

Collars.

D 50
Strong Screw Duplex Collar,
18/- gross.

D 51
Bayonet Duplex Collar,
30/- gross.

D 52
Strong Bayonet Collar,
turned up edge,
36/- gross.

D 53
Extra Strong Cork lined Bayonet
Collar,
6/- dozen.

D 54
Strong Princess Socket
with Steel Clips.
36/- gross.

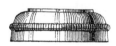

No.	Diameter.	Size.		
00	$1\frac{5}{16}$	-	$\frac{5}{8}$	**4/6** gro.
0	$1\frac{3}{8}$	-	$\frac{5}{8}$	**5/6** ,,
1	$1\frac{5}{8}$	-	$\frac{5}{8}$	**7/6** ,,
2	$1\frac{7}{8}$	-	$\frac{5}{8}$	**9/-** ,,
2	,,	-	$\frac{7}{8}$	**9/-** ,,
3	$2\frac{3}{8}$	-	$\frac{7}{8}$	**14/-** ,,
4	$2\frac{1}{2}$	-	$\frac{7}{8}$	**16/-** ,,
1 in. Screwed, 10''' Kos.				**9/-** ,,

Cut Threads.

Strong Collar	-		$\frac{5}{8}$	**18/-** ,,
,,	,,	-	$\frac{7}{8}$	**24/-** ,,

D 55
Strong Brass Can Corks,
21A Small size - **20/-** gross.
22A Large ,, - **25/-** ,,

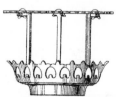

D 57
Duplex Chimney Coronet, with mica
5/- dozen.

D 56
Wick Scissors,
6 in. - **2/6** each.
Superior Sheffield make, N.P. finish.

Globe Galleries.

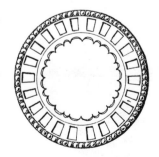

No. 1
Flat Gallery,
For 1 in. and Duplex Burners,
36/- gross.

No. 2
Raised Duplex Gallery,
36/- gross.
No. **0** Raised Bijou Gallery, 3 in. fitting,
33/- gross.

No. 3
Strong Raised Gallery,
For Duplex and Sun Burners,
48/- gross.

No. 4
Strong Flat Duplex Gallery,
with 3 set screws for ship lamps,
4 in. fitting - **12/-** dozen.

SHERWOODS LAMPS.

Smoke Bells.

D 58
Black Iron Smoke Bell with Hook,
2/- doz.
Polished Brass Bell with Hook,
5/- doz.

D 59
Corrugated Brass Bell with Hook,
3½ in. dia. - **30/-** gro.

D 60
Polished Brass Bell with Hook,
2½ in. - **1/6** doz.
3 in. - **2/6** ,,
4 in. - **4/-** ,,
5 in. - **6/6** ,,

D 61
4 in. China Bell, with Hook,
6/- doz.

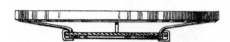

D 62
Polished Brass Shade Holder,
7½ in.	9¼ in.	12 in.
8/-	**12/-**	**36/-** doz.

D 63
Strong Tin Fluted Smoke Consumers with Strong Cast
Japanned Hooks and Loops.
6 in.	7 in.	8 in.	9 in.	10 in.	12 in.
5/-	**6/-**	**6/6**	**8/-**	**8/6**	**10/6**

D 64
Strong Brass Shade Holder,
with cast ring and clips.
9¼ in.	10 in.	11 in.	12 in.	14 in.
30/-	**30/-**	**33/-**	**36/-**	**42/-** doz.

D 65
Polished Brass Basket,
36/- doz.

D 66
Polished Brass Basket,
42/- doz.

D 67
Brass Duplex Shade Holder,
with clips,
13/- doz.

D 68
⅜ in. Brass Stripping Basket,
42/- doz.

D 69
½ in. Brass Stripping Basket,
48/- doz.

When ordering please state fittings of Founts the Baskets
are required to fit.

Strong SPUN Shade Rings.

D 70
Brass Pearled Shade Ring.
9¼ in.	10 in.	11 in.	12 in.	14 in.
10/-	**13/-**	**13/-**	**14/-**	**18/-** doz.

D 71
Brass O.G. Shade Ring.
12 in.	14 in.	16 in.
18/-	**24/-**	**33/-** doz.

D 72
Brass Pierced Straight sided Shade Ring.
12 in.	14 in.	16 in.
36/-	**48/-**	**60/-** doz.

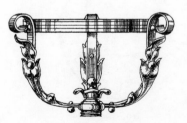

D 73
Polished Cast Brass Basket,
7/6 each.

D 74
Strong Brass Stripping Basket,
with cast centre.
10/- each.

D 75
Strong Brass Stripping Basket
with Copper leaves,
8/- each.

Air Diffusers.

D 76
Sun Diffuser,
10‴ 12‴ 16‴ 20‴
4/- 5/- 6/- 10/- doz.

D 77
Belge Diffuser,
12/- doz.

D 78
Defries' Diffuser,
No. 1 - **15/-** doz.
„ 2 - **18/-** „

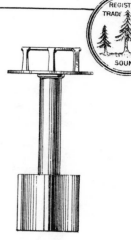

D 79
30‴ Sun Diffuser,
15/- doz.

Brass Feeder Screws.

D 80
Small Brass Cup Feeder
with
Cast Screw Top.
6/- doz.

D 81
Brass Feeder with Collar,
18/- gross.

D 82
SMALL SIZE.
24/- gro.

D 83
LARGE SIZE.
36/- gro.

Machine—made seamless Feeders with Collars.

D 84
Large Brass Cup Feeder
with
Cast Screw Top.
7/- doz.

Chimney Cleaner.

D 85
Strong Double Flue Mop,
13/- doz.

Supplied empty   to be fitted
with Shot to   required weight.

D 86
Slide Balance Weights,
Polished Brass, with Iron weights,
6 lb.   8 lb.   12 lb.
10/-   15/-   24/- each.

D 87
Strong Bright Tin Oil Can,
2 pints - **12/-** doz.
3 „   - **15/-** „

D 88
Slide Balance Weights,
Polished Brass, will balance up to 16 lbs.
15/- each.

SHERWOODS LAMPS.

Reflectors.

Scale. ¼"

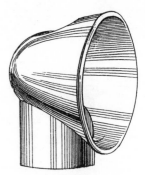

D 89
Nickel Plated Parabolic Reflector,
To fit 6''' cos. Burner, **18/-** doz.

D 90
To fit 10''' cos. Burner, **24/-** doz.

D 91
Large Nickel Plated Parabolic Reflector
with Neck,
To fit 6''' cos. Burner, **30/-** doz.

D 92
Nickel Plated Parabolic Deep Reflector
with Neck.

D 92 to fit	6''' cos. Burner,	**30/-** doz
D 93	,,	10'''	,,	**36/-** ,,
D 94	,,	14'''	,,	**42/-** ,,

D 95
Bright Tin Reflector,
6 in.
14/- gross.

D 96
Strong Polished Tin Reflector,
7 in.
36/- gross.

D 97
Bright Tin Reflector,
8½ in.
30/- gross.

D 98
Silver Glass Reflector.
5"   6"   7"   8"   9"   10"   12"
12/- 14/- 15/- 20/- 30/- 36/- 48/- doz

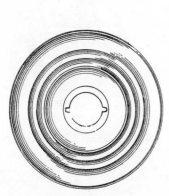

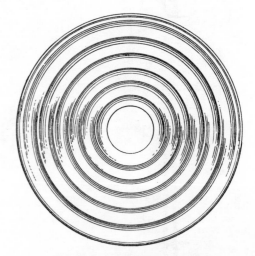

D 99
Bright Tin Spun Reflector,
12 in. - **9/-** doz.
15 in. - **10/6** ,,

D 100
Japanned Iron Plain Spun Reflector,
16 in. - **30/-** doz.
18 in. - **36/-** ,,

D 101
Japanned Iron Spun Reflector,
12 in. - **9/-** doz.   18 in. - **21/-** doz.
15 in. - **14/-** ,,   22 in. - **30/-** ,,
16 in. - **16/-** ,,   24 in. - **48/-** ,,

D 101A   Real Patent Enamelled.
18 in. - **48/-** doz.
22 in. - **72/-** ,,

BURNERS.
Patent "Lynlight" and "Sherlyn" Burners,
Particularly recommended for
Guards' Hand Signal, Engine Head, and Brake Van Lamps.

Scale ½

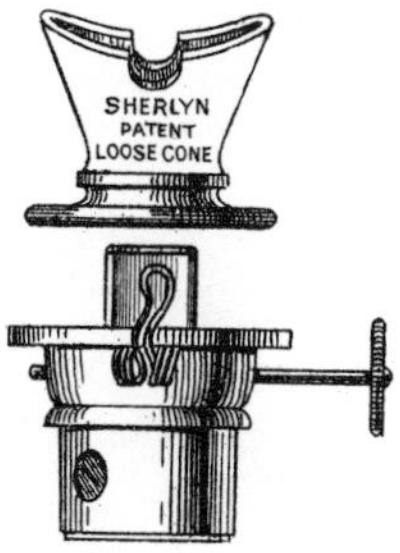

102B

PATENT " LYNLIGHT " BURNER.
Porcelain Cone.
No. 1 size, ¼ in. wick.   No. 2 size, ⅜ in. wick
12/- doz.   **15/-** doz.
Plug or Screw Fitting.

128B

PATENT "SHERLYN" BURNER,
with
Porcelain loose cone.
No. 1 size, ¼ in. wick.   No. 2 size, ⅜ in. wick.
17/- doz.   **20/-** doz.
Spare Adaptable Porcelain Cones,
No. 1 size, **8/6** doz.   No. 2 size, **10/·** doz.

103B

PATENT " LYNLIGHT " BURNER.
Metal Cone.
No. 1 size, ¼ in. wick.   No. 2 size, ⅜ in. wick.
15/6 doz.   **18/6** doz.
Plug or Screw Fitting.

129 B

PATENT " SHERLYN " BURNER,
with
Brass Metal Loose Cones.
No. 1 size, ¼ in. wick,   No. 2 size, ⅜ in. wick.
21/- doz.   **24/-** doz.
Spare Adaptable Metal Cones,
No. 1 size, **10/6** doz.   No. 2 size, **12/-** doz.
The above Burners are specially constructed for Engine Head and Brake Van Lamps.

Sherwoods "Patent Loose Cone Vaporite" Burners.

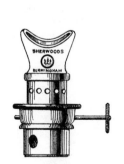 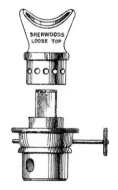 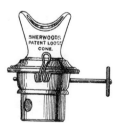  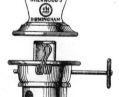

95B

Sherwoods " Loose Top Vaporite " Burner,
Porcelain Cones,
With **Brass Tube Slide Collars** to hold Tops in position
No. 1 size, ¼ in. wick.   No. 2 size, ⅜ in. wick.
11/- doz.   **14/-** doz.
Spare adaptable loose Porcelain Cones,
No. 1 size, **5/-** doz. No. 2 size, **6/-** doz.

96B

Sherwoods " Loose Top Vaporite " Burner,
Brass Metal Cones.
No. 1 size, ¼ in. wick.   No. 2 size, ⅜ in. wick.
15/- doz.   **18/-** doz.
Spare adaptable loose Metal Cones.
No. 1 size, **6/-** doz. No. 2 size, **8/-** doz.

119B

Sherwoods " Patent Loose Cone Vaporite " Burner,
Porcelain Cones,
Strong Brass Side Springs to hold Cones in position.
No. 1 size, ¼ in. wick.   No. 2 size, ⅜ in. wick.   No. 3 size, ⅝ in. wick.
13/- doz.   **15/-** doz.   **22/-** doz.
Spare Adaptable Loose Cones.
No. 1 size, **5/-** doz.   No. 2 size, **6/-** doz.   No. 3 size, **9/-** doz.

120B

Sherwoods " Patent Loose Cone Vaporite " Burner,
Brass Metal Cones.
With **Two Strong Brass Side Springs** to hold Cones in position.
No. 1 size, ¼ in. wick.   No. 2 size, ⅜ in. wick.   No. 3 size, ⅝ in. wick.
16/- doz.   **20/-** doz.   **24/-** doz.
Spare Adaptable Loose Metal Cones.
No. 1 size, **7/-** doz.   No. 2 size, **9/-** doz.   No. 3 size, **12/-** doz.

SHERWOODS LAMPS.

BURNERS.

Sherwoods "Vaporite" Burners.

Specially prepared Vitreous Porcelain Tops, Vapour Burners.

Scale ½

118B

Sherwoods " Vaporite " Burner.
No. **1** size, ¼ in. wick.
7/- doz.
Plug or Screw Fitting.

118B

Sherwoods " Vaporite " Burner.
No. **2** size, ⅜ in. wick.
10/- doz.
Plug or Screw Fitting.

118B

Sherwoods " Vaporite " Burner.
No. **3** size, ⅝ in. wick.
18/- doz.
Plug or Screw Fitting.

118B No. **4** size, ɪ in. wick, **30**/- doz. plug fitting.

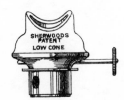

125B

Sherwoods Patent " Low Cone " Vapour Burner.
No. 1 size, ¼ in. wick; **12**/- doz.
No. 2 size, ⅜ in. wick., **15**/- doz.
No. 3 size, ⅝ in. wick., **21**/- doz.

126B

Patent " Metal Low Cone " Vapour Burner.
No. 1 size, ¼ in. wick, **15**/- doz.
No. 2 size, ⅜ in. wick, **18**/- doz.
No. 3 size, ⅝ in. wick, **24**/- doz.
Plug or Screw Fitting.

143B

Sherwoods " Vaporite " Burner,
with Screw down.
(for Engine Head Lamps).
No. 2 size, ⅜ in. wick.
25/- doz.
Plug or Screw Fitting.

97B

Sherwoods Patent "Low Loose Cone " Vapour Burr
No. 1 size, ¼ in. wick.
15/- doz.

98B

Patent " Metal Low Loose Cone " Vapour Burne
No. 1 size, ¼ in. wick.
18/- doz.
Plug or Screw Fitting.

106B

Sherwoods " Metal Cone " Vapour Burner.
(Cast Brass Cones).
No. 1 size, ¼ in. wick, **12**/- doz.
No. 2 size, ⅜ in. wick, **14**/- doz.
No. 3 size, ⅝ in. wick, **20**/- doz
106B Improved.
With Safety Cased Tube Spindles,
2/- doz. extra.
Plug or Screw Fitting.

118B

Sherwoods " Vaporite " Burner.
No. 1 size, ¼ in wick.   No. 2 size, ⅜ in. wick.
9/- doz.   **12**/- doz.
With Single grooved Tube Sockets.

107B

Sherwoods " Metal Cone " Vapour Burner.
(Stamped Brass Cones).
No. 1 size, ¼ in. wick.   No. 2 size, ⅜ in. wick.
12/- doz.   **14**/- doz.
107B Improved.
With Safety Cased Tube Spindles as drawn.
2/- doz. extra.
Plug or Screw Fitting.

BURNERS.
Motor Side and Tail Lamp Burners.

Scale ½

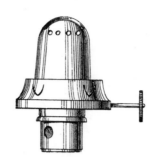

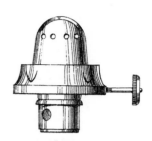

137B
Motor-tail Lamp Burner,
Nickel Plated.
⅜ in. wick, **13**/– doz.
Plug or Screw Fitting.

49B
MEDIUM CONE.
Motor Side Lamp Burner,
Nickel Plated.
½ in. wick, **15**/– doz.

48B
Extra Strong make, with Cast Buttons,
Nickel Plated.
½ in. wick, **18**/– doz.
Plug or Screw Fitting.

54B
LOW CONE.
Motor Side Lamp Burner,
Nickel Plated,
½ in. wick, **15**/– doz.
Plug or Screw Fitting.

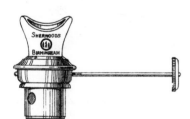

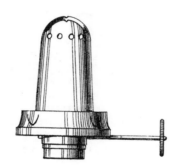

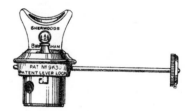

58B
Sherwoods "VAPORITE" Burner.
Motor Tail Lamp Burner.
Patent Ratchet arrangement,
with extra strong spindles.
No. 1 size, ¼ in. wick.   No. 2 size, ⅜ in. wick.
11/– doz.   **13**/– doz.
Plug or Screw Fitting.

94B
LONG CONE.
Motor Head and Side Lamp Burner,
Nickel Plated.
Extra Strong with Cast Buttons.
½ in. wick, **30**/– doz.
Plug or Screw Fitting.

112B
Sherwoods "VAPORITE" Burner.
Motor Tail Lamp Burner.
Patent Lever Lock Collar & Ratchet arrangement
with Extra Strong Spindles
No. 1 size, ¼ in. wick.   No. 2 size, ⅜ in. wick.
13/– doz.   **15**/– doz.
Plug or Screw Fitting.

Miner Safety Lamp Burners.

108B
Tin Burner with Safety Tube.
10/– gross.

with Strong Brass Plates and
Safety Tubes.
18/– gross.

Strong Copper Burner.
36/– gross.

118B
CHINA CONE Burner.
No. **0** short, ¼ in. wick.
9/– doz.

73B
Double Tube Burner
with Cast Screw Collar
42/– gross.

118B
CHINA CONE Burner.
No. **00** long, ¼ in. wick.
10/– doz.

65B
Brass round wick Burner
with Screw Collar.
9/– doz.
Special price per 1,000.
7/– doz.

SHERWOODS LAMPS.

BURNERS.
Sherwoods "Ship Lamp" Burners.

Scale ½

WEDGE

14 B Burner, with Screw Collar.
⅝ in. Wick - **48**/- gross.
Special Price 50 doz. lots.
36/- gross, without Collars **32**/- gross.
Special Price 100 doz. lots.
34/- gross, without Collars **30**/- gross

WEDGE

5 B Burner, with Grooved Sockets.
⅝ in. Wick - **6/6 doz.**
Special Price 12 doz. lots **6**/- doz.

WEDGE

14 B Burner with Screw Collar,
1 in. Wick - **72**/- gross.
Special Price 50 doz. lots.
62/- gross, without Collars **56**/- gross.
Special Price 100 doz. lots.
60/- gross, without Collars **54**/- gross.

WEDGE

7 B Burner with Grooved Sockets.
1 in. Wick - **11**/- doz.
Special Price 12 doz. lots, **10**/- doz.

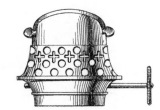

TRINITY

15 B Burner with Screw Collar.
1 in. Wick - **18**/- doz.
1¼ ,, - **21**/- ,,
Burner Cast Body with Cast Collar
1 in. Wick - **24**/- doz.
1¼ ,, - **30**/- ,,

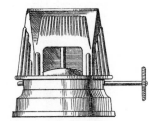

MARITIME

14 B Burner with Screw Collar.
1¼ in. Wick - **12**/- doz.
Special Price 12 doz. lots, **11**/- doz.

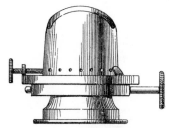

MASTHEAD

140 B Strong Cast Burner
with Screw Collar.
1 in. Wick - **9**/- each

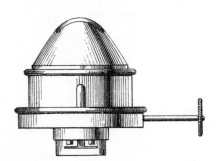

DAN

41 B Burner, plug fitting without collar.
¾ in. & 1 in. wick - **30**/- doz.
Special price, 12 doz. lots, **24**/- doz.

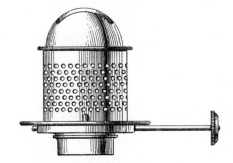

CONE

100 B Burner with Plug Collar.
¾ in. & 1 in. wick - **21**/- doz.
Special price 25 doz. lots, **19**/- doz.

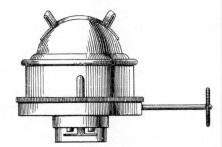

BUOY,

with two ears rivetted on cone.
68 B Burner, Plug fitting without Collars.
¾ in. and 1 in. wick - **36**/- doz.
Special price 12 doz. lots, **30**/- doz.

BURNERS.

Sherwoods "Ship Lamp" Burners.

Scale ½

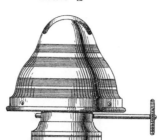

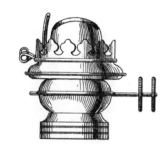

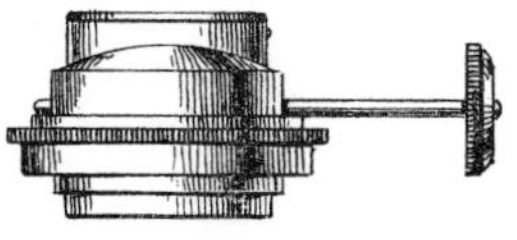

COLZA

28B Burner with Cast Screw Collar
(as drawn).

¾ in.   1 in. wick.
7/- doz.   **11/- doz.**

28B Burner, with Stamped Lock Collar.

¾ in. ½ in. ¾ in. 1 in.
24/- 30/- 36/- 54/- gross.

Long Spindles **6/-** gross extra.

ZENITH

60 B Burner with Strong Cast Thread Collars.
⅝ in. wick **13/6** doz., without Collar **12/-** doz.
1 ,, **21/-** doz.   ,,   **19/-** ,,

COLZA

71 B Strong Cast Brass Burner with Cast
Screw Collars.

                                1¾ in. and
½ in. ¾ in. 1 in. 1⅛ in. 1¼ in. 1½in. 2 in. wick
10/- 11/- 14/- 15/- 16/- 18/- 33/- doz.

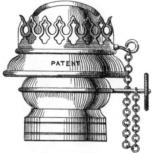

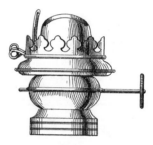

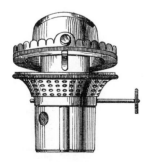

DUAL

DOUBLE WINDER.

86 B Burner, with Strong Cut Thread Collar.
⅝ in. wick **16/6** doz., without collars **15/-** doz.
⅞ ,, **22/-** doz.   ,,   **20/-** doz.

Special price 25 doz. lots,

⅝ in. wick, **13/6** doz., without collars **12/-** doz.
⅞ ,, **18/-** doz.   ,,   **16/-** doz.

ADMIRALTY

135 B Burner with PATENT pin cone attachment,
Strong Cut Thread Collars.
⅞ in. wick - **48/-** doz.

DUAL

SINGLE WINDER.

86 B Burner with Strong Cut Thread Collars.
⅝ in. wick **17/6** doz., without collars **16/-** doz.
⅞ ,, **23/-** doz.   ,,   **21/-** doz.

Special price 25 doz. lots.

⅝ in. wick **14/6** doz., without collars **13/-** doz.
⅞ ,, **19/-** doz.   ,,   **17/-** doz.

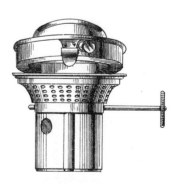

HINGE

214 B Burner, Hinge Cone with Screw Collar.
¾ in. wick - **10/-** doz.
1 in. wick - **13/-** doz.

215B with Single Grooved Tube Sockets
(as drawn).

¾ in. wick - **13/-** doz.
1 ,,   - **16/-** doz.

ZENITH

145B Burner with Grooved Tube Sockets.
⅝ in. wick - **16/-** doz.
1 ,,   - **23/-** doz.

HINGE

139 B Burner, Hinged Cone, with Screw Collar.
1¼ in wick - **15/-** doz.

89B with Grooved Tube Sockets
(as drawn).

1¼ in. wick - **17/-** doz.

BURNERS.
Sherwoods "Magic Diamond" Burners.
Chimneyless.
Scale ½

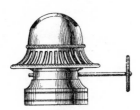

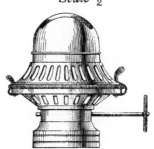

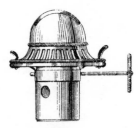

16B

MAGIC DIAMOND.
Fixed Cone.
⅜ in. wick, **12/-** doz.
Plug or Screw Fitting.

24B

MAGIC DIAMOND.
Loose Cone,
with Steel Clips and Springs.
½ in. wick, **15/-** doz.
With Strong Screw Collar.

27B

MAGIC DIAMOND.
Loose Cone,
with Steel Clips and Springs.
Long Spindles.
⅜ in. wick, **15/-** doz.

27B improved,
with Safety Capped and Cased Tube Spindles.
(Guaranteed Fireproof).
⅜ in. wick, **18/-** doz.
Plug Tube Sockets.

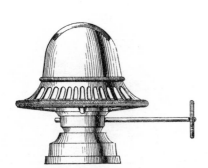

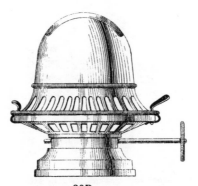

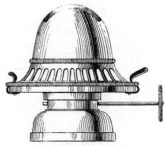

18B

MAGIC DIAMOND.
Fixed Cone.
⅝ in. wick, **13/-** doz.
Plug Collar.

20B

MAGIC DIAMOND.
Loose Cone,
with Steel Clips and Springs.
1 in. wick, **24/-** doz.
With Strong Cut Thread Screw Collar.

17B

MAGIC DIAMOND.
Loose Cone,
with Steel Clips and Springs.
⅝ in. wick, **18/-** doz.

17B improved,
with Safety Capped and Cased Tube Spindles.
(Guaranteed Fireproof).
⅝ in. wick, **24/-** doz.
With Strong Screw Collar.

Sherwoods "Beacon Light" Burners.
Chimneyless.

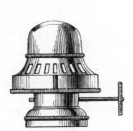

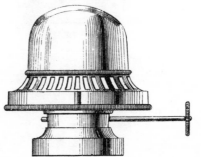

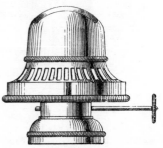

61B

BEACON LIGHT,
with Removable Cone.
⅜ in. wick, **10/-** doz.
With Screw Collar.

116B

BEACON LIGHT,
with Removable Cone.
1 in. wick, **20/-** doz.
With Screw Collar.

115B

BEACON LIGHT,
with Removable Cone.
⅜ in. wick, **15/-** doz.
With Screw Collars.

BURNERS.
Sherwoods "Railway Lamp" Burners.
Scale ½

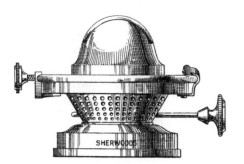

84 B

Heavy 1 in. Chimneyless Burner.
Movable Cone.
36/- doz.
with Large Screw Collar.

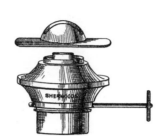

55 B

Chimneyless Roof Lamp Burner,
Ridsdale Pattern,
Complete with Cone.
24/- doz.
Spare Cones only
2/6 doz.

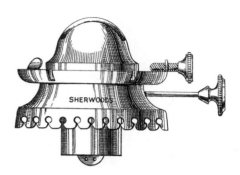

36 B

Heavy Cast Gallery, Eclipse Burner,
Movable Cone.
No. 5 ⅝ in. wick - **36/-** doz.
No. 7 ¾ ,, - **42/-** ,,
No. 10 1 ,, - **48/-** ,,
with Plug Socket Collars.

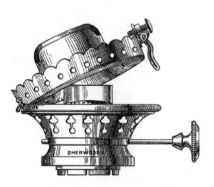

67

Heavy 1 in. Chimneyless Burner
Hinged Globe Holder for Lighting.
66/- doz.
Plug or Screw Collars.

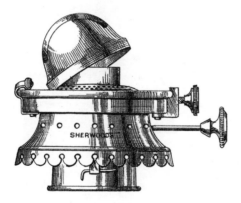

109

Heavy 1 in. Chimneyless Burner
(Indian Platform Pattern)
with Hinged Cone,
60/- doz.
Bayonet Catch Collar.

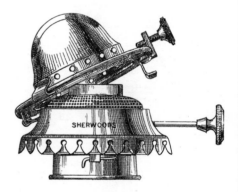

66 B

Heavy 1 in. Chimneyless Burner.
Hinged Globe Holder for Lighting.
54/- doz.
Bayonet Catch Collar.

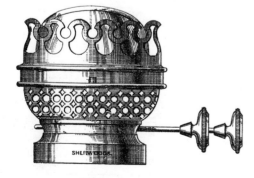

142 B
VICTOR

Heavy Duplex Burner.
For Street and Railway Station Lighting.
Movable Cone.
5/- each.
with Cut Thread Screw Collar.

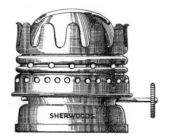

121 B
PARAGON

Heavy 1½ in. Single Wick Burner.
For Railway Station and Signal Cabin Lighting,
Movable Cone.
4/- each.
with Cut Thread Screw Collar.

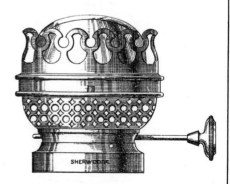

74 B
TIGER

Heavy 1½ in. Single Wick Burner,
For Street and Railway Station Lighting,
Movable Cone,
5/- each.
with Cut Thread Screw Collar.

SHERWOODS LAMPS.

Burners.

Scale ½

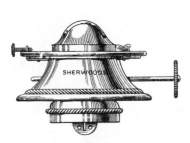

36 B
No. 5. ⅝ in. Wick.
Strong Eclipse Burner.
With Brass Buttons,   With White Buttons,
16/6 doz.   **17/6** doz.

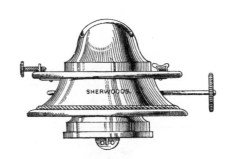

36 B
No. 7. ¾ in. Wick.
Strong Eclipse Burner.
With Brass Buttons,   With White Buttons.
19/- doz.   **20/-** doz.

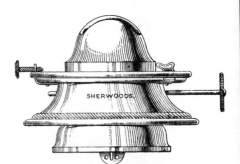

36 B
No. 10. 1 in. Wick.
Strong Eclipse Burner.
with Brass Buttons   with White Buttons
22/- doz.   **23/-** doz.

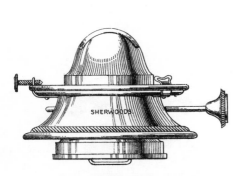

36 B
No. 10. 1 in. Wick.
Extra Strong Eclipse Burner,
with large collar and white button,
24/- doz.

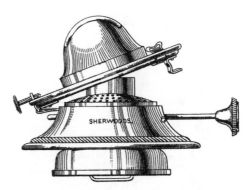

69 B
No. 10. 1 in. Wick.
Extra Strong Eclipse Burner,
Hinged cone for lighting and white buttons,
36/- doz.

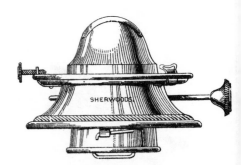

87 B
No. 10. 1 in. Wick.
Extra Strong Eclipse Burner,
with white buttons and Bayonet-catch collar,
36/- doz.

Indian Platform Founts and Burners.

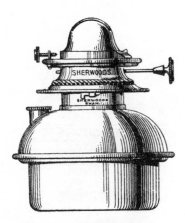

87 B/168
Polished Brass Container,
1 in. Strong Eclipse Burner, Bayonet fitting,
with cast feeder screw,
5/6 each.
No. 168 Brass container without collars,
2/6 each.

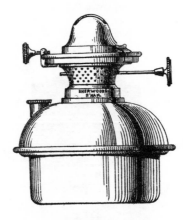

84 B/168
Polished Brass Container,
1 in. Heavy Chimneyless Hinge Cone Burner,
with cast feeder screw,
5/6 each.
No. 168 Brass container without collars,
2/6 each.

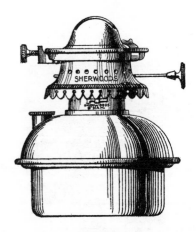

109B/168
Polished Brass Container,
1 in. Extra Strong Eclipse Burner, Hinge Cone,
with cast feeder screw,
7/6 each.
Special price 12 dozen lots,
7/- each.

Burners.

Scale. ½"

1 A
Fine thread
Benzo Burner with cap. and chain,
without collar,
21/- gross.
Without cap or chain **1/6** gross less.

1 B
Fine thread,
Strong Quality Benzo Burner with
cap and chain,
without collar,
24/- gross.
Without cap or chain **1/6** gross less.

45 B
Fine thread,
Extra Strong Quality Benzo Burner,
with cap and chain, without collar,
30/- gross.
43 B
Coarse W.B. thread,
36/9 gross.

2 B
Fine thread,
Extra Strong Quality Double Tube
Benzo Burner,
with cap and chain, without collar,
48/- gross.

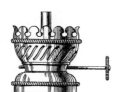

104 B
Strong Night Light Burner,
36/- gross.
Without collars,
33/- gross.

4 B
Strong Benzo Burner with china cone,
with cap and chain, without collar,
50/- gross.

93 B
Strong Gem Arctic Burner,
40/- gross.
Without collars,
36/- gross.

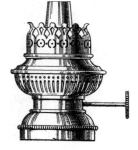

76 B
Strong Quality Cosmos Burner.
'' with collar, **10**/- doz., white buttons, **12**/- doz.
'' ,, ,, **15**/- ,, with 7¼" Shade ring **18**/- ,,
'' ,, ,, **21**/- ,, with 9¼" Shade ,, **28**/- ,,

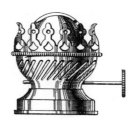

13 B
½ in. Bijou Burner with Extinguisher,
7/- doz.
With White Buttons,
8/- doz.

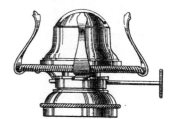

83 B
Strong Eureka Burner.
English make.
No. 0 ½ in. **5/6** doz., 5 gross, **5**/- doz.
No. 1A ¾ in. **7**/- ,, 5 gross, **6/6** ,,
No. 2B 1 in. **9/6** ,, 5 gross, **9**/- ,,

Without collars,
No. 0 ½ in. **5**/- doz., 5 gross, **4/6** doz.
No. 1A ¾ in. **6/6** ,, ,, **6**/- ,,
No. 2B 1 in. **8/6** ,, ,, **8**/- ,,

SHERWOODS LAMPS.

Burners.

Scale. ½″

11 B

¾ in. Strong Slip Burner and Collar,
48/- gross.

Without Collars,
40/- gross.

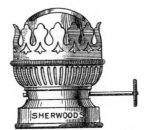

11 B

1 in. Strong Slip Burner collar,
66/- gross.

Without Collars,
54/- gross.

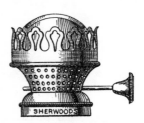

12 B

¾ in. Extra Strong Slip Burner and
Collar, with China Button,
7/- doz.

With Brass Buttons,
72/- gross.

Without Collar,
64/- gross.

12 B

1 in. Extra Strong Slip Burner and
Collar, with China Button,
9/6 doz.

With Brass Buttons,
102/- gross.

Without Collar,
90/- gross.

88 B

Strong Bijou Burner and Collar,
with China Button,
8/- doz.

Made for ½ in. and ¾ in. wick.

88 B

Strong Bijou Burner and Collar,
3 in. Gallery with China Button,
9/- doz.

Made for ½ in. or ¾ in. wick.

110 B

Strong Duplex Bijou Burner and Collar,
with 3 in. Gallery,
24/- doz.
With ½ in. wick tubes.

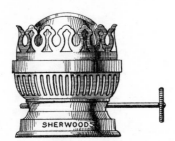

21 B

1 in. Extra Strong Slip Burner and Collar,
16/- doz.

Ditto   made with Extinguisher,
19/- doz.

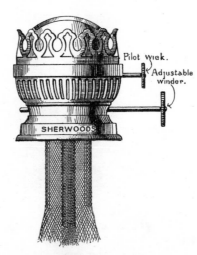

37 B

1 in. Extra Strong Slip Burner and Collar,
with burning pilot wick attachment for
re-lighting burner,
36/- doz.

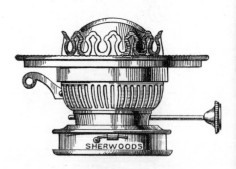

25 B

1 in. Extra Strong Slip Burner, with Gallery,
with Duplex Bayonet fitting collar,
and Extinguisher,
with China Button,
48/- doz.

Duplex Burners.

Strong Quality with Double Bar Winder.

Scale ½

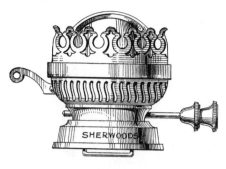

29 B
Strong Extinguisher Duplex Burner,
double winder,
21/- doz.
with Screw Collar.

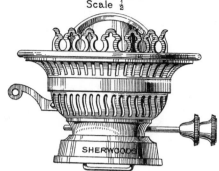

23 B
Strong Extinguisher Duplex Burner,
double winder,
with raised gallery,
24/- doz.
with Screw Collar

133 B
Strong Extinguisher Duplex Burner,
double winder,
with fixed raised gallery,
30/- doz.
with Screw Collar.

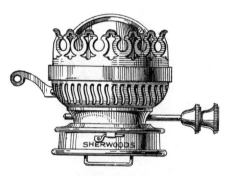

22 B
Strong Extinguisher Duplex Burner,
double winder,
27/- doz.
Bayonet catch collar.

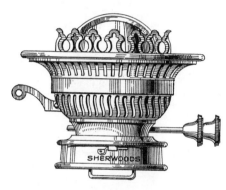

32 B
Strong Extinguisher Duplex Burner,
double winder,
with raised gallery,
30/- doz.
Bayonet catch collar.

134B
Strong Extinguisher Duplex Burner,
double winder,
with fixed raised gallery,
36/- doz.
Bayonet catch collar.

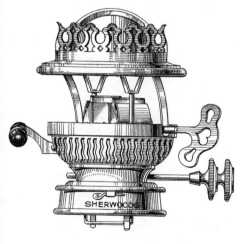

92 B
Strong Extinguisher Raiser Duplex Burner,
double winder,
72/- doz.
Made with screw or bayonet catch collar.

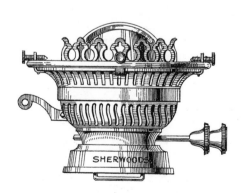

44 B
Strong Extinguisher Duplex Burner,
double winder,
with three set screws on gallery,
for ship lamps,
33/- doz.
with Screw Collar,

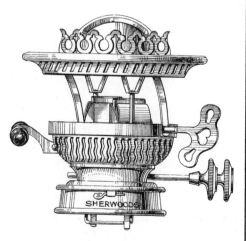

92 B
Strong Raiser Extinguisher Duplex Burner,
double winder,
with fixed raised gallery,
78/- doz.
Made with screw or bayonet catch collar.

SHERWOODS LAMPS.

Duplex Burners.

Strong Quality, with Single Bar Winder.

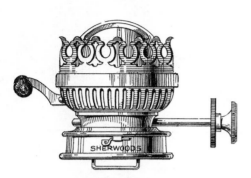

Scale ½

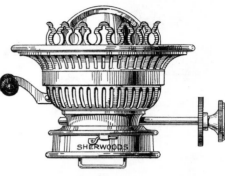

22 B S.W.
Heavy Extinguisher Duplex Burner,
single winder,
4/- each.
Bayonet catch collar.

23 B S.W.
Heavy Extinguisher Duplex Burner,
single winder,
with heavy raised gallery,
4/6 each.
Bayonet catch collar.

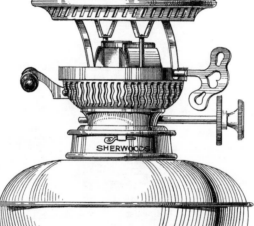

30 B S.W.
Heavy Extinguisher Duplex Burner,
single winder,
4/9 each.
with Screw Collar.

122 B S.W.
Heavy Extinguisher Duplex Burner,
single winder,
with fixed raised gallery,
5/- each.
Bayonet catch collar.

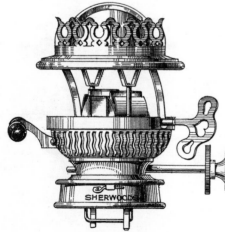

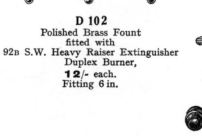

D 102
Polished Brass Fount
fitted with
92B S.W. Heavy Raiser Extinguisher
Duplex Burner,
12/- each.
Fitting 6 in.

92 B S.W.
Heavy Raiser Extinguisher Duplex Burner,
single winder,
7/- each.
Bayonet catch collar.

92 B S.W.
Heavy Raiser Extinguisher Duplex Burner,
single winder,
with raised gallery,
7/6 each.
Bayonet catch collar.

Sherwoods "SUN" Central Draught Burners.

Strong Quality English Make,

Scale ½

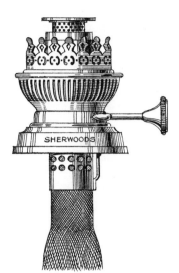

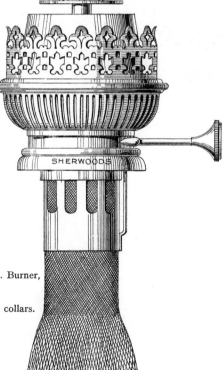

57 B/12''' Sun

Sherwoods' 30 c.p. 12''' Sun C.D. Burner,
with air diffuser,
3/- each.

Brass central air way tubes and collars.

57 B/16''' Sun

Sherwoods' 45 c.p. 16''' Sun Burner,
with air diffuser,
4/- each.

Brass central air way tubes and collars.

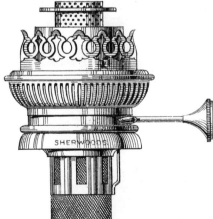

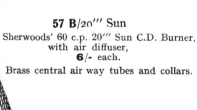

D 103

Polished Brass Fount
fitted with
Sherwoods' 60 c.p. 20''' Sun Raiser,
C.D. Burner,
13/6 each.

Sherwoods' 60 c.p. 20''' Sun Raiser
C.D. Burners only,
8/- each.

57 B/20''' Sun

Sherwoods' 60 c.p. 20''' Sun C.D. Burner,
with air diffuser,
6/- each.

Brass central air way tubes and collars.

57 B/30''' Sun

Sherwoods' 100 c.p. 30''' Sun C.D. Burner,
with air diffuser,
10/- each.

Brass central air way tubes and collars.

To obtain the best results from our Sun Central Draught Burners it is imperative that only our Sun Chimneys
be used. They are specially moulded to suit our burners, and will ensure a perfect steady,
clear and brilliant light, which cannot be obtained by using other chimneys.

SHERWOODS LAMPS.

Polished Brass Founts

fitted with

Strong ¾ in. and 1 in. Extinguisher Duplex Burners.

D 104
Polished Brass Fount
fitted with
12B ¾ in. Burner,
20/- doz.
No. **7** Screw Under Mount.

D 105
Polished Brass Fount
fitted with
Strong 12B ¾ in. Burner and 3 in. Gallery,
22/- doz.
No. **7** Screw Under Mount.

D 106
Polished Brass Fount
fitted with
12B 1 in. Burner and 4 in. Gallery,
30/- doz.
No. **7** or No. **10** Screw under Mount.

Scale ¼ th.

D 107
Polished Brass Fount
fitted with
23B Extinguisher Duplex Burner
and Gallery,
42/- doz.
No. **10** Screw Under Mount.

D 108
Polished Brass Fount
fitted with
23B Extinguisher Duplex Burner
and Gallery,
50/- doz.
No. **10** Screw Under Mount.

D 109
Polished Brass Fount
fitted with
23B Extinguisher Duplex Burner
and Gallery,
48/- doz.
No. **10** Screw Under Mount.

D 110
Polished Brass Fount
fitted with
133B Extinguisher Duplex Burner
and Gallery,
5/- each.
No. **10** Screw Under Mount.

D 111
Polished Brass Fount
fitted with
133B Extinguisher Duplex Burner
and Gallery.
6/- each.
No. **10** Screw Under Mount.

D 112
Polished Brass Fount
fitted with
133B Extinguisher Duplex Burner,
and Gallery,
5/6 each.
No. **10** Screw Under Mount.

Polished Brass Founts
fitted with
Heavy Single Winder Extinguisher Duplex Burners.

D 113

Polished Brass Fount
fitted with
30B S.W. Heavy Extinguisher
Duplex Burner,
9/- each.
No. **10** Screw Under Mount.

D 114

Polished Brass Fount
fitted with
30B S.W. Heavy Extinguisher
Duplex Burner,
8/6 each.
No. **10** Screw Under Mount.

Scale $\frac{1}{4}$ th.

D 115

Polished Brass Fount
fitted with
30B S.W. Heavy Extinguisher
Duplex Burner,
8/- each.
No. **10** Screw Under Mount.

D 116

Polished Brass Fount
fitted with
92B S.W. Heavy Raiser Extinguisher
Duplex Burner,
fixed raised gallery,
12/- each.
No. **10** Screw Under Mount.

D 117

Polished Brass Fount
fitted with
92B S.W. Heavy Raiser Extinguisher
Duplex Burner,
fixed raised gallery,
12/6 each.
No. **10** Screw Under Mount.

D 118

Polished Brass Fount
fitted with
92B S.W. Heavy Raiser Extinguisher
Duplex Burner,
fixed raised gallery,
13/- each.
No. **10** Cast Screw Under Mount.

D 119

Polished Brass Fount
fitted with
92B S.W. Heavy Raiser Extinguisher
Duplex Burner,
12/- each.
No. **10** Screw Under Mount.

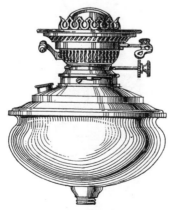

D 120

Polished Brass Fount
fitted with
92B S.W. Heavy Raiser Extinuisher
Duplex Burner,
14/- each.
No. **10** Cast Screw Under Mount.

D 121

Polished Brass Fcunt
fitted with
92B S.W. Heavy Rasier Extinguisher,
Duplex Burner,
13/- each.
No. **10** Cast Screw Under Mount.

SHERWOODS LAMPS.

Polished Brass Drop-in Founts

fitted with

Strong Duplex Extinguisher Burners.

Scale ¼th.

D 122

Polished Brass Fount
fitted with
23ʙ Duplex Extinguisher Burner and Gallery,
45/- doz.
Fittings 4 in., 4¼ in., 4¾ in., 5⅛ in.

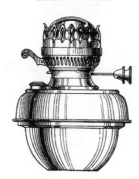

D 123

Polished Brass Fount
fitted with
29ʙ Duplex Extinguisher Burner,
42/- doz.
Fittings 4½ in., 5 in.

D 124

Polished Brass Fount
fitted with
23ʙ Duplex Extinguisher Burner and Gallery,
50/- doz.
Fittings 4¼ in., 4¾ in., 5 in., 5¼ in.

D 125

Polished Brass Fount
fitted with
133ʙ Duplex Extinguisher Burner,
fixed Gallery,
5/- each.
Fittings 5¼ in., 5⅞ in., 6¼ in.

D 126

Polished Brass Fount
fitted with
133ʙ Duplex Extinguisher Burner, Fixed Gallery,
6/6 each.
Fittings 5 in., 5⅝ in., 6 in., 6½ in.

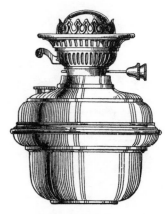

D 127

Polished Brass Fount
fitted with
133ʙ Duplex Extinguisher Burner,
fixed Gallery,
6/6 each.
Fittings 5 in., 5⅝ in.

Polished Copper Founts.

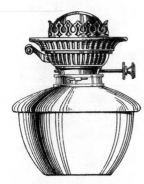

D 128

Polished Copper Fount
fitted with
122ʙ S.W. Heavy Duplex Extg. Burner,
8/6 each.
Fitting, 5¼ in.

D 129

Polished Copper Fount
fitted with
122ʙ S.W. Heavy Duplex Extg. Burner,
9/- each.
Fittings 6 in. and 6¼ in.

D 130

Polished Copper Fount
fitted with
122ʙ S.W. Heavy Duplex Extg. Burner,
10/- each.
Fitting 6½ in.

Polished Brass Drop in Founts

fitted with

Strong Duplex Extinguisher Burners.

Scale ¼ th.

D 131

Polished Brass Fount,
fitted with
133B Duplex Extinguisher Burner,
fixed Gallery,
7/- each.
Fitting 6 in.

D 132

Polished Brass Fount,
fitted with
122B S.W. Heavy Duplex Extinguisher Burner,
fixed Gallery,
8/- each.
Fitting 4⅞ in.

D 133

Polished Brass Fount,
fitted with
92B S.W. Heavy Raiser Extinguisher,
Duplex Burner,
12/- each.
Fitting 6¼ in.

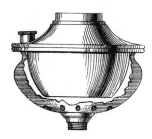

D 134

Polished Brass Fount,
14‴ Cosmos Screw or Bayonet Duplex Collar,
with
Spun Brass Basket.
7/- each.

D 135

Cut Crystal Fount,
fitted with
Bayonet Duplex Collar.
4/- each.
5¼ in. Fitting.

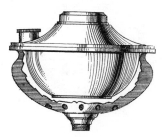

D 136

Polished Brass Fount,
14‴ Cosmos Screw or Bayonet Duplex Collar,
with
Spun Brass Basket.
8/6 each.

D 137

Single Cut Crystal Fount,
fitted with
Bayonet Duplex Collar and Mount.
2/6 each.
5¼ in. diameter.

D 138

Heavy Fancy Cut Crystal Fount,
fitted with
Bayonet Duplex Collar and Cast Mount.
9/- each.
6 in. diameter.

D 139

Double Cut Crystal Fount,
fitted with
Bayonet Duplex Collar and Mount.
2/6 each.
5¼ in. diameter.

SHERWOODS LAMPS.

Polished Brass Founts.
fitted with
Sherwoods 30 c.p. 12''' and 45 c.p. 16''' Sun C.D. Burners.

Scale ¼ th.

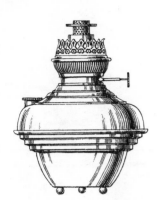

D 140
Polished Brass Fount
fitted with
Sherwoods' 30 c.p. 12''' Sun C.D. Burner,
5/6 each.
Fittings 4¼″, 4¾″, 5″ and 5¼″.

D 141
Polished Brass Fount
fitted with
Sherwoods' 30 c.p. 12''' Sun C.D. Burner,
6/- each.
Fittings 5½ in.

D 142
Polished Brass Fount
fitted with
Sherwoods' 30 c.p. 12''' Sun C.D. Burner,
6/- each.
Fittings 4¼ in. and 5 in.

D 143
Polished Brass Fount,
fitted with
Sherwoods' 30 c.p. 12''' Sun C.D. Burner,
with 3″ or 4″ fitting gallery,
6/3 each.
No. 10 Screw Under Mount.

D 144
Polished Brass Fount
fitted with
Sherwoods' 45 c.p. 16''' Sun C.D. Burner,
7/- each.
Fittings 5 in., 5½ in.

D 145
Polished Brass Fount
fitted with
Sherwoods' 30 c.p. 12''' Sun C.D. Burner,
3 in. or 4 in. fitting gallery.
6/3 each.
No. 10 Screw Under Mount.

D 146
Polished Brass Fount,
fitted with
Sherwoods' 45 c.p. 16''' Sun C.D. Burner,
with 4″ fitting gallery,
8/- each.
No. 10 Screw Under Mount.

D 147
Polished Brass Fount,
fitted with
Sherwoods' 45 c.p. 16''' Sun C.D. Burner,
7/6 each.
Fittings 5¼ in., 5⅞ in., 6¼ in.

D 148
Polished Brass Fount
fitted with
Sherwoods' 45 c.p. 16''' Sun C.D. Burner,
with 4 in. fitting gallery.
8/6 each.
No. 10 Screw Under Mount.

SHERWOODS LAMPS.

Polished Brass Founts,

fitted with

Sherwoods 60 c.p. 20''' Sun and 100 c.p. 30''' Sun. C.D. Burners.

Scale ¼ th.

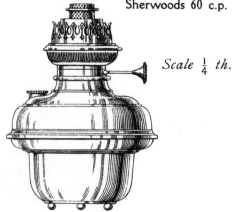

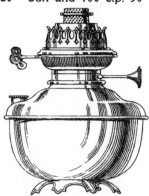

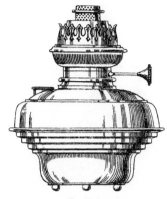

D 149
Polished Brass Fount
fitted with
Sherwoods' 60 c.p. 20''' Sun C.D. Burner,
10/- each.
Fitting **5¼ in.**

D 150
Polished Brass Fount,
fitted with
Sherwoods' 60 c.p. Raiser, 20''' Sun C.D. Burner,
Cast leaf piece.
15/6 each.
Polished Copper,
16/6 each.
Fitting **6 in.**

D 151
Polished Brass Fount,
fitted with
Sherwoods' 60 c.p. 20''' Sun C.D. Burner,
11/- each.
Fittings **5 in., 5¼ in., 6 in. and 6¼ in.**

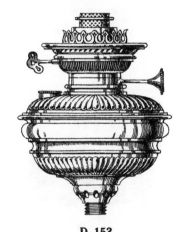

D 152
Polished Brass Fount
fitted with
Sherwoods' 60 c.p. 20''' Sun C.D. Burner,
12/- each.
No. **10** Cast Screw Under Mount.

D 153
Polished Brass Fount
fitted with
Sherwoods' 60 c.p. Raiser 20''' Sun
C.D. Burner.
14/- each.
No. **10** Cast Screw Under Mount.

D 154
Polished Brass Fount
fitted with
Sherwoods' 60 c.p. 20''' Sun C.D. Burner,
13/- each.
No. **10** Cast Screw Under Mount.

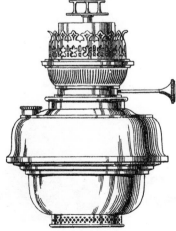

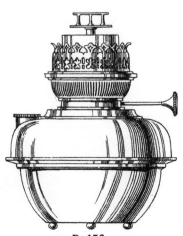

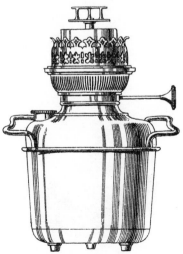

D 155
Polished Copper Fount
fitted with
Sherwoods' 100 c.p. 30''' Sun C.D. Burner,
21/- each.
Fitting **5⅜ in., 5¾ in., 6 in., 6¼ in.**

D 156
Polished Brass Fount
fitted with
Sherwoods' 100 c.p. 30''' Sun C.D. Burner,
16/- each.
Fitting **6¼ in., 6½ in.**

D 157
Polished Brass Fount
fitted with
Sherwoods' 60 c.p. 20''' Sun C.D. Burner,
18/- each.
100 c.p. 30''' Sun C.D. Burner,
21/- each.
Fitting **6¼ in.**

SHERWOODS LAMPS.

Polished Brass Low Stands.

With Marble Bases.

Scale ⅕th.

D 158
Polished or Steel Bronzed Stand.
"B" 6 in. Black Base,
22/- doz.

D 160
Polished Bright or Relieved Stand.
"H" 7 in. Black Base,
24/- doz.

D 161
Polished Bright or Relieved Stand,
"H" 7 in. Black Base,
24/- doz.

D 162
Polished or Steel Bronzed Stand.
"B" 6 in. Black Base,
22/- doz.

D 159
"I" 6 in. Green Coloured Base,
26/- doz.

D 163
"I" 6 in. Green Coloured Base,
26/- doz.

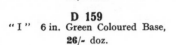

Approx. weights and measurements per No. 3 Cask, 4 doz. assorted patterns

Gross   2   0   12
                        28 × 28
Net   1   2   8

Prices do not include Under Mounts, see page **11**.

D 164
Polished or Steel Bronzed Stand.
"A" 7 in. Black Base,
25/- doz.

D 165
Polished or Steel Bronzed Stand,
"A" 7 in. Black Base,
25/- doz.

D 166
Polished or Steel Bronzed Stand.
"A" 7 in. Black Base.
25/- doz.

Approximate weights and measurements :—

Per No. 3 Cask, 3 doz. assorted patterns.

Gross   1   3   20
                        28 × 28
Net   1   1   4

Per No. 1 Cask, 6 doz. assorted patterns.

Gross   3   1   12
                        40 × 30
Net   2   2   8

D 167
Polished or Steel Bronzed Stand.
"A" 7 in. Black Base,
27/- doz.

D 169
Polished or Steel Bronzed Stand.
"D" 7½ in. Black Base,
42/- doz.

D 170
Polished or Steel Bronzed Stand.
"E" 8¼ in. Black Base,
48/- doz.

D 172
Polished or Steel Bronzed Stand.
"A" 7 in. Black Base.
36/- doz

D 168
"J" 7 in. Brown Coloured Base.
33/- doz.

D 171
"K" 8¼ in. Green Coloured Base.
60/- doz.

D 173
"J" 7 in. Brown Coloured Base,
42/- doz.

SHERWOODS LAMPS.

Polished Brass Pillar Stands.

With Marble Bases.

Scale ⅕th.

D 174

Polished Pillar Stand,
" C " 6½ in. Black Base,
26/- doz.

D 175

" L " 6½ in. Green Coloured Base.
32/- doz.

D 176

Polished Pillar Stand,
"A" 7 in. Black Base,
30/- doz.

Prices do not include Under Mounts, see page 11.

D 177

Polished Pillar Stand.
" C " 6½ in. Black Base,
27/- doz.

D 178

" L " 6½ in. Green Coloured Base,
33/- doz.

D 179

Polished Pillar Stand.
"A" 7 in. Black Base,
36/- doz.

D 180

Polished Pillar Stand.
"A" 7 in. Black Base,
36/- doz.

D 181

Polished Pillar Stand.
"A" 7 in. Black Base,
36/- doz.

Approx. weights and measurements per No. 2 Cask, 3 doz. assorted patterns.

Gross 2 1 6
                   36 × 31
Net   1 1 24

D 182

Polished Pillar Stand.
"A" 7 in. Black Base,
42/- doz.

D 183

" J " 7 in. Brown Coloured Base.
48/- doz.

D 184

Polished Pillar Stand.
" D " 7½ in. Black Base,
54/- doz.

D 185

Polished Pillar Stand.
"A" 7 in. Black Base,
48/- doz.

D 186

" J " 7 in. Brown Coloured Base.
54/- doz.

SHERWOODS LAMPS.

Polished Brass Stands.

Scale ⅕th.

D 187
Polished Brass Stand.
18/- doz.

D 188
Polished Brass Stand.
45/- doz.

D 190
Polished Brass Stand.
50/- doz.

D 192
Polished Brass Stand.
54/- doz.

D 189
Polished Brass with Copper Shell,
50/- doz.

D 191
Polished Brass with Copper Shell,
55/- doz.

Prices do not include Under Mounts, see page Nº 11.

D 193
Polished Brass Pillar Stand.
" J " 7 in. Brown Coloured Base.
45/- doz.

D 194
Polished Brass Pillar Stand.
" F " 7 in. Green Coloured Base.
54/- doz.

D 195
Polished Brass Pillar Stand.
" F " 7 in. Green Coloured Base,
60/- doz.

 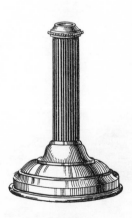  

D 196
Polished Brass Pillar Stand,
54/- doz.

D 198
Polished Brass Pillar Stand.
40/- doz.

D 200
Polished Brass Pillar Stand.
7/- each.

D 202
Polished Brass Tripod Stand,
14/- each.

D 197
Oxidized Copper,
72/- doz.

D 199
Polished Brass with Copper Shell,
45/- doz.

D 201
Oxidized Copper,
9/- each.

D 203
Oxidized Copper,
18/- each.

SHERWOODS LAMPS.

Polished Brass Pillar Stands.

Scale ⅕th.

D 204
Polished Brass Pillar Stand,
5/- each.

D 205
Polished Brass Pillar Stand,
5/6 each.

D 206
Polished Brass Pillar Stand,
6/- each.

D 207
Polished Brass Pillar Stand,
9/- each.

Prices do not include Under Mounts, see page Nº 11.

D 208
Polished Brass Pillar Stand,
6/6 each.

D 209
Oxidized Copper,
8/- each.

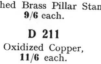

D 210
Polished Brass Pillar Stand,
9/6 each.

D 211
Oxidized Copper,
11/6 each.

D 212
Polished Brass Pillar Stand,
10/- each.

D 213
Oxidized Copper,
12/- each.

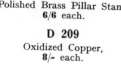

D 214
Polished Brass Telescopic Stand,
"A" 7 in. Black Base,
8/- each.

D 215
Large size, "D" 7½ in. Black Base,
10/- each.
Height 10¾ in., full extension 16½ in.

D 216
Heavy Polished Brass Pillar Stand,
with cast foot,
13/- each.

D 217
Polished Brass Telescopic Stand,
9/- each.

D 218
Oxidized Copper,
12/- each.
Height 11 in., full extension 17 in.

SHERWOODS LAMPS.

Polished Brass Corinthian Pillar Stands.

Scale ⅕th.

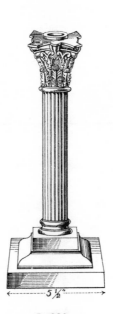

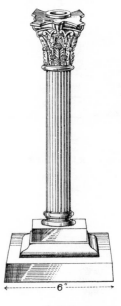

D 219
Polished Brass Corinthian Stand.
7/- each.

D 220
Polished Brass Corinthian Stand,
9/- each.

D 221
Polished Brass Corinthian Stand.
11/- each.

These Stands are also supplied Steel Bronzed and Relieved finish.

Prices do not include Under Mounts, see page Nº 11.

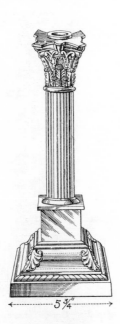

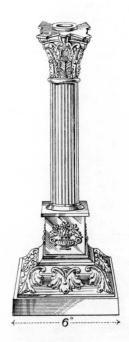

D 222
Polished Brass Corinthian Stand.
12/- each.

D 223
Polished Brass Corinthian Stand,
15/- each.

D 224
Polished Brass Corinthian Stand,
13/- each.

SHERWOODS LAMPS.

Polished Brass Corinthian Pillar Stands.

Scale ⅕th.

D 225
Polished Brass Corinthian Stand,
14/- each.

D 226
Polished Brass Corinthian Stand,
with cast foot,
40/- each.

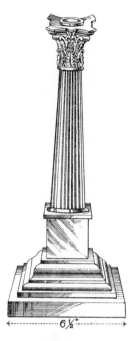

D 227
Polished Brass Corinthian Stand,
15/- each.

These Stands are also supplied Steel Bronzed and Relieved finish.

Prices do not include Under Mounts, see page 11.

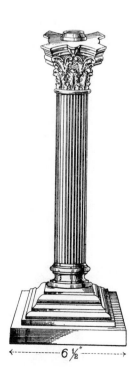

D 228
Polished Brass Corinthian Stand,
20/- each.

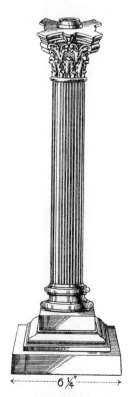

D 229
Polished Brass Corinthian Stand,
with cast foot.
36/- each.

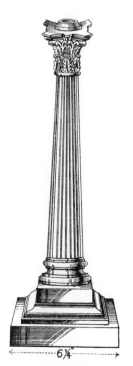

D 230
Polished Brass Corinthian Stand,
with cast foot,
36/- each.

SHERWOODS LAMPS.

Polished Brass Drop in Founts

and

Brass Table Lamps.

Scale ⅕ th.

D 231
Polished Brass Fount.
14′′′ Cosmos or Screw Duplex Collar
26/- doz.
Fittings 4¼ in., 4¾ in. 5 in., 5¼ in.

D 232
Polished Brass Fount.
14′′′ Cosmos Screw or Bayonet Duplex Collar.
30/- doz.
Fittings 5¼ in., 5⅞ in., 6¼ in.

D 233
Polished Brass Fount.
14′′′ Cosmos Screw or Bayonet Duplex Collar.
46/- doz.
Fittings 5 in., 5⅝ in., 6 in., 6½ in.

D 234
Polished Brass Table Lamp.
⅝ in. Screw Collar.
21/- doz.

D 235
Polished Brass Table Lamp.
14′′′ Cosmos or Screw Duplex Collar.
24/- doz.

D 236
Polished Brass Table Lamp.
14′′′ Cosmos or Screw Duplex Collar.
33/- doz.

D 237
Polished Brass Table Lamp.
14′′′ Cosmos or Screw Duplex Collar.
3/- each.

D 238
Polished Brass Table Lamp.
14′′′ Cosmos Screw or Bayonet Duplex Collar.
3/6 each.

D 239
Polished Brass Table Lamp.
14′′′ Cosmos Screw or Bayonet Duplex Collar.
4/- each.

Polished Brass Table Lamps,

Scale ⅕ th.

D 240
Polished Brass Table Lamp.
Black Marble Base.
14''' Cosmos Screw or Bayonet Duplex Collar.
8/- each.

D 241
Polished Brass Table Lamp.
Iron loaded foot.
14''' Cosmos Screw or Bayonet Duplex Collar.
5/- each.

D 242
Polished Brass Table Lamp.
Fancy cast foot.
14''' Cosmos Screw or Bayonet Duplex Collar.
11/- each.

D 243
Polished Brass Table Lamp.
Embossed.
14''' Cosmos Screw or Bayonet Duplex Collar.
3/6 each.

D 244
Polished Brass Table Lamp,
Iron loaded foot.
14''' Cosmos Screw or Bayonet Duplex Collar.
7/6 each.

D 245
Polished Brass Table Lamp.
Embossed.
14''' Cosmos Screw or Bayonet Duplex Collar.
4/- each.

D 246
Polished Brass Table Lamp.
Iron loaded foot.
14''' Cosmos Screw or Bayonet Duplex Collar.
7/- each.

D 247
Polished Brass Table Lamp.
Iron loaded foot.
14''' Cosmos Screw or Bayonet Duplex Collar.
9/- each.

D 248
Polished Brass Table Lamp.
Iron loaded foot.
14''' Cosmos Screw or Bayonet Duplex Collar.
8/- each.

Extra Strong Copper Bronzed
WALL LAMPS.

ENGLISH MAKE THROUGHOUT.

Scale $\frac{1}{5}$ th.

Special Export Lines.

All Lamps are

Priced without Chimneys.

Special Export Lines.

D 249
Miniature Wall Lamp,
with Gem Burner, Bright Tin Reflector;
Assorted colors, Red, Blue, and Green.
7/6 doz.
Special price 50 doz. lots
7/- doz.
Special price, 100 doz. lots,
6/6 doz.
Packed 50 doz. Lamps per case,
Approximate weights and measurement
Gross   2   2   24 ⎱
             ⎰ 40 × 37 × 27
Net   1   3   4 ⎰

D 250
Strong Copper Bronzed Wall Lamp
with $\frac{3}{4}$ in. 11B Burner,
6 in. Bright Tin Reflector,
10/- doz.
Special price 100 doz. lots,
9/- doz.
Special price 200 doz. lots,
8/6 doz.

D 250A
With 1 in. 11B Burner,
Copper Bronzed or Assorted Colors,
6 in. Bright Tin Reflector,
12/- doz.
Packed 25 doz. Lamps per case.
Approximate weights and measurement
Gross   2   1   10 ⎱
             ⎰ 47 × 35 × 25
Net   1   1   24 ⎰

D 251
Miniature Wall Lamp
with Gem Burner, Glass Mirror Reflector.
Assorted colors, Red, Blue and Green,
7/9 doz.
Special price 50 doz. lots,
7/3 doz.
Special price 100 doz. lots.
6/9 doz.
Packed 50 doz. Lamps per case.
Approximate weights and measurement
Gross   2   2   24 ⎱
             ⎰ 40 × 37 × 27
Net   1   3   4 ⎰

Copper Bronzed Wall Lamps.

Fitted with ¾ in. and 1 in. English Make Burners.

Scale ⅕ th.

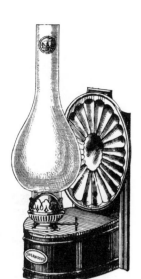

D 252

Copper Bronzed Wall Lamps.

fitted with strong ¾ in. 11B Burner, 6 in. Bright Reflector,

11/- doz.

D 253

Extra strong ¾ in. 12B Burner 6 in. Bright Reflector,

13/6 doz.

D 254

Copper Bronzed Wall Lamp

fitted with strong 1 in. 11B Burner, 6 in. Bright Reflector,

15/6 doz.

D 255

Extra strong 1 in. 12B Burner, 6 in. Bright Reflector,

19/6 doz.

D 256

Copper Bronzed Wall Lamp

fitted with strong 1 in. 12B Burner, 7 in. Bright Reflector,

20/- doz.

D 257

Assorted colours, Bronzed, Red and Green with Gold lines,

22/- doz.

Above Lamps supplied with Feeder 1/- doz. extra.

All Lamps are Priced without Chimneys.

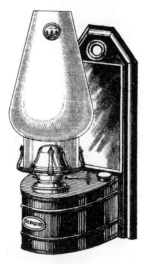

Copper Bronzed Wall Lamp fitted with 6 in. Bright Reflector.

D 258

¾ in. (A) English make Eureka Burner,

13/- doz.

Special price 50 doz. lots, **12/6** doz.

D 259

with ⅝ in. (A) Collars (without Burners),

6/- doz.

D 260

1 in. (B) English make Eureka Burner,

15/- doz.

Special price 50 doz. lots, **14/6** doz.

D 261

with ⅞ in. (B) Collars (without Burners)

6/6 doz.

D 262

Copper Bronzed Wall Lamp fitted with 1 in. English make Eureka Burner. Glass Mirror Reflector.

26/- doz

Special price·50 doz. lots, **25/-** doz.

D 263

with ⅞ in. (B) Collars (without Burners),

17/6 doz.

Copper Bronzed Wall Lamp fitted with 7 in. Bright Reflector.

D 264

¾ in. (A) English make Eureka Burner

17/- doz.

Special price 50 doz. lots, **16/-** doz.

D 265

with ⅝ in (A) Collars (without Burners)

10/6 doz.

D 266

1 in. (B) English make Eureka Burner,

19/6 doz.

Special price 50 doz. lots, **18/6** doz

D 267

with ⅞ in. (B) Collars (without Burners)

11/- doz.

SHERWOODS LAMPS.

Copper Bronzed Wall Lamps.

Scale $\frac{1}{5}$ th.

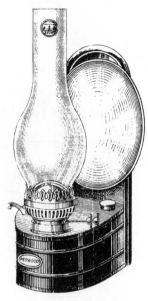

D 268

Copper Bronzed Wall Lamps
fitted with
Strong Duplex Burner, 7 in. Bright Reflector,
36/- doz.

D 269

with 6 in. Silvered Glass Reflector,
48/- doz.

D 270

Copper Bronzed Wall Lamp
fitted with
Strong Duplex Burner, Glass Mirror Reflector,
40/- doz.

D 271

Copper Bronzed Wall Lamps
fitted with
Strong Duplex Burner, 7 in. Bright Reflector,
42/- doz.

D 272

with 7 in. Silvered Glass Reflectors,
60/- doz.

Strong Hand Made Wall Lamps,

With Wired Backs

All Lamps are priced without Chimneys.

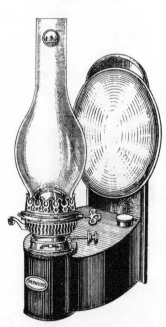

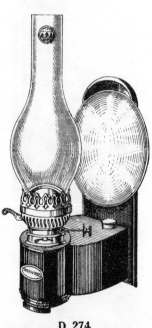

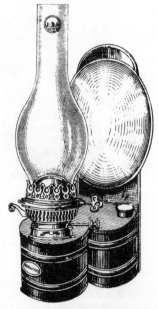

D 273

Strong Hand made, wired back, Bronzed
Wall Lamps, fitted with
Heavy 92B S.W. Raiser Duplex Burner,
7 in. Silvered Glass Reflector.
11/- each.

D 274

Strong Hand made, wired back, Bronzed
Wall Lamp, fitted with
Heavy 22B S.W. Duplex Burner.
6 in. Silvered Glass Reflector.
7/- each.

D 275

Strong Hand made, wired back, Bronzed
Wall Lamps, fitted with
Heavy 92B S.W. Raiser Duplex Burner,
7 in. Silvered Glass Reflector.
13/- each.

Polished Brass Wall Lamps.

Scale $\frac{1}{5}$ th.

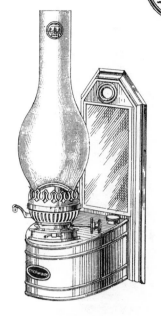

D 276

Polished Brass Wall Lamp
fitted with
Strong 1 in. 12B Burner,
5 in. Silvered Glass Reflector.
5/- each.

D 277

Polished Brass Wall Lamp
fitted with
Extra Strong 1 in. 21B Burner,
6 in. Silvered Glass Reflector.
6/6 each.

D 278

Polished Brass Wall Lamp
fitted with
Strong 22B S.W. Duplex Burner,
Glass Mirror Reflector.
11/- each.

Strong Hand Made Bronzed Wall Lamps,
fitted with
Sherwoods Sun C.D. Burners.

All Lamps are priced without Chimneys.

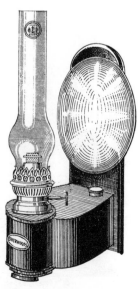

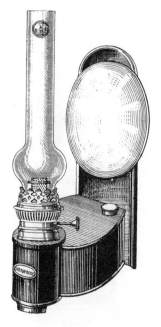

D 279

Strong Hand made Bronzed Wall Lamp
fitted with
Sherwoods 12‴ Sun 30 c.p. C.D. Burner,
6 in. Silvered Glass Reflector,
6/6 each.

D 280

Strong Hand made Black and Gold Wall Lamp
fitted with
Sherwoods 20‴ Sun 60 c.p. C.D. Burner,
7 in. Silvered Glass Reflector.
11/6 each.

D 281

Strong Hand made Bronzed Wall Lamp
fitted with
Sherwoods 16‴ Sun 45 c.p. C.D. Burner,
6 in. Silvered Glass Reflector.
7/6 each.

SHERWOODS LAMPS.

Contractors' Road Lanterns.

Scale ⅛ th.

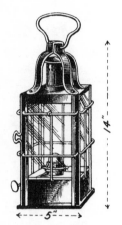

D 282
Strong Red Japanned Lantern
fitted with
⅝ in. no Chimney Burner,
48/- doz.

D 283
with 2 Ruby and 2 clear panes,
60/- doz.

D 284
Strong Red Japanned Lantern
fitted with
¾ in. English make, Eureka Burner,
45/- doz.

D 285
1 in. English make Eureka Burner,
48/- doz.

D 286
Strong Red Japanned Lantern,
fitted with
⅝ in. no Chimney Burner,
66/- doz.

D 287
Strong Red Japanned Lantern,
fitted with
⅝ in. no Chimney Burner.
2 Ruby and 2 clear panes,
84/- doz.

All Lanterns are priced without Chimneys.

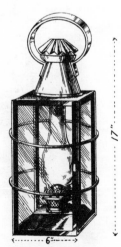

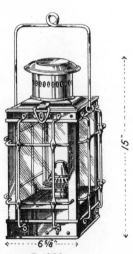

D 288
Strong Green Japanned Lantern
with Galvanized rivetted Top,
fitted with
¾ in. 12B Burner, clear panes,
60/- doz.

D 289
⅝ in. no Chimney Burner,
66/- doz.

D 290
Extra Strong Copper Rivetted Hand made
Galvanized Lantern
with Hinged Top and Container to slide out,
2 Ruby and 2 clear panes,
fitted with
⅝ in. no Chimney Burner,
12/- each.

D 291
Strong Green Japanned Lantern
fitted with
1 in. 12B Burner, clear panes,
78/- doz.

D 292
1 in. no Chimney Burner,
90/- doz.

SHERWOODS LAMPS.

Yard and Contractors' Lanterns.

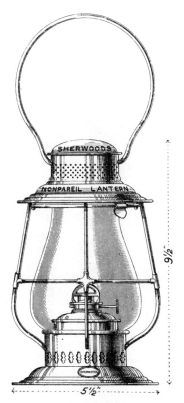

No. 1828

Sherwoods "Nonpareil" Lantern,
complete with globe,
26/- doz.
Packed 3 doz. per case.

Gross ... 1 0 18 ⎫
⎬ L39 W27 D26
Net ... 0 1 20 ⎭

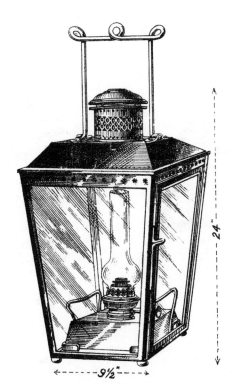

D 293

Extra Strong Green Japanned Lantern to hang up,
with four clear side panes,
fitted with
22B S.W. Heavy Extinguisher Duplex Burner complete,
32/- each.

D 294

Sherwoods 20''' Sun 60 c.p. C.D. Burner complete,
36/- each.

No. 1824

Sherwoods "Defiance" Lantern
complete with globe,
36/- doz.
Packed 3 doz. per case.

Gross ... 1 1 0 ⎫
⎬ L39 W27 D26
Net ... 0 2 4 ⎭

Strong Contractors' Lanterns.

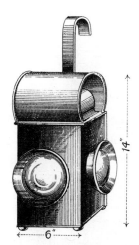

D 295

Strong Contractors' Red Japanned Lantern
fitted with
Sherwoods ⅝ in. Vapour Burner.
One 3½ in. Ruby and two 3½ in. clear lenses,
14/- each.

D 296

Two 3½ in. Ruby and one 3½ in. clear lenses,
16/- each.

D 297

Three 3½ in Ruby lenses.
18/- each.

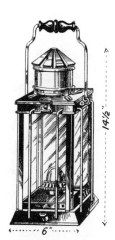

D 298

Strong Contractors' Red Japanned Lantern
with Hinged Top to open,
fitted with
⅝ in. Chimneyless Burner.
2 Ruby and 2 clear glasses,
10/- each.

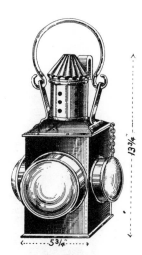

D 299

Heavy Contractors' Red Japanned Lantern.
Extra Strong make with hook strap at back,
fitted with
Sherwoods ⅝ in. Vapour Burner.
One 5 in. Ruby and two 4 in. clear lenses,
16/6 each.

D 300

Two 5 in. Ruby and one 4 in. clear lenses,
18/- each.

Yard and Passage Lanterns.

Scale ⅛ th.

D 301
Strong Green Japanned Lantern
fitted with
¾ in. 12B Burner, 6 in. Reflector,
5/6 each.

D 302
Strong Green Japanned Lantern
fitted with
⅝ in. no Chimney Burner,
6 in. Reflector,
6/- each.

D 303
As above, size larger, (17″ × 9″ × 9″),
fitted with
I in. no Chimney Burner, 8½ in. Reflector.
8/6 each.

D 304
Strong Green Japanned Lantern
fitted with
1 in. 12B Burner, 8½ in. Reflector,
10/- each.

D 305
Strong Green Japanned Lantern
fitted with
Duplex Extinguisher Burner,
8½ in. Reflector,
14/- each.

D 306
Extra Strong Galvanized,
20/- each.

All Lanterns are priced without Chimneys.

D 307
Strong Green Japanned Lantern
Iron Straps at back to nail against wall,
fitted with
1 in. 12B Burner, 8½ in. Reflector,
11/- each.

D 308
Strong Japanned Passage Gas Lantern.
Iron straps at back to nail against wall,
7 in. Silvered Glass Reflector.
(Burner and Chimney extra),
17/- each.

D 309
Strong Green Japanned Lantern.
Iron Straps at back to nail against wall.
fitted with
Duplex Extinguisher Burner. 8½ in. Reflector,
14/- each.

Street Lamps and Accessories.

D 310

Strong Wrought Iron Cradle,
Japanned Black, with Set Screw.
15/- each.

D 311

Strong Wrought Iron Wall Bracket,
Japanned Black.
27/- each.

D 312

Strong Wrought Iron Socket for Post
can be supplied fitted
on Nos. **D 313** and **D 315** Street Lamps, extra Cost.
6/- each.

D 313

Square Top.
Extra Strong Wind proof Street Lamp
fitted with
Raiser 92ʙ S.W. Duplex Burner and chimney,
26 oz. Opal Top and 21 oz. Clear Side Panes.
36/- each

Extra Cost with 1 lettered pane
(name of Station or Town).
5/- each.

Full length 12 ft. 7 in.

37″

9′ 5½″

1′ 9″

D 314

Strong Cast Iron Street Lamp Column
fitted with
Complete Lamp as Drawn.
£6 each.

D 314 A

Cast Iron Column only,
72/- each

Spare sets of glass for Nos. D 313, D 315.
4 26 ozs. Opal top panes and 4 21 ozs. clear side panes.
9/- per set.

D 315

Extra Strong Wind proof Street Lamp
with Copper Top.
20‴ Sun, 60 c.p. C D. Burner and Chimney.
26 oz. Opal Top, 21 oz. Clear Side Panes.
40/- each.

Extra Cost with 1 lettered Pane
(name of Station or Town).
5/- each.

SHERWOODS LAMPS.

Spirit Lamps and Stoves.

Scale $\frac{1}{5}$ th.

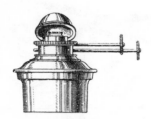

D 316

Polished Brass Spirit Lamp,
fitted with
136B $\frac{1}{2}$ in. round Wick Burner, with Extinguisher.
30/- doz.

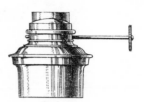

D 317

Polished Brass Spirit Lamp,
fitted with
31B 1 in. Flat Wick Burner.
21/- doz.

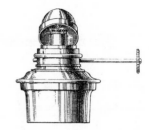

D 318

Polished Brass Spirit Lamp,
fitted with
42B $\frac{1}{2}$ in. round Wick Burner with Extinguisher.
24/- dozen.

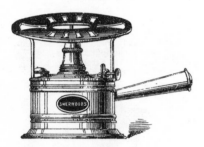

D 319

Small Size,
Bright Tin Spirit Stove with Plate,
with Feeder, Extinguisher Cap and Wick
15/- doz.

D 320

Strong Polished Brass Spirit Lamp,
with Plate Protector.
1 in. Flat Wick Burner, with Safety Capped
and Cased Tube Spindles
(guaranteed not to fire).
6/- each.

D 321

Large Size.
Bright Tin Spirit Stove with Plate,
with Feeder, Extinguisher Cap and Wick.
17/- doz.

Spare Steel Stove Plates, 2/- doz.

D 322

Small Size.
Bright Tin Spirit Stove with Plate,
with Feeder, Extinguisher Cap and Wick,
with Black Wood Handle.
19/- doz.

D 323

Polished Brass Spirit Stove with Plate,
with Feeder, Extinguisher Cap and Wick
with Black Wood Handle.
6/- each.

This stove is boxed singly complete
with detachable screw handle for packing.

D 324

Large Size.
Bright Tin Spirit Stove with Plate,
with Feeder, Extinguisher Cap and Wick,
with Black Wood Handle
21/- doz.

SHERWOODS LAMPS.
Tin Hand Lamps.

D 325
Large Bright Tin Hand Lamp
Tin Burner and Wick.
36/- gross.
Special price 10 Gross lots,
33/- gross

Scale ¼ th.

D 326
Pillar Benzo Lamp,
Japanned assorted colours, Red, Blue and Green.
7/- doz.
Special price 10 gross lots,
6/6 doz.
Approximate Weights and Measurement.
Packed 25 doz. per case.

Gross 1 3 8 }
Net   1 0 0 }   L37 W29 D33

D 327
Large Bright Tin Hand Lamp
with Dish,
Tin Burner and Wick,
48/- gross.
Special price 10 gross lots.
45/- gross.

D 328
Bright Tin Hand Lamp
with Dish.
Brass Burner with Cap and Chain
48/- gross.
Special price 10 gross lots,
45/- gross.

D 329
Bright Tin Hand Lamp.
Brass Burner with Cap and Chain
45/- gross.
Special price 10 gross lots.
42/- gross.

D 330
Bright Tin Hand Lamp,
Tin Burner and Wick.
36/- gross.
Special price 10 gross lots.
33/- gross.

D 331
Bright Tin Hand Lamp,
Tin Burner and Wick.
33/- gross.
Special price 10 gross lots,
30/- gross.

D 332
Bright Tin Hand Lamp.
Tin Burner and Wick.
30/- gross.
Special price 10 gross lots.
27/- gross.

The above lamps electro coppered finish
12/- gross extra

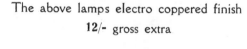

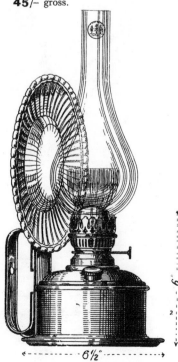

D 333
Strong Copper Bronzed Hand or Wall Lamp,
fitted with
1 in. 11B Burner, 8½ in. Bright Tin Reflector
with Chimney, complete as drawn.
30/- doz.

D 334
Strong Tin Hand Lamp,
Japanned assorted colours, Red, Blue and Green,
fitted with
¾ in. 11B Burner and Chimney,
Complete as drawn.
16/- doz.

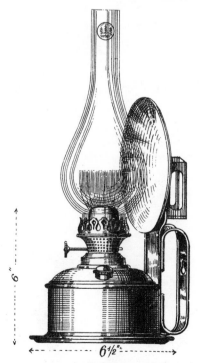

D 335
Strong Copper Bronzed Hand or Wall Lamp,
fitted with
1 in. 12B Burner, 7 in. Glass Reflector,
with Chimney, complete as drawn,
40/- doz.

SHERWOODS LAMPS.

SHERWOODS "LION" BRAND.
Brass Benzo Kaffir Lamps.

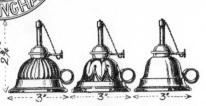

490   **491**   **489**

Set No. 0.
Assorted three patterns in boxes of 1 doz.
3/6 doz.
Case quantity 120 doz. lots, **3/3** doz.

425

O. K. Burner,
three sizes.

424	$3\frac{1}{2} \times 4$	**7/6** doz.
425	$4 \times 4\frac{3}{4}$	**9/6** ,,
426	$4\frac{1}{2} \times 5$	**11/-** ,,

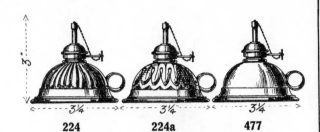

224   **224a**   **477**

Set No. 1.
Assorted three patterns in boxes of 1 doz.
4/- doz.
Case quantity 120 doz. lots, **3/9** doz.

If required with White Buttons on Handles, 6/- gross extra.

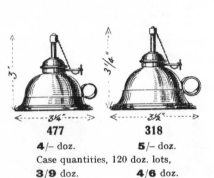

477   **318**

4/- doz.   **5/-** doz.
Case quantities, 120 doz. lots,
3/9 doz.   **4/6** doz.

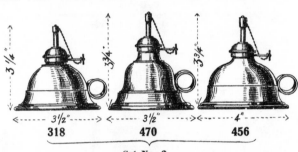

318   **470**   **456**

Set No. 2.
Assorted three patterns in boxes of 1 doz.
5/6 doz.
Case quantity 120 doz. lots, **5/-** doz.

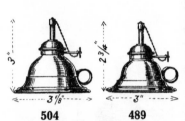

504   **489**

3/8 doz.   **3/6** doz.
Case quantities,   120 doz. lots,
3/5 doz.   **3/3** doz.

When ordering specify SHERWOODS "LION" BRAND Brass Benzo Lamps.

All Lamps are tested by Machinery before leaving our Works, and Guaranteed not to leak.

554   **84**   **470**   **518**   **456**   **555**   **474**

3/3 doz.   **5/6** doz.   **5/6** doz.   **5/9** doz.   **6/-** doz.   **6/-** doz.   **6/6** doz.
240 doz. lots,   120 doz. lots,   120 doz. lots,   120 doz. lots.   120 doz. lots,   120 doz. lots,   120 doz. lots,
3/- doz.   **5/-** doz.   **5/-** doz.   **5/3** doz.   **5/6** doz.   **5/6** doz.   **6/-** doz.

Without cap and chain,
1/6 gross less.

Specially Prepared Benzo Wicks, per gross packets, 6 in. long, 2/6 gross.

All Lamps are boxed dozens.

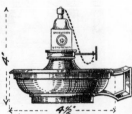

250   **280**   **551**   **93c**   **319**   **301a**

5/6 doz.   **5/6** doz.   **5/9** doz.   China top burner   China top Burner,   China top Burner,
120 doz. lots,   120 doz. lots,   120 doz. lots,   **11/-** doz.   **11/-** doz.   **13/-** doz.
5/- doz.   **5/-** doz.   **5/3** doz.   30 doz. lots,   30 doz. lots,   30 doz. lots.
 | | | **10/-** doz.   **10/-** doz.   **12/-** doz.

SHERWOODS LAMPS.

SHERWOODS "LION" BRAND.
Brass Pillar Benzo Kaffir Lamps.

358
8/- doz.
30 doz. lots,
7/- doz.

355
9/- doz.
30 doz. lots,
8/- doz.

429
11/- doz.
30 doz. lots,
10/- doz.

362
10/6 doz.
30 doz. lots,
9/6 doz.

248
8/- doz.
30 doz. lots,
7/- doz.

247
9/6 doz.
30 doz. lots,
8/- doz.

245
10/- doz.
30 doz. lots,
9/- doz.

537
10/- doz.
30 doz. lots,
9/- doz.

All Lamps are tested by Machinery before leaving our Works, and Guaranteed not to leak.

468
12/- doz.
30 doz. lots,
11/- doz.

366
11/6 doz.
30 doz. lots,
10/- doz.

510 **511** **512**
Set No. 3.
Assorted three patterns in boxes of ¼ doz.
9/6 doz.
Case quantity 30 doz. lots, **8/6** doz.

428
11/6 doz.
30 doz. lots,
10/6 doz.

430
13/- doz.
30 doz. lots.
12/- doz.

Specially Prepared Benzo Wicks, per gross packets, 6 in. long, 2/6 gross.

When ordering specify SHERWOODS "LION" BRAND Brass Benzo Lamps

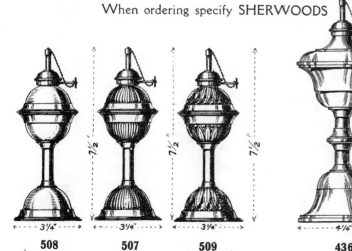
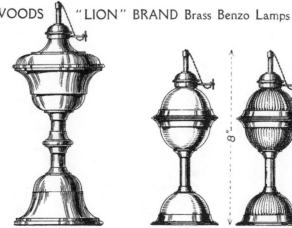
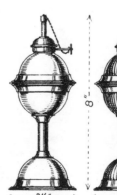

508 **507** **509**
Set No. 4.
Assorted three patterns in boxes of ¼ doz.
10/6 doz.
Case quantity 30 doz. lots, **9/6** doz.

436
18/- doz.

440 **219** **219a**
Set No. 5.
Assorted three patterns in boxes of ¼ doz.
11/6 doz.
Case quantity 30 doz. lots, **10/6** doz.

The "MAGIC"
Safety Night Light Lamps.

SHERWOODS
(all Brass)
Magic Night Light Lamps
are the best
value and quality on the markets.

Each lamp boxed complete.

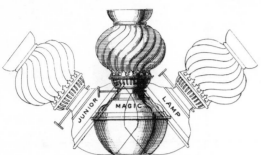

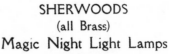

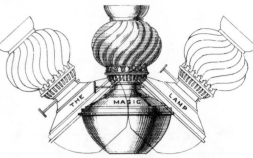

D 336
JUNIOR MAGIC LAMP.
Polished Brass Self-Righting Lamp,
Iron loaded,
with Ribbed Opal Globe complete,
10/- doz.

Scale ⅓ rd.

D 337
THE MAGIC LAMP.
Polished Brass Self-Righting Lamp,
Iron loaded,
with Ribbed Opal Globe complete,
14/- doz.

(Shown as Table Lamp.)

(Shown as Wall Bracket Lamp.)

D 338
Polished Brass Hand Lamp,
Night Light Burner,
with Ribbed Opal Globe complete,
11/- doz.

D 339
THE LUNA LAMP.
Polished Brass Table or Wall Lamp,
Night Light Burner,
with Ribbed Opal Globe complete,
13/- doz.
Copper or Nickel Plated complete,
16/- doz.

D 340
Polished Brass Hand Lamp,
Night Light Burner,
With Ribbed Opal Globe complete.
11/6 doz.

(Shown as Table Lamp.)

(Shown as Wall Bracket Lamp.)

(Shown as Wall Bracket Lamp.)

(Shown as Table Lamp.)

D 341
THE "UNO" LAMP.
Polished Brass Table or Wall Swing Lamp.
Iron loaded Container,
with Ribbed Opal Globe complete.
17/- doz.

D 342
THE GIMBAL LAMP.
Polished Brass Table or Wall Swing Lamp.
Iron loaded Container and foot,
with Ribbed Opal Globe complete.
21/- doz.

These lamps are boxed singly in cardboard boxes.

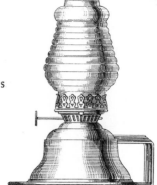

"ELVELIT"
Safety Night Light Lamps.

Fitted with

Gem Burners and New Shape large Ribbed Opal Globes

Scale ⅓ rd.

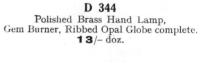

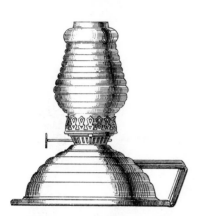

D 343
Polished Brass Hand Lamp,
Gem Burner, Ribbed Opal Globe complete.
12/3 doz.

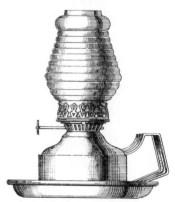

D 344
Polished Brass Hand Lamp,
Gem Burner, Ribbed Opal Globe complete.
13/- doz.

D 345
Polished Brass Hand Lamp,
Gem Burner, Ribbed Opal Globe complete.
14/- doz

D 346
Wall Night Light Lamp.
Japanned Assorted colours, Red, Blue and Green,
Gem Burner, Ribbed Opal Globe complete,
with Bright Tin Reflector.
10/6 doz.
Special price 12 doz. lots,
10/- doz.

D 347
Polished Brass Hand Lamp,
Gem Burner, Ribbed Opal Globe
17/- doz.

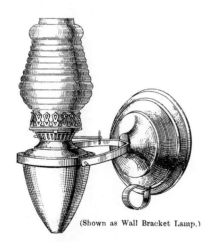

(Shown as Wall Bracket Lamp.)

D 348
Polished Brass Table or Wall Swing Lamp,
Iron loaded Container and foot,
Gem Burner, Ribbed Opal Globe complete.
22/6 doz

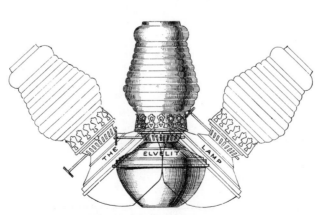

D 349
THE "ELVELIT" LAMP.
Polished Brass Self-righting Lamp,
Iron loaded
Gem Burner, Ribbed Opal Globe.
15/6 doz.

(Shown as Table Lamp.)

D 348
Polished Brass Table or Wall Swing Lamp,
Iron loaded Container and foot.
Gem Burner, Ribbed Opal Globe complete.
22/6 doz.

These lamps are boxed singly in cardboard boxes.

SHERWOODS LAMPS.

Polished Brass Hand Lamps.

D 351
Polished Brass Hand Lamp,
fitted with
Gem Burner and Chimney.
9/6 doz.

D 352
Polished Brass Hand Lamp,
fitted with
Gem Burner and Chimney.
10/6 doz.

D 353
Polished Brass Hand Lamp,
fitted with
Gem Burner and Chimney.
11/– doz.

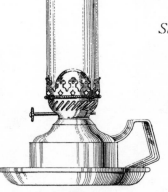

Scale ⅓ rd

D 354
Polished Brass Hand Lamp,
fitted with
13B ½ in. Bijou Extinguisher Burner and Chimney,
21/– doz.

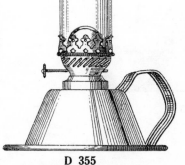

D 355
Polished Brass Hand Lamp,
fitted with
13B ½ in. Bijou Extinguisher Burner and Chimney,
24/– doz.

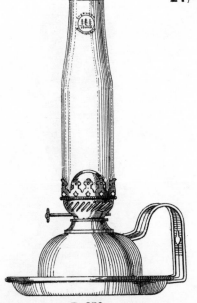

D 356
Polished Brass Hand Lamp,
fitted with
13B ½ in. Bijou Extinguisher Burner and Chimney.
25/– doz.

D 357
Polished Brass Safety Hand Lamp,
Iron loaded.
fitted with
13B ½ in. Bijou Extinguisher Burner and Chimney.
30/– doz.

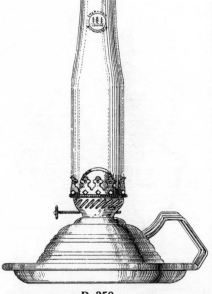

D 358
Polished Brass Hand Lamp,
fitted with
13B ½ in. Bijou Extinguisher Burner and Chimney.
26/– doz.

SHERWOODS LAMPS.

Polished Brass Hand Lamps.

D 359
Polished Brass Hand Lamp,
fitted with
88B ¾ in. Bijou Burner and Chimney
27/- doz.

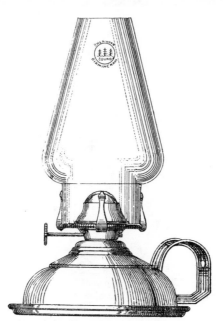

D 360
Polished Brass Hand Lamp,
fitted with
83B ¾ in. Eureka Burner and Chimney,
26/- doz.

D 361
Polished Brass Hand Lamp,
fitted with
88B ¾ in. Bijou Burner and Chimney,
26/- doz.

Scale ⅓ rd

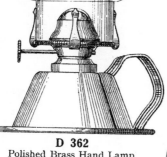

D 362
Polished Brass Hand Lamp,
fitted with
83B ¾ in. Eureka Burner and Chimney
25/- doz.

D 363
Polished Brass Hand Lamp,
fitted with
83B ¾ in. Eureka Burner and Chimney,
27/- doz.

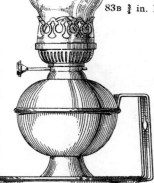

D 364
Polished Brass Hand Lamp,
fitted with
B ¾ in. Bijou Burner and Chimney,
28/- doz.

D 365
Polished Brass Hand Lamp,
fitted with
88B ¾ in. Bijou Burner and Chimney,
32/- doz.

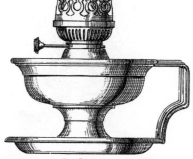

D 366
Polished Brass Hand Lamp,
fitted with
88B ¾ in. Bijou Burner and Chimney,
31/- doz.

SHERWOODS LAMPS.

Polished Brass Hand Lamps.

Scale ⅓ rd.

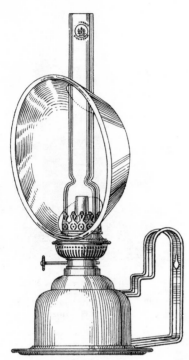

D 367
Polished Brass Hand Lamp,
Nickel Plated Hood Reflector.
6‴ Cosmos Burner and Chimney,
42/- doz.

D 368
Nickel Plated Hand Lamp complete,
48/- doz.

D 369
Polished Brass Hand Lamp,
Nickel Plated Hood Reflector.
6‴ Cosmos Burner and Chimney,
48/-doz.

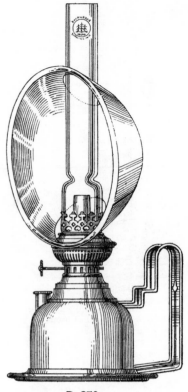

D 370
Polished Brass Hand Lamp,
Nickel Plated Hood Reflector.
10‴ Cosmos Burner and Chimney,
60/- doz.

D 371
Nickel Plated Hand Lamp complete.
72/- doz.

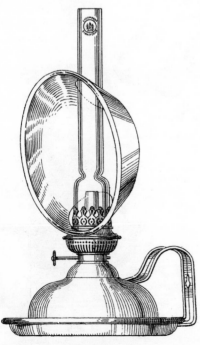

D 372
Polished Brass Hand Lamp,
Nickel Plated Hood Reflector,
6‴ Cosmos Burner and Chimney,
45/- doz.

D 373
Polished Brass Hand Lamp.
Nickel Plated Hood Reflector,
10‴ Cosmos Burner and Chimney,
66/- doz.

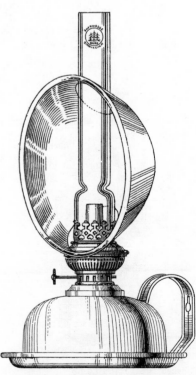

D 374
Polished Brass Hand Lamp.
Nickel Plated Hood Reflector.
10‴ Cosmos Burner and Chimney.
60/- doz.

Chamber Candle Lamps.

Scale ⅕th.

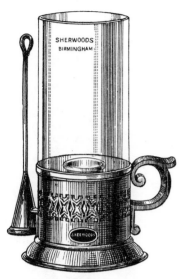

D 375
Chamber Candle Lamp.
Japanned Assorted colours, Red, Blue and Green,
fitted with
6 in. × 3 in. Cylinder and Extinguisher,
21/6 doz.

D 376
Chamber Candle Lamp with Dish.
Japanned Assorted colours, Red, Blue and Green,
fitted with
7 in. × 1 11/16 in. Cylinder and Extinguisher,
24/– doz

D 376 A
Polished Brass or Steel Bronzed
complete.
48/– doz.

D 377
Chamber Candle Lamp.
Japanned Assorted colours, Red, Blue and Green,
fitted with
7 in. × 3⅜ in. Cylinder and Extinguisher,
28/– doz.

Crystal Glass Cylinders.

6 in. × 3, **8/–** doz.
Gross lots, **6/–** doz.

7 in. × 1 11/16 in., **9/–** doz
Gross lots, **8/–** doz.
Brass Mounts for same, **5/–** doz.

7 in. × 3⅜ in, **8/–** doz.
Gross lots, **6/–** doz.

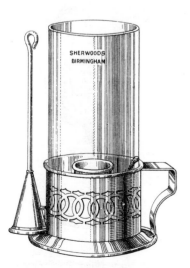

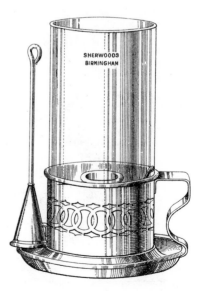

D 378
Chamber Candle Lamp.
Polished Brass or Steel Bronzed,
fitted with
6 in. × 3 in. Cylinder and Extinguisher,
40/– doz.

D 379
Chamber Candle Lamp,
Polished Brass or Steel Bronzed,
fitted with
7 in. × 3⅜ in. Cylinder and Extinguisher,
54/– doz.

D 380
Chamber Candle Lamp with Dish.
Polished Brass or Steel Bronzed,
fitted with
7 in. × 3⅜ in. Cylinder and Extinguisher,
56/– doz.

SHERWOODS LAMPS.

Brass and Copper Bijou Lamps.

Scale ⅕th.

D 381

Fancy Copper and Brass Bijou Lamp
fitted with
88B Burner, Assorted English made
Globes and Chimney complete,
9/– each.

D 382

Polished Brass Bijou Table Lamp
fitted with
88B Burner, Silk Shade, Shade holder & Chimney
complete,
10/– each.

D 383

Fancy Copper and Brass Bijou Lamp
fitted with
88B Burner, Assorted English made Globes
and Chimney complete,
9/6 each.

All Lamps are priced. complete as drawn.

D 384

Polished Brass Bijou Table Lamp
fitted with
88B Burner, Silk Shade, Shade Holder,
and Chimney complete,
11/– each.

D 385

Fancy Copper and Brass Bijou Lamp
fitted with
88B Burner, Assorted English made Globes
and Chimney complete.
10/6 each.

D 386

Polished Brass Bijou Table Lamp
fitted with
88B Burner, Silk Shade, Shade Holder
and Chimney complete.
11/– each.

Brass and Copper Bijou Lamps.

Scale ⅕th.

D 387
Fancy Copper Bijou Lamp
fitted with
88ʙ Burner, Silk Shade, Shade Holder
and Chimney complete.
10/6 each.

D 388
Fancy Bijou Lamp
fitted with
88ʙ Burner, Assorted English made Globes
and Chimney complete.

Polished Brass.	Polished Copper.
8/- each	**9**/- each.

D 389
Fancy Copper Bijou Lamp
fitted with
88ʙ Burner, Silk Shade, Shade Holder
and Chimney complete.
11/6 each.

All Lamps are priced complete as drawn.

D 390
Fancy Copper and Brass Bijou Lamp
fitted with
88ʙ Burner, Assorted English made Globes
and Chimney complete.
13/- each.

D 391
Bijou Table Lamp
fitted with
88ʙ Burner, Silk Shade, Shade Holder
and Chimney complete.

Polished Brass	Polished Copper.
11/- each.	**12**/- each.

D 392
Fancy Copper and Brass Bijou Lamp
fitted with
88ʙ Burner, Assorted English made Globes
and Chimney complete.
13/- each.

Polished Brass Table Lamp,

with extra strong

¾ in. ENGLISH MAKE BURNER.

The "BRITISH" Lamp.

Scale ¼ th.

SPECIAL EXPORT LINE.

SPECIAL EXPORT LINE.

PACKING.
Approximate weight and measurements.
Case containing
6 doz. Table Lamps, Burners and Shade Holders.

Gross ... **1 2 26**
L36 W23 D42
Net ... **0 3 24**

PACKING.
Approximate weight and measurements,
Case containing
4 doz. Table Lamps, Burners and Shade Holders
5 doz. 7¼ Opal Shades.
6 doz. ¾ in. Straight Chimneys.
6 rolls ¾ in. Wick.

Gross ... **2 1 24**
L47 W36 D32
Net ... **1 1 26**

Approximate weight and measurements.
Case containing
6 doz. 7¼ Opal Shades.
7 doz. ¾ in. Bulge Chimneys.
12 rolls ¾ in. Wick.

Gross ... **2 2 10**
L42 W33 D34
Net ... **0 3 8**

D 393
Polished Brass Table Lamp.
fitted with
Strong ¾ in. ENGLISH MAKE Burner.
7¼ in. Opal Shade and Chimney complete.
55/- doz.
Special price 6 doz. lots,
50/- doz.

D 394
With 7¼ in. Green cased Opal Shade and Chimney.
77/- doz.

All Lamps are tested by Machinery
before leaving our Works,
and are
Guaranteed not to leak.

All Lamps are tested by Machinery
before leaving our Works,
and are
Guaranteed not to leak.

Polished Brass Table Lamps.

Scale ⅕ th.

with extra strong
¾ in. ENGLISH MAKE BURNER

with extra strong
¾ in. ENGLISH MAKE BURNER

D 395
Polished Brass Table Lamp
with ¾ in. ENGLISH MAKE Burner.
27/- doz.
Special price 6 doz. lots,
25/- doz.

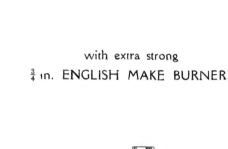

All Lamps are   Priced without Glass.

D 396
Polished Brass Table Lamp,
with ¾ in. ENGLISH MAKE Burner, 3 in. Gallery.
30/- doz.

D 397
Polished Brass Table Lamp,
Black Marble Base.
with ¾ in. ENGLISH MAKE Burner, 3 in. Gallery.
50/- doz.

D 398
Polished Brass Table Lamp
Black Marble Base.
with ¾ in. ENGLISH MAKE Burner, 7¼ in. Shade Holder,
60/- doz.

When ordered with Green Cased Opal Shades, Lamps are mounted on Green Marble Bases to match.

SHERWOODS LAMPS.

Polished Brass Table Lamp,

with extra strong

1 in. ENGLISH MAKE BURNER.

The "SERVICE" Lamp.

Scale ¼ th.

SPECIAL EXPORT LINE

SPECIAL EXPORT LINE.

PACKING.
Approximate weight and measurements.
Case containing
3 doz. Table Lamps, Burners, and Shade Holders.
4 doz. 7¼ Opal Shades.
5 doz. 1 in. Straight Chimneys.
6 doz. 1 in. Wicks.

Gross ... **1 2 24**
Net ... **0 3 18**   47 × 30 × 31

PACKING.
Approximate weight and measurements.
Case containing
6 doz. Table Lamps, Burners, and Shade Holders.

Gross ... **1 3 0**
Net ... **0 3 20**   39 × 28 × 28

Approximate weight and measurements.
Case containing
6 doz. 7¼ Opal Shades.
9 doz. 1 in. Straight Chimneys.
12 doz. 1 in. Wicks.

Gross ... **2 2 18**
Net ... **0 3 8**   42 × 33 × 34

D 399
Polished Brass Table Lamp
fitted with
Strong 1 in. ENGLISH MAKE Burner.
7¼ in. Opal Shade and Chimneys complete
60/– doz.
Special price 6 doz. lots.
55/– doz.

D 400
With 7¼ in. Green cased Opal Shade and Chimney,
82/- doz.

All Lamps are tested by Machinery
before leaving our Works,
and are
Guaranteed not to leak.

All Lamps are Tested by Machinery
before leaving our Works,
and are
Guaranteed not to leak.

SHERWOODS LAMPS.

Polished Brass Table Lamps.

Scale ⅕ th.

with extra strong

1 in. ENGLISH MAKE BURNERS.

with extra strong

1 in. ENGLISH MAKE BURNERS.

D 401
Polished Brass Table Lamp
with 1 in ENGLISH MAKE Burner,
32/- doz.
Special price 6 doz. lots.
29/- doz.

All Lamps are   Priced without Glass.

D 402
Polished Brass Table Lamp,
with 1 in. ENGLISH MAKE Burner, **3** in. Gallery.
35/- doz.

D 403
Polished Brass Table Lamp,
Black Marble Base.
with 1 in. ENGLISH MAKE Burner, **3** in. Gallery
54/- doz.

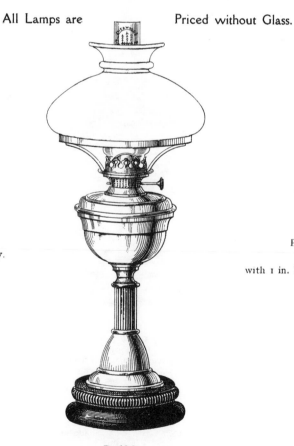

D 404
Polished Brass Table Lamp,
with Black Marble Base.
1 in. ENGLISH MAKE Burner, 7¼ in. Shade Holder
72/- doz.

When ordered with Green Cased Opal Shades, Lamps are mounted on Green Marble Bases to match.

SHERWOODS LAMPS.

Polished Brass Table Lamp,

with 10''' Cosmos Burner.

The "AFRICAN" Lamp.

Scale ¼ th.

SPECIAL EXPORT LINE.

Approximate weights and measurements.
Case containing
3 doz. Table Lamps, Burners, and Shade Holders
Gross ... **1 0 10**
$33 \times 25 \times 25$
Net ... **0 2 4**

Approximate weights and measurements.
Case containing
4 doz. 7¼ in. Opal Shades.
6 doz. 10''' Cosmos Chimneys.
6 rolls 10''' Cosmos Wicks.
Gross ... **1 0 20**
$39 \times 27 \times 27$
Net ... **0 1 14**

All Lamps are tested by Machinery
before leaving our Works,
and are
Guaranteed not to leak.

SPECIAL EXPORT LINE.

Approximate weights and measurements.
Case containing
6 doz. Table Lamps, Burners, and Shade Holders.
Gross ... **1 3 16**
$43 \times 25 \times 34$
Net ... **1 0 12**

Approximate weights and measurements
Case containing
6 doz. 7¼ in. Opal Shades.
9 doz. 10''' Cosmos Chimneys.
1 doz. rolls 10''' Cosmos Wick.
Gross ... **2 0 6**
$42 \times 33 \times 22$
Net ... **0 2 8**

All Lamps are tested by Machinery
before leaving our Works,
and are
Guaranteed not to leak.

D 405
Polished Brass Table Lamp
fitted with
10'''Cosmos Burner, 7¼ in. Opal Shade & Chimney
complete as drawn.
54/- doz.
Special price 6 doz. Lamps complete
50/- doz.

D 406
With 7¼ in. Green Cased Opal Shade and Chimney,
75/- doz.

SHERWOODS LAMPS.

Polished Brass Table Lamps,

Fitted with 10''' Cosmos Burners.

Scale ⅕ th.

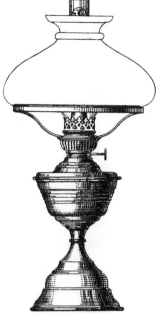

D 407
Polished Brass Table Lamp,
fitted with
10''' Cosmos Burner, 7¼ in. Shade Holder.
39/- doz.
6 doz. lots **36/-** doz.

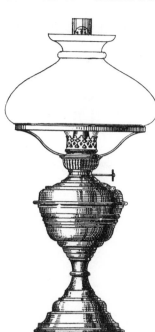

D 408
Polished Brass Table Lamp,
fitted with
10''' Cosmos Burner, 7¼ in. Shade Holder.
42/- doz.
6 doz. lots **39/-** doz.

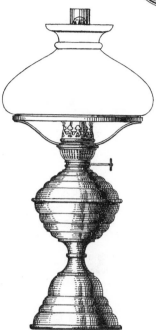

D 409
Polished Brass Table Lamp,
fitted with
10''' Cosmos Burner, 7¼ in. Shade Holder.
45/- doz.
6 doz. lots **42/-** doz.

All Lamps are Priced without Glass.

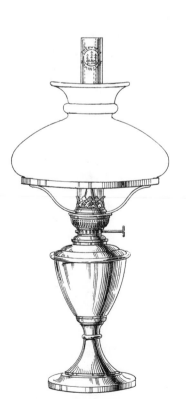

D 410
Superior Polished Table Lamp,
fitted with
10''' Cosmos Burner, 7¼ in. Shade Holder.
Brass   Copper
60/– doz.   **66/–** doz.

D 411
Polished Brass Table Lamp,
with Black Marble Base.
fitted with
10''' Cosmos Burner, 7¼ in. Shade Holder.
6/6 each.
When ordered with Green Cased Opal Shade
Lamp is mounted on Green Marble Base to match.

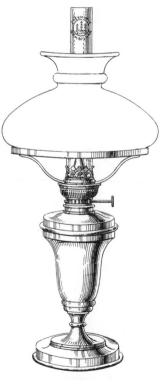

D 412
Superior Polished Table Lamp,
fitted with
10''' Cosmos Burner, 7¼ in. Shade Holder.
Brass.   Copper.
66/– doz.   **72/–** doz.

SHERWOODS LAMPS.

Polished Brass Duplex Table Lamp,
with Black Marble Base Stand.

The "COUNTY" Lamp.

Scale ¼ th.

SPECIAL EXPORT LINE.

SPECIAL EXPORT LINE.

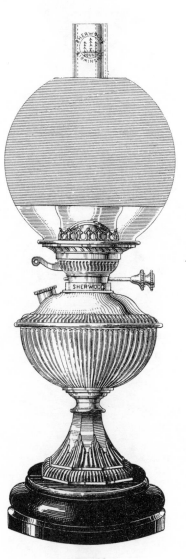

Approximate weights and measurements.
Packed in No. 3 CASKS.
3 doz. Marble Base Stands
Gross ... **1 3 20**
Net ... **1 1 4**   28 × 28

Approximate weights and measurements,
packed in No. 1 CASKS.
6 doz. Marble Base Stands.
Gross ... **3 1 12**
Net ... **2 2 8**   40 × 31

Approximate case weights and measurements.
3 doz. Brass Founts, and Duplex Burners.
Gross ... **1 1 4**
Net ... **0 2 4**   33 × 25 × 25

Approximate case weights and measurements.
6 doz. Brass Founts and Duplex Burners.
Gross ... **1 1 20**
Net ... **0 3 12**   39 × 27 × 29

Approximate case weights and measurements.
4 doz. ¾ Frosted 7½ × 4 in. Mono Duplex Globes.
6 doz. Duplex Chimneys.
9 doz. Duplex Wicks.
Gross ... **2 0 16**
Net ... **0 2 18**   50 × 37 × 24

Approximate case weights and measurements,
(original case quantities).
8 doz. 7½ × 4 in. Mono Globes.
Gross ... **2 2 4**
Net ... **0 3 12**   60 × 39 × 36
24 doz. Duplex Chimneys.
Gross ... **2 0 26**
Net ... **0 3 12**   48 × 34 × 35

D 413
Polished Brass Table Lamp,
"H" 7 in. Black Base.
No. 23B Extinguishing Duplex Burner and Gallery,
7½ × 4 in. Mono Frosted Globe and Chimney,
complete as drawn.
10/6 each.
Special price 3 doz. lamps complete,
10/- each.
Special price 6 doz. lamps complete,
9/6 each.

All Lamps are Tested by Machinery
before leaving our Works,
and are
Guaranteed not to leak.

All Lamps are Tested by Machinery
before leaving our Works,
and are
Guaranteed not to leak.

Polished Brass Duplex Table Lamps.

Scale ⅕ th.

D 414

Polished Brass or Steel Bronzed Table Lamp,
"A" 7 in. Black Base.
No. 23B Exting. Duplex Burner and Gallery.
6/6 each.

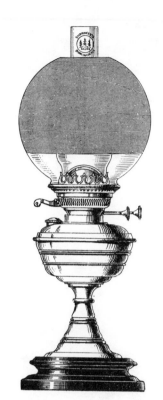

D 415

Polished Brass or Steel Bronzed Table Lamp,
"A" 7 in. Black Base.
No. 23B Exting. Duplex Burner and Gallery,
5/6 each.

D 416

Polished Brass or Steel Bronzed Table Lamp,
"A" 7 in. Black Base.
No. 23B Exting. Duplex Burner and Gallery.
6/6 each.

All Lamps are Priced without Glass.

D 417

Polished Brass Table Lamp,
Cut Glass Crystal Fount,
"A" 7 in. Black Base.
No. 23B Exting. Duplex Burner and Gallery.
6/7 each.

D 418

Polished Brass Table Lamp,
Cut Glass Crystal Fount,
"H" 7 in. Black Base.
No. 23B Exting. Duplex Burner and Gallery.
6/6 each.

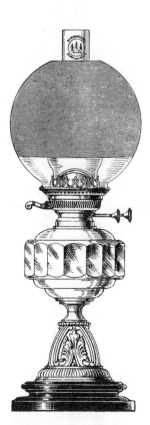

D 419

Polished Brass Table Lamp,
Cut Glass Crystal Fount,
"A" 7 in. Black Base.
No. 23B Exting. Duplex Burner and Gallery,
6/7 each.

SHERWOODS LAMPS.
Polished Brass Duplex Table Lamps.

REGISTERED TRADE MARK SOUND

Scale ⅕ th.

D 420

Polished Brass Table Lamp.
" A " 7 in. Black Base.
No. 23B Exting. Duplex Burner and Gallery.
7/3 each.

D 421

Polished Brass Table Lamp.
" A " 7 in. Black Base.
No. 23B Exting. Duplex Burner and Gallery.
8/6 each.

D 422

Polished Brass Table Lamp.
" A " 7 in. Black Base.
No. 23B Exting. Duplex Burner and Gallery.
7/6 each.

All Lamps are Priced without Glass.

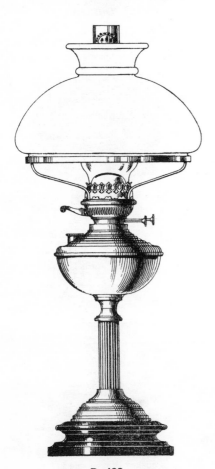

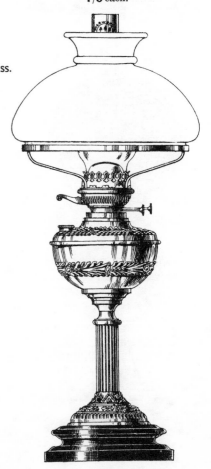

D 423

Polished Brass Pillar Table Lamp.
" A " 7 in. Black Base.
No. 29B Exting. Duplex Burner, 9¼in. Shade holder
7/9 each.

D 424

Polished Brass Table Lamp.
" D " 7½ in. Black Base.
No. 133B Exting. Duplex Burner, fixed Gallery.
12/9 each.

D 425

Polished Brass Pillar Table Lamp.
" A " 7 in. Black Base.
No. 29B Exting. Duplex Burner, 9¼in. Shade holder
8/- each.

SHERWOODS LAMPS.

Polished Brass   Duplex Table Lamps.

Scale ⅕ th.

D 426

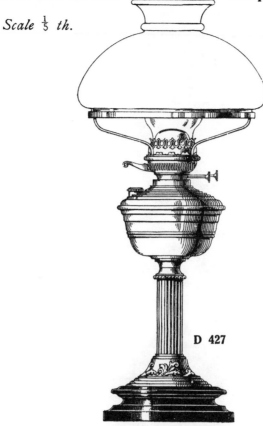

D 427

D 428

Polished Brass Pillar Table Lamp.
" A " 7 in. Black Base.
No. 23ʙ Exting. Duplex Burner and Gallery.
8/- each.

Polished Brass Pillar Table Lamp.
" A " 7 in. Black Base.
No. 29ʙ Exting. Duplex Burner, 9¼ in. Shade holder
9/- each.

Polished Brass Pillar Table Lamp.
" A " 7 in. Black Base.
No. 23ʙ Exting. Duplex Burner and Gallery.
8/6 each.

All Lamps are   Priced without Glass.

D 429

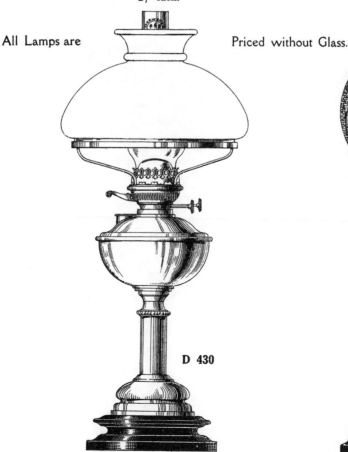

D 430

D 431

Polished Brass Pillar Table Lamp.
" A " 7 in. Black Base.
No. 23ʙ Exting. Duplex Burner and Gallery.
9/- each.

Polished Brass Pillar Table Lamp.
" A " 7 in. Black Base.
No. 29ʙ Exting. Duplex Burner, 9¼in. Shade holder
10/- each.

Polished Brass Pillar Table Lamp.
Cut Crystal Fount.
" A " 7 in. Black Base.
No. 23ʙ Exting. Duplex Burner and Gallery.
9/6 each.

SHERWOODS LAMPS.
Polished Brass Duplex Table Lamps.

Scale ⅕th.

D 432
Polished Brass Table Lamp.
" F " 7 in. Green Coloured Base.
No. 23B Extg. Duplex Burner and Gallery.
7/6 each.

D 433
Polished Brass Table Lamp.
" F " 7 in. Green Coloured Base.
No. 23B Extg. Duplex Burner and Gallery.
8/6 each.

D 434
Polished Brass Table Lamp.
" F " 7 in. Green Coloured Base.
No. 23B Extg. Duplex Burner and Gallery.
8/- each.

All Lamps are   Priced without Glass.

D 435
Polished Brass Pillar Table Lamp.
" J " 7 in. Brown coloured Base.
No. 133B Extg. Duplex Burner, fixed Gallery.
10/- each.

D 436
Polished Brass Pillar Table Lamp.
" F " 7 in. Green coloured Base.
No. 133B Extg Duplex Burner, fixed Gallery.
12/- each.

D 437
Polished Brass Pillar Table Lamp.
" F " 7 in. Green coloured Base.
No. 133B Extg Duplex Burner, fixed Gallery.
11/- each

Polished Brass Duplex Table Lamps.

Scale $\frac{1}{5}$ th.

D 438
Polished Brass Table Lamp.
Brass Base, Iron Loaded.
. 133B Extg. Duplex Burner, fixed Gallery.
11/- each.

D 439
Polished Brass Table Lamp.
Brass Base, Iron Loaded.
No. 133B Extg. Duplex Burner, fixed Gallery.
10/- each.

D 440
Polished Brass Table Lamp.
Brass Base, Iron Loaded.
No. 133B Extg. Duplex Burner, fixed Gallery.
12/- each.

All Lamps are   Priced without Glass.

D 441
Polished Brass Pillar Table Lamp.
Brass Base, Iron Loaded.
. 133B Extg. Duplex Burner fixed Gallery.
12/- each.

D 442
Polished Brass Table Lamp.
Brass Base, Iron Loaded.
No. 133B Extg. Duplex Burner, fixed Gallery.
9/6 each.

D 443
Polished Brass Pillar Table Lamp.
Brass Base, Iron Loaded.
No. 133B Extg. Duplex Burner, fixed Gallery.
12/- each.

Polished Brass Duplex Table Lamps.

The "SCOTT" Lamp.

Scale ¼ th.

SPECIAL EXPORT LINE.

SPECIAL EXPORT LINE.

PACKING.
Approximate weights and measurements.
Case containing
3 doz. Brass Table Lamps, Burners, and Shade holders.

Gross ... **1 3 20**
34 × 27 × 28
Net ... **1 0 2**

PACKING.
Approximate Weights and measurements.
Case containing.
6 doz. Brass Table Lamps, Burners, and Shade holders.

Gross ... **2 3 18**
47 × 30 × 34
Net ... **2 0 4**

Approximate weights and measurements.
Case containing
(Original Case Quantity).
6 doz. 9¼ in. Opal Shades.

Gross ... **2 0 10**
46 × 27 × 40
Net ... **0 2 4**

Approximate weights and measurements.
Case containing
4 doz. 9¼ in. Opal Shades.
6 doz. Duplex Chimneys.
9 doz. Duplex Wicks.

Gross ..., **1 1 18**
47 × 27 × 31
Net ... **0 2 2**

Approximate weights and measurements.
Case containing
9 doz. Duplex Chimneys and 12 doz. Duplex Wicks.

Gross ... **1 0 20**
39 × 27 × 29
Net ... **0 1 14**

D 444
Polished Brass Table Lamp
fitted with
No. 29B Duplex Extinguisher Burner.
9¼ in. Shade Holder, Opal Shade and Chimney
complete as drawn.
8/- each.
Special price 6 doz. lots,
7/6 each.

D 445
9¼ in. Green Cased Opal Shade and Chimney.
10/- each.

All lamps are tested by Machinery
before leaving our Works,
and are
Guaranteed not to leak.

All lamps are tested by Machinery
before leaving our Works,
and are
Guaranteed not to leak.

Polished Brass Duplex Table Lamps.

Scale $\frac{1}{5}$ th.

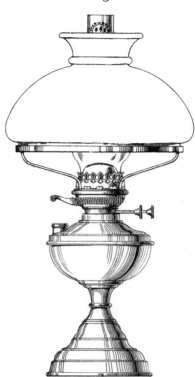

D 446
Polished Brass Table Lamp
fitted with
No. 23B Exting. Duplex Burner and Gallery
48/- doz.

D 447
Polished Brass Table Lamp
fitted with
No. 29B Exting. Duplex Burner, 9¼ in. Shade holder.
6/- each.

D 448
Polished Brass Table Lamp
fitted with
No. 23B Exting. Duplex Burner and Gallery,
54/- doz.

All Lamps are Priced without Glass.

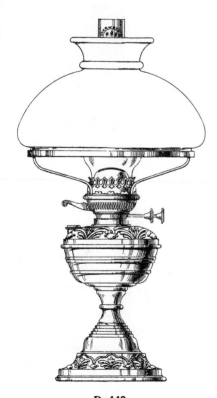

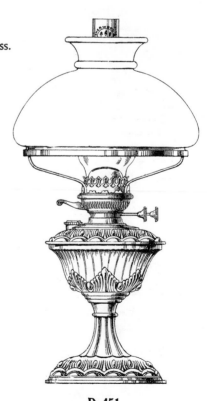

D 449
Polished Brass Table Lamp,
fitted with
No. 29B Exting. Duplex Burner, 9¼ in. Shade holder.
6/- each.

D 450
Polished Brass Table Lamp,
fitted with
No. 23B Exting. Duplex Burner and Gallery.
6/- each.

D 451
Polished Brass Table Lamp,
No. 29B Exting. Duplex Burner, 9¼ in. Shade holder.
7/- each.

SHERWOODS LAMPS.

Polished Brass Duplex Table Lamps.

All Lamps are Priced without Glass.

Scale $\frac{1}{5}$ *th.*

D 452

Polished Brass Table Lamp
fitted with
No. 23B Extg. Duplex Burner
and Gallery.
5/- each.

D 453

Polished Brass Table Lamp
fitted with
No. 23B Extg. Duplex Burner
and Gallery.
5/3 each.

D 454

Polished Brass Table Lamp
fitted with
No. 133B Extinguisher Duplex Burner,
fixed Gallery.
5/6 each.

D 455

Polished Brass Table Lamp
fitted with
No. 133B Extg Duplex Burner, fixed Gallery.
6/- each.

D 456

Polished Brass Table Lamp
fitted with
No. 133B Extinguisher Duplex Burner
fixed Gallery.
6/6 each.

Polished Brass Duplex Table Lamps.

All Lamps are Priced without Glass.

Scale ⅕ th.

D 457
Polished Brass Table Lamp
fitted with
No. 133B Extg. Duplex Burner,
fixed Gallery.
7/6 each.

D 458
No. 30B S.W. Extg. Duplex Burner,
fixed Gallery.
9/6 each.

D 459
Polished Brass Table Lamp
fitted with
No. 133B Extg. Duplex Burner,
fixed Gallery.
8/- each.

D 460
No. 30B S.W. Extg. Duplex Burner,
fixed Gallery.
10/- each.

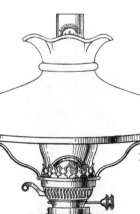

D 461
Polished Brass Table Lamp
fitted with
133B Extg. Duplex Burner,
fixed Gallery.
7/- each.

D 462
Polished Brass Table Lamp
fitted with
No. 29B Extinguisher Duplex Burner,
9¼ in. Shade Holder.
6/3 each.

D 463
Polished Brass Table Lamp
fitted with
No. 133B Extg. Duplex Burner,
fixed Gallery.
7/6 each.

SHERWOODS LAMPS.

Polished Brass Duplex Table Lamps.

All Lamps are Priced without Glass.

Scale $\frac{1}{5}$ *th.*

D 464
Polished Brass Table Lamp
fitted with
No. 30B S.W. Extg. Duplex Burner,
fixed Gallery.
12/- each.

D 465
Polished Brass Table Lamp
fitted with
No. 30B S.W. Extg. Duplex Burner,
fixed Gallery.
12/6 each.

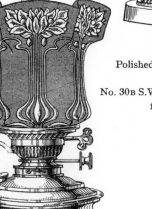

D 466
Polished Brass Table Lamp
fitted with
No. 30B S.W. Extg. Duplex Burner,
fixed Gallery.
11/6 each.

D 467
Polished Brass Table Lamp
fitted with
No. 92B S.W. Raiser Extinguisher Duplex Burner,
fixed Gallery.
16/6 each.

D 468
Polished Brass Table Lamp
fitted with
No. 30B S.W. Extg. Duplex Burner,
fixed Gallery.
13/- each.

Polished Brass Duplex Table Lamps.

All Lamps are Priced without Glass.

Scale ⅕ th.

D 469
Polished Brass Table Lamp
fitted with
No. 30B S.W. Extg. Duplex Burner,
fixed Gallery.
12/6 each.

D 470
No. 92B S.W. Raiser Gallery,
Extinguisher Duplex Burner.
15/6 each.

D 471
Polished Brass Table Lamp
fitted with
No. 30B S.W. Extg. Duplex Burner.
fixed Gallery.
15/6 each.

D 472
No. 92B S.W. Raiser Gallery,
Extinguisher Duplex Burner.
18/6 each.

D 473
Polished Brass Table Lamp
fitted with
No. 92B S.W. Raiser Gallery,
Extinguisher Duplex Burner.
15/- each.

D 474
Polished Brass Table Lamp
fitted with
No. 122B S.W. Extinguisher Duplex Burner,
fixed Gallery.
12/- each.

D 475
Polished Brass Table Lamp
fitted with
No. 92B S.W. Raiser Gallery,
Extinguisher Duplex Burner.
15/- each.

SHERWOODS LAMPS.

Polished Brass Duplex Table Lamps.

All Lamps are Priced without Glass.

Scale $\frac{1}{5}$ *th.*

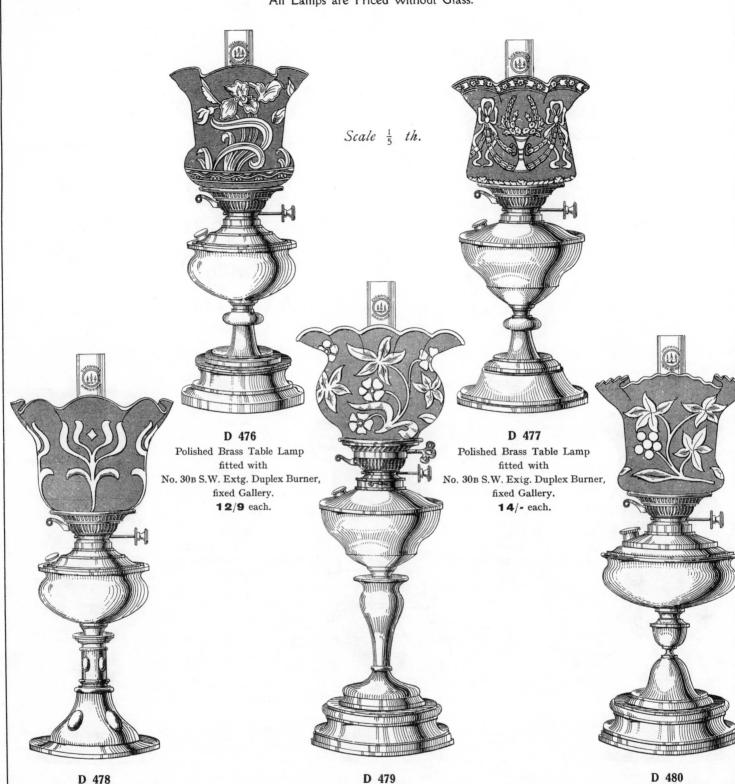

D 476
Polished Brass Table Lamp
fitted with
No. 30B S.W. Extg. Duplex Burner,
fixed Gallery.
12/9 each.

D 477
Polished Brass Table Lamp
fitted with
No. 30B S.W. Exig. Duplex Burner,
fixed Gallery.
14/- each.

D 478
Polished Brass Table Lamp
fitted with
No. 30B S.W. Extg. Duplex Burner,
fixed Gallery,
13/6 each.

D 479
Polished Brass Table Lamp
fitted with
No. 92B S.W. Raiser Gallery,
Extinguisher Duplex Burner.
20/- each.

D 480
Polished Brass Table Lamp
fitted with
No. 30B S.W. Extg. Duplex Burne
fixed Gallery.
17/- each.

Polished Brass Duplex Table Lamps.

All Lamps are Priced without Glass.

Scale $\frac{1}{5}$ th.

D 481

Polished Brass Table Lamp
fitted with
No. 122B S.W. Extg. Duplex Burner,
fixed Gallery.
15/- each.

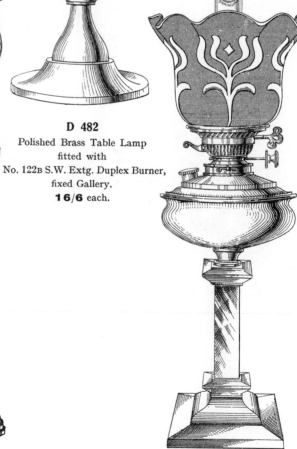

D 482

Polished Brass Table Lamp
fitted with
No. 122B S.W. Extg. Duplex Burner,
fixed Gallery.
16/6 each.

D 483

Polished Brass Table Lamp
fitted with
No. 92B S.W. Raiser Gallery,
Extinguisher Duplex Burner.
18/- each.

D 484

Polished Brass Table Lamp
fitted with
No. 92B S.W. Raiser Gallery,
Extinguisher Duplex Burner.
26/- each.

D 485

Polished Brass Table Lamp
fitted with
No. 92B S.W. Raiser Gallery,
Extinguisher Duplex Burner.
25/- each.

SHERWOODS LAMPS.

Nickel Plated Hood Reflector Reading Lamps,

fitted with

6''' and 10''' Cosmos and 30 c.p. 12''' Sun C.D. Burners.

Scale ⅕ th.

All Lamps are Priced complete.

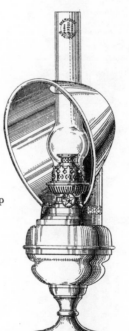

D 486
Adjustable
Hood Reflector N.P. Reading Lamp
fitted with
6''' Cosmos Burner and Chimney.
15/- each.

D 487
Adjustable
Hood Reflector N.P. Reading Lamp
fitted with
10''' Cosmos Burner and Chimney.
18/- each.

D 488
Hood Reflector N.P. Reading Lamp
fitted with
6''' Cosmos Burner and Chimney.
11/6 each.

D 489
10''' Cosmos Burner and Chimney.
12/- each.

D 490
Hood Reflector N.P. Reading Lamp
fitted with
Sherwoods 30 c.p. 12''' Sun. C.D. Burner
and Chimney.
15/- each.

D 491
Hood Reflector N.P. Reading Lamp
fitted with
10''' Cosmos Burner and Chimney.
14/- each.

D 492
14''' Cosmos Burner and Chimney.
15/- each.

ENGLISH MAKE.

These Lamps are made fitted with Detachable Iron Loadings for Packing Purposes.

Polished Brass Adjustable Reading Lamps,

fitted with

Duplex and 30 c.p. 12''' Sun C.D. Burners.

Scale $\frac{1}{5}$ th.

All Lamps are Priced without Glass.

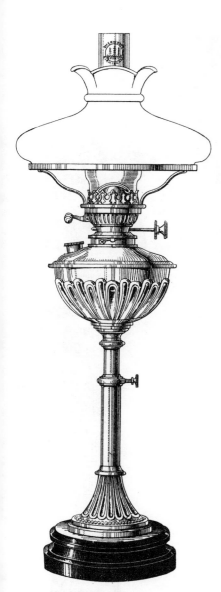

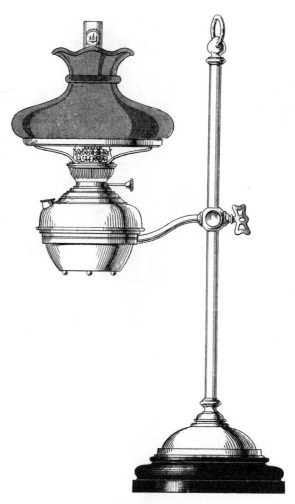

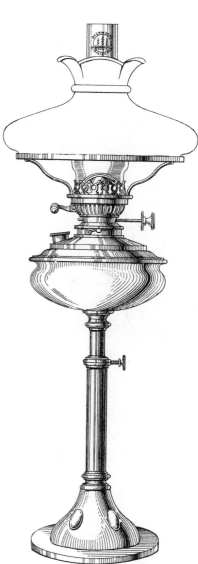

D 493

Polished Brass Adjustable Reading Lamp
fitted with
No. 22B S.W. Extinguisher Duplex Burner,
9¼ in. Shade Holder.
Large size " D," 7¼ in. Black Base.
18/- each.

D 494

One Light Single Arm
Polished Brass Adjustable Reading Lamp
fitted with
Sherwood's 30 c.p. 12''' Sun. C.D. Burner,
7¼ in. Shade Holder.
Large Size " E," 7¼ in. Black Base.
24/- each.

D 495

Two Light Double Arm.
33/- each.

D 496

Polished Brass Adjustable Reading Lamp,
fitted with
No. 22B S.W. Extinguisher Duplex Burner,
9¼ in. Shade Holder.
Heavy Loaded Brass Foot.
20/- each.

SHERWOODS LAMPS.

Polished Brass Duplex Corinthian Table Lamps.

All Lamps are Priced without Glass.

Scale $\frac{1}{5}$ *th.*

D 497
Polished Brass Table Lamp
fitted with
No. 133B Extinguisher Duplex Burner,
fixed Gallery.
11/- each.

D 498
Polished Brass Table Lamp
fitted with
No. 133B Extinguisher Duplex Burner,
fixed Gallery.
12/- each.

D 499
Polished Brass Corinthian Table Lamp
fitted with
No. 30B S.W. Extg. Duplex Burner,
fixed Gallery.
15/- each.

D 500
Polished Brass Corinthian Table Lamp
fitted with
No. 92B S.W. Raiser Gallery,
Extinguisher Duplex Burner.
26/- each.

D 501
Polished Brass Corinthian Table Lamp
fitted with
No. 30B S.W. Extinguisher Duplex Burner,
fixed Gallery.
21/- each.

Polished Brass Duplex Corinthian Table Lamps.

All Lamps are Priced without Glass.

Scale ⅕ th.

D 502
Polished Brass Table Lamp
fitted with
No. 122ʙ S.W. Extg. Duplex Burner,
fixed Gallery.
20/- each.

D 503
Polished Brass Table Lamp
fitted with
No. 122ʙ S.W. Extg. Duplex Burner,
fixed Gallery.
22/- each.

D 504
Polished Brass Corinthian Table Lamp
fitted with
No. 92ʙ S.W. Raiser Gallery,
Extinguisher Duplex Burner.
24/- each.

D 505
Polished Brass Corinthian Table Lamp
fitted with
No. 92ʙ S.W. Raiser Gallery,
Extinguisher Duplex Burner.
30/- each.

D 506
Polished Brass Corinthian Table Lamp
fitted with
No. 92ʙ S.W. Raiser Gallery,
Extinguisher Duplex Burner.
26/- each.

SHERWOODS LAMPS.

Polished Brass Table Lamps,

fitted with

Heavy Raiser S.W. Extinguisher Duplex Burners.

Scale $\frac{1}{5}$ th.

All Lamps are Priced Complete

with Shade, Shade Holder and Chimney.

D 507

Polished Brass Table Lamp
fitted with
No. 92B S.W. Raiser Extinguisher Duplex Burner,
D 25 12 in. Silk Shade.
Shade Holder and Chimney complete
31/- each.

D 508

Polished Brass Corinthian Table Lamp
fitted with
No. 92B S.W. Raiser Extinguisher Duplex Burner,
D 28 15 in. Silk Shade.
Shade Holder and Chimney complete.
42/- each.

D 509

Polished Brass Table Lamp
fitted with
No. 92B S.W. Raiser Extinguisher Duplex Burner,
D 27 12 in. Silk Shade.
Shade Holder and Chimney complete.
39/- each.

SHERWOODS LAMPS.

Polished Brass Table Lamps,

fitted with

Heavy Raiser S.W. Extinguisher Duplex Burners.

Scale $\frac{1}{5}$ th.

All Lamps are Priced Complete

with Shade, Shade Holder and Chimney.

D 510

Polished Brass and Copper Table Lamp
fitted with
No. 92B S.W. Raiser Extinguisher Duplex Burner,
D 25   12 in. Silk Shade.
Shade Holder and Chimney complete.
50/- each

D 511

Polished Brass Table Lamp
fitted with
No. 92B S.W. Raiser Extinguisher Duplex Burner,
D 30   15 in. Silk Shade.
Shade Holder and Chimney complete.
55/- each.

D 512

Polished Brass and Copper Table Lamp
fitted with
No. 92B S.W. Raiser Extinguisher Duplex Burner,
D 27   12 in. Silk Shade.
Shade Holder and Chimney complete.
60/- each.

SHERWOODS LAMPS.

Polished Brass Table Lamps,

fitted with

Heavy Raiser S.W. Extinguisher Duplex Burners.

Scale $\frac{1}{5}$ th.

All Lamps are Priced Complete   with Shade, Shade Holder and Chimney.

D 513	**D 514**	**D 515**
Polished Brass Table Lamp	Polished Brass Table Lamp	Polished Brass Table Lamp
fitted with	fitted with	fitted with
No. 92B S.W. Raiser Extinguisher Duplex Burner,	No. 92B S.W. Raiser Extinguisher Duplex Burner,	No. 92B S.W. Raiser Duplex Burner,
D 25 12 in. Shade.	**D 30** 15 in. Shade.	**D 27** 12 in. Shade.
Shade Holder and Chimney.	Shade Holder and Chimney.	Shade Holder and Chimney.
42/- each.	**72/-** each.	**54/-** each.

Polished Brass Table Lamps,

fitted with

Heavy Raiser S.W. Extinguisher Duplex Burners.

Scale $\frac{1}{5}$ th.

All Lamps are Priced Complete   with Shade, Shade Holder and Chimney.

D 516	**D 517**	**D 518**
Polished Brass Table Lamp	Polished Brass Table Lamp	Polished Brass Table Lamp
fitted with	fitted with	fitted with
No. 92B S.W. Raiser Extinguisher Duplex Burner,	No. 92B S.W. Raiser Extinguisher Duplex Burner,	No. 92B S.W. Raiser Extinguisher Duplex Burner,
D 25 12 in. Shade.	**D 29** 15 in. Shade.	**D 27** 12 in. Shade.
Shade Holder and Chimney.	Shade Holder and Chimney.	Shade Holder and Chimney.
52/- each.	**84/-** each.	**56/-** each.

SHERWOODS LAMPS.

Superior Quality

Superior Polished Brass Telescopic Floor Lamps,

Scale $\frac{1}{9}$ th.

All lamps are   priced without shades.

D 519

Polished Brass and Copper Floor Lamp
fitted with
No. 92B S.W. Raiser Extinguisher Duplex Burner,
D 74 Basket and Shade Holder.
80/- each
D 28 18 in. Shade.
18/- each.

D 520

Polished Brass Floor Lamp
fitted with
No. 92B S.W. Raiser Extinguisher Duplex Burner,
D 74 Basket and Shade Holder.
95/- each.
D 29 18 in. Shade.
36/- each.

D 521

Polished Brass Floor Lamp
fitted with
No. 92B S.W. Raiser Extinguisher Duplex Burner,
D 74 Basket and Shade Holder.
90/- each.
D 30 18 in. Shade.
24/- each.

Superior Quality
Polished Brass Telescopic Floor Lamps,

Scale $\frac{1}{9}$ th.

All lamps are   priced without shades.

D 522
Polished Brass Floor Lamp
fitted with
No. 92B S.W. Raiser Extinguisher Duplex Burner,
D 74 Basket and Shade Holder.
85/- each.
D 28 18 in. Shade.
18/- each.

D 523
Polished Brass Cast Floor Lamp
fitted with
No. 92B S.W. Raiser Extinguisher Duplex Burner,
D 74 Basket and Shade Holder.
120/- each.
D 29 18 in. Shade.
36/- each.

D 524
Polished Brass Floor Lamp
fitted with
No. 92B S.W. Raiser Extinguisher Duplex Burner,
D 74 Basket and Shade Holder.
100/- each.
D 30 18 in. Shade.
24/- each.

Polished Brass Table Lamp,

fitted with

Sherwoods 12''' 30 c.p. Sun C.D. Burner.

The "EMPIRE" Lamp.

Scale $\frac{1}{4}$ th.

SPECIAL EXPORT LINE,

PACKING,
Approximate weight and measurements.
Case containing
3 doz. Table Lamps, Burners and Shade Holders.

Gross ... **1 0 0**
33 × 24 × 23
Net ... **0 1 18**

Approximate weight and measurements.
Case containing
4 doz. 7¼ in. Opal Shades.
6 doz. 12''' Sun Chimneys.
9 doz. 12''' Sun Wicks.

Gross ... **1 0 20**
43 × 23 × 27
Net ... **0 1 22**

SPECIAL EXPORT LINE.

PACKING.
Approximate weight and measurements.
Case containing
6 doz. Table Lamps, Burners and Shade Holders.

Gross ... **1 3 20**
34 × 34 × 30
Net ... **1 0 20**

Approximate weight and measurements.
Case containing
8 doz. 7¼ in. Opal Shades.
9 doz. 12''' Sun Chimneys.
12 doz. 12''' Sun Wicks.

Gross ... **2 1 16**
42 × 34 × 42
Net ... **0 3 0**

D 525
Polished Brass Table Lamps,
fitted with
Sherwoods 12''' 30 c.p. Sun C.D. Burner,
7¼ in. Shade Holder, Opal Shade and Chimney,
complete as drawn,
78/- doz.
Special price 3 doz. lamps complete,
75/- doz.
Special price 6 doz. lamps complete,
72/- doz.

D 526
With 7¼ in. Green Cased Opal Shade and Chimney.
8/- each.

All Lamps are tested by Machinery
before leaving our Works,
and are
Guaranteed not to leak.

All Lamps are tested by Machinery
before leaving our Works,
and are
Guaranteed not to leak.

Polished Brass Table Lamp,

fitted with

Sherwoods 12''' 30 c.p. Sun C.D. Burner.

The "COLONIAL" LAMP.

Scale ¼ th.

SPECIAL EXPORT LINE.

Approximate weight and measurements.
Case containing
3 doz. Table Lamps, Burners and Shade Holders.

Gross ... **1 0 10**

Net ... **0 2 0**   **34 × 27 × 28**

Approximate weight and measurements.
Case containing
4 doz. 7¼ in. Opal Shades.
6 doz. 12''' Sun Chimneys.
9 doz. 12''' Sun Wicks.

Gross ... **1 0 20**

Net ... **0 1 22**   **43 × 23 × 27**

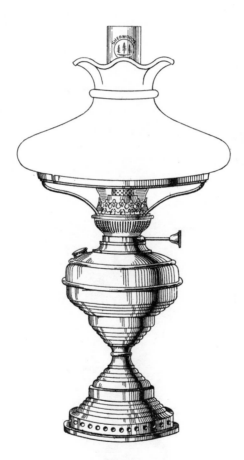

D 527
Polished Brass Table Lamps,
fitted with
Sherwoods 12''' 30 c.p. Sun C.D. Burner,
7¼ in. Shade Holder, Opal Shade and Chimney,
complete as drawn,
90/- doz.
Special price 3 doz. lamps complete,
87/- doz.
Special price 6 doz. lamps complete,
84/- doz.
D 528
With 7¼ in. Green Cased Opal Shade and Chimney.
9/- each.

SPECIAL EXPORT LINE,

Approximate weight and measurements.
Case containing
6 doz. Table Lamps, Burners and Shade Holders.

Gross ... **2 0 20**

Net ... **1 1 13**   **38 × 29 × 33**

Approximate weight and measurements.
Case containing
8 doz. 7¼ in. Opal Shades.
9 doz. 12''' Sun Chimneys.
12 doz. 12''' Sun Wicks.

Gross ... **2 1 16**

Net ... **0 3 0**   **42 × 34 × 42**

All Lamps are tested by Machinery
before leaving our Works,
and are
Guaranteed not to leak.

All Lamps are tested by Machinery
before leaving our Works,
and are
Guaranteed not to leak.

SHERWOODS LAMPS.

Polished Brass Table Lamp,

fitted with

Sherwoods 12''' 30 c.p. Sun C.D. Burner.

Scale ⅕ th.

D 529
Polished Brass Table Lamp,
fitted with
Sherwoods 12''' Sun 30 c.p. C.D. Burner,
3 in. Gallery.
60/- doz.

D 530
Polished Brass Table Lamp,
fitted with
Sherwoods 12''' Sun 30 c.p. C.D. Burner,
3 in. Gallery.
66/- doz.

All Lamps are   Priced without Glass.

D 531
Polished Brass Table Lamp,
fitted with
Sherwoods 12''' Sun 30 c.p. C.D. Burner,
7¼ in. Shade Holder.
6/- each.

D 532
Polished Brass Table Lamp,
fitted with
Sherwoods 12''' Sun 30 c.p. C.D. Burner,
7¼ in. Shade Holder.
60/- doz.
Special price 6 doz. lots,
57/- doz.

D 533
Polished Brass Table Lamp,
fitted with
Sherwoods 12''' Sun 30 c.p. C.D. Burner,
7¼ in. Shade Holder.
6/6 each.

Polished Brass Table Lamp,

fitted with

Sherwoods 12‴ 30 c.p. Sun C.D. Burner.

Scale ⅕ th.

D 534
Polished Brass Table Lamp,
fitted with
Sherwoods 12‴ Sun 30 c.p. C.D. Burner,
3 in. Gallery.
7/- each.

D 535
Polished Brass Table Lamp,
fitted with
Sherwoods 12‴ Sun 30 c.p. C.D. Burner,
3 in. Gallery.
7/3 each.

All Lamps are   Priced without Glass.

D 536
Polished Brass Table Lamp,
Black Marble Base.
Sherwoods 12‴ Sun 30 c.p. C.D. Burner,
7¼ in. Shade Holder.
7/9 each.

D 537
Polished Brass Table Lamp,
fitted with
Sherwoods 12‴ Sun 30 c.p. C.D. Burner,
7¼ in. Shade Holder.
9/- each.

D 538
Polished Brass Table Lamp,
Black Marble Base.
Sherwoods 12‴ Sun 30 c.p. C.D. Burner,
7¼ in. Shade Holder.
8/- each.

SHERWOODS LAMPS.

Polished Brass Table Lamp.

Fitted with

Sherwoods 16''' 45 c.p. Sun C.D. Burner.

The "FRONTIER" Lamp.

Scale ¼ th.

SPECIAL EXPORT LINE.

Approximate weight and measurements.
Case containing
3 doz. Table Lamps, Burners and Shade Holders.

Gross ...	1 3 20		38 × 30 × 28
Net ...	1 0 2		

Approximate case weights and measurements.
4 doz. 9¼ in. Opal Shades.
6 doz. 16''' Sun Fireproof Chimneys.
9 doz. 16''' Sun Wicks.

Gross ...	1 1 18	47 × 27 × 31
Net ...	0 2 2	

SPECIAL EXPORT LINE.

Approximate weights and measurements.
Case containing
6 doz. Table Lamps, Burners and Shade Holders.

Gross ...	2 2 20	44 × 30 × 31.
Net	1 2 10	

Approximate case weights and measurements.
(Original case quantity).
6 doz. 9¼ in. Opal Shades.

Gross ...	2 3 18	47 × 30 × 34
Net ...	2 0 4	

Approximate case weights and measurements
9 doz. 16''' Sun Chimneys.
12 doz. 16''' Sun Wicks.

Gross ...	1 0 10	36 × 20 × 29
Net ...	0 1 18	

D 539

Polished Brass Table Lamps
fitted with
Sherwood's 16''' 45 c.p. Sun C.D. Burner.
9¼ in. Shade Holder, Opal Shade and Chimney.
9/6 each.
Special price 6 doz. lots.
9/- each.

D 540

With 9¼ in. Opal Green Cased Shade and Chimney.
11/6 each.

All Lamps are tested by Machinery
before leaving our Works,
and are
Guaranteed not to leak.

All Lamps are tested by Machinery
before leaving our Works,
and are
Guaranteed not to leak.

Polished Brass Table Lamp.

Black Marble Base Stand,

Fitted with

Sherwoods 16''' 45 c.p. Sun C.D. Burner.

The "BRIGADIER" Lamp.

Scale ¼ th.

SPECIAL EXPORT LINE.

Approximate weights and measurements.
Packed in No. 3 cask.
3 doz. Black Marble Base Stands.
Gross ... **1 3 20**
28 × 28
Net ... **1 1 4**

Approximate weights and measurements.
3 doz. Brass Founts and Burners.
Gross ... **1 1 4**
33 × 25 × 25
Net ... **0 2 4**

Approximate weights and measurements.
4 doz. ¾ in. Frosted 7½ × 4in. Mono Globes.
6 doz. 16''' Sun Fireproof Chimneys.
9 doz. 16''' Sun Wicks.
Gross ... **2 0 16**
50 × 37 × 24
Net ... **0 2 18**

SPECIAL EXPORT LINE.

Approximate weights and measurements.
Packed in No. 1 Cask.
6 doz. Black Marble Base Stands.
Gross ... **3 1 22**
40 × 31
Net ... **2 2 8**

Approximate weights and measurements.
6 doz. Brass Founts and Burners.
Gross... **1 3 20**
39 × 27 × 29
Net ... **1 0 0**

Approximate weights and measurements.
(Original case quantities).
8 doz. ¾ in. Frosted 7½ × 4 in. Mono Globes.
Gross ... **2 2 4**
60 × 39 × 36
Net ... **0 3 12**
Approximate weights and measurements.
9 doz. 16''' Sun Fireproof Chimneys.
12 doz. 16''' Sun Wicks.
Gross ... **1 0 10**
36 × 20 × 29
Net ... **0 1 18**

D 541

Polished Brass Table Lamp
A 7 in. Black Marble Base,
fitted with
Sherwood's 16''' 45 c.p. Sun C.D. Burner and
gallery.
Frosted 7½ × 4 in. Mono Globe and Chimney
Complete, as drawn,
12/6 each.
Special price 3 doz. lamps complete.
12/- each.
Special price 6 doz. lamps complete.
11/6 each.

All Lamps are tested by Machinery
before leaving our Works,
and are
Guaranteed not to leak.

All Lamps are tested by Machinery
before leaving our Works,
and are
Guaranteed not to leak.

SHERWOODS LAMPS.

Polished Brass Table Lamp.

Fitted with

Sherwoods 16''' 45 c.p. Sun C.D. Burner.

Scale $\frac{1}{5}$ *th.*

D 542

Polished Brass Table Lamp
fitted with
Sherwood's 16''' 45 c.p. Sun C.D. Burner.
4 in. gallery.
7/6 each.

D 543

Polished Brass Table Lamp
fitted with
Sherwood's 16''' 45 c.p. Sun C.D. Burner.
4 in. gallery.
8/- each.

All Lamps are   Priced without Glass.

D 544

Polished Brass Table Lamp.
fitted with
Sherwood's 16''' 45 c.p. Sun C.D. Burner
4 in. gallery.
9/6 each.

D 545

Polished Brass Table Lamp
fitted with
Sherwood's 16''' 45 c.p. Sun C.D. Burner.
9¼ in. Shade Holder.
8/6 each.

D 546

Polished Brass Table Lamp
fitted with
Sherwood's 16''' 45 c.p. Sun C.D. Burner,
4 in. gallery.
10/6 each.

SHERWOODS LAMPS.

Polished Brass Table Lamps.

Fitted with

Sherwoods 16‴ 45 c.p. Sun C.D. Burner.

Scale ⅕ th.

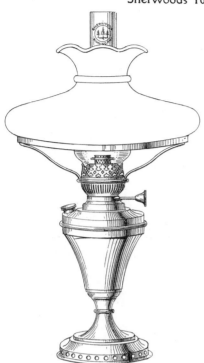

D 547

Polished Brass Table Lamp
fitted with
Sherwood's 16‴ 45 c.p. Sun C.D. Burner.
9¼ in. Shade Holder.
9/6 each.

D 548

Polished Brass Table Lamp
fitted with
Sherwood's 16‴ 45 c.p. Sun C.D. Burner.
9¼ in. Shade Holder.
9/6 each.

All Lamps are   Priced without Glass.

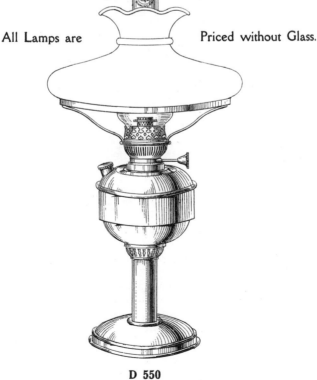

D 549

Polished Brass Table Lamp
fitted with
Sherwood's 16‴ 45 c.p. Sun C.D. Burner.
4 in. gallery.
10/6 each.

D 550

Polished Brass Table Lamp
fitted with
Sherwood's 16‴ 45 c.p. Sun C.D. Burner.
9¼ in. Shade Holder.
9/9 each.

D 551

Polished Brass Table Lamp
fitted with
Sherwood's 16‴ 45 c.p. Sun C.D. Burner.
4 in. gallery
12/- each.

SHERWOODS LAMPS.

Polished Brass Table Lamp

fitted with

Sherwoods 20''' Sun 60 c.p. C.D. Burner.

The "UNITED" Lamp.

Scale ¼ th.

SPECIAL EXPORT LINE.

Approximate weights and measurements.
Case containing
3 doz. Table Lamps, Burners and Shadeholders.

Gross   2 1 14
                      48 × 29 × 27
Net ... 1 2   0

Approximate weights and measurements.
4 doz. 9¼ in. Opal Shades.
6 doz. 20''' Sun Fireproof Chimneys.
9 doz. 20''' Sun Wicks.

Gross ... 1 3 14
                      47 × 27 × 40
Net   ... 0 2   8

SPECIAL EXPORT LINE.

Approximate weights and measurements.
case containing
6 doz. Table Lamps, Burners and Shade Holders.

Gross ... 4 0 6
                      48 × 43 × 33
Net   ... 3 0 0

Approximate weights and measurements.
(Original case quantity).
6 doz. 9¼ in. Opal Shades.

Gross ... 2 3 18
Net   ... 2 0   4

Approximate weights and measurements.
Case containing
9 doz. 20''' Sun Chimneys.
12 doz. 20''' Sun Wicks.

Gross ... 1 0 20
                      39 × 27 × 29
Net   ... 0 1 14

D 552
Polished Brass Table
fitted with
Sherwoods 20''' Sun 60 c.p. C.D. Burner.
9¼ in. Shade Holder, Opal Shade and Chimney.
Complete, as drawn,
15/- each.
Special price 3 doz. Lamps complete.
14/6 each.
Special price 6 doz. Lamps complete.
14/- each.

D 553
With 9¼ in. Green Cased Opal Shade and Chimney.
17/- each.

All Lamps are tested by Machinery
before leaving our Works,
and are
Guaranteed not to leak.

All Lamps are tested by Machinery
before leaving our Works,
and are
Guaranteed not to leak.

Polished Brass Table Lamps

fitted with

Sherwoods 20''' Sun 60 c.p. C.D. Burner.

All Lamps are priced without Glass.

Scale $\frac{1}{5}$ th.

D 554

Polished Brass Table Lamp
fitted with
Sherwoods 20''' Sun 60 c.p.
C.D. Burner. 4 in. gallery.
10/6 each.

D 555

Nickel plated finish.
13/- each.

D 556

Polished Brass Table Lamp
fitted with
Sherwoods 20''' Sun 60 c.p.
C.D. Burner. 4 in. gallery.
10/9 each.

D 557

Nickel plated finish.
13/6 each.

D 558

Polished Brass Table Lamp.
fitted with
Sherwoods 20''' Sun 60 c.p. C.D. Burner.
9¼ in. Shade Holder.
13/6 each.

D 559

Polished Brass Table Lamp
fitted with
Sherwoods 20''' Sun 60 c.p. C.D. Burner.
4 in. gallery.
10/- each.
Special price 50 Lamps.
9/6 each.

D 560

Polished Brass Table Lamp
fitted with
Sherwoods 20''' Sun 60 c.p. C.D. Burner.
9¼ in. Shade Holder.
14/- each.

SHERWOODS LAMPS.

Polished Brass Table Lamps

fitted with

Sherwoods 20''' Sun 60 c.p. C.D. Burner.

All Lamps are priced without Glass.

Scale $\frac{1}{5}$ th.

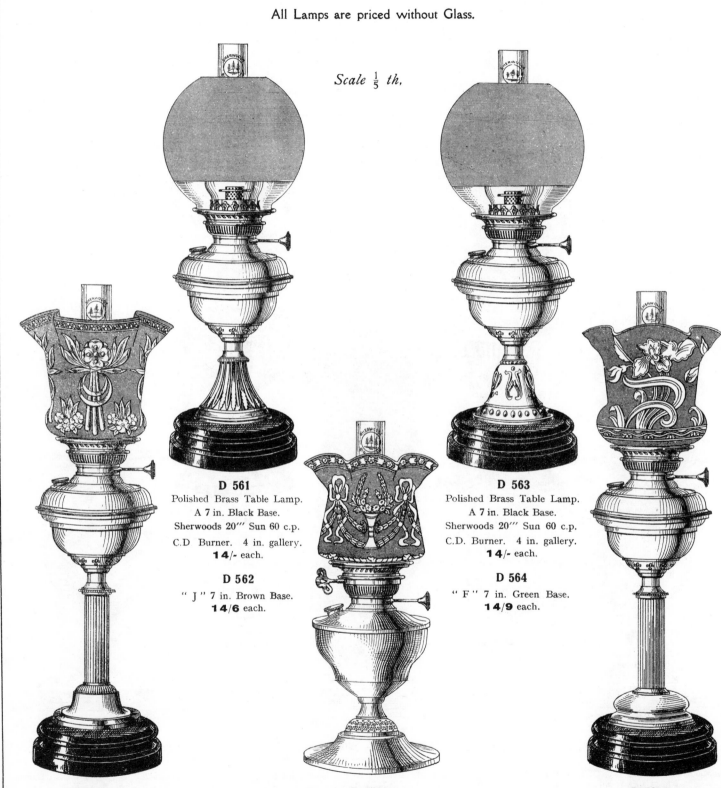

D 561
Polished Brass Table Lamp.
A 7 in. Black Base.
Sherwoods 20''' Sun 60 c.p.
C.D Burner. 4 in. gallery.
14/- each.

D 562
" J " 7 in. Brown Base.
14/6 each.

D 563
Polished Brass Table Lamp.
A 7 in. Black Base.
Sherwoods 20''' Sun 60 c.p.
C.D. Burner. 4 in. gallery.
14/- each.

D 564
" F " 7 in. Green Base.
14/9 each.

D 565
Polished Brass Table Lamp.
A 7 in. Black Base.
Sherwoods 20''' Sun 60 c.p. C.D. Burner.
4 in. Gallery.
15/- each.

D 566
Polished Brass Table Lamp
fitted with
Sherwoods Raiser 20''' Sun 60 c.p. C.D. Burner.
4 in. gallery.
18/- each.

D 567
Polished Brass Table Lamp.
" A " 7 in. Black Base.
Sherwoods 20''' Sun 60 c.p. C.D. Burne
4 in. gallery.
15/6 each.

SHERWOODS LAMPS.

Polished Brass Table Lamps

fitted with

Sherwoods 20''' Sun 60 c.p. C.D. Burner.

All Lamps are priced without Glass.

Scale ⅕ th.

D 568
Polished Brass Table Lamp
fitted with
Sherwoods Raiser 20''' Sun
60 c.p. C.D. Burner.   4 in. gallery.
19/- each.

D 569
Polished Brass Table Lamp
fitted with
Sherwoods Raiser 20''' Sun
60 c.p. C.D. Burner.   4 in. gallery.
20/- each.

D 570
Polished Brass Table Lamp
fitted with
rwoods Raiser 20''' Sun 60 c.p. C.D. Burner,
4 in. gallery.
25/- each.

D 571
Polished Brass Table Lamp
fitted with
Sherwoods Raiser 20''' Sun 60 c.p. C.D. Burner,
4 in. gallery.
18/6 each.

D 572
Polished Brass Table Lamp
fitted with
Sherwoods Raiser 20''' Sun 60 c.p. C.D. Burner,
4 in. gallery.
30/- each.

SHERWOODS LAMPS.

Sherwoods "GRANVILLE BELGE" Burner.

60 c.p. Central Draught Burner.

The "PRESIDENT" Lamp.

Scale ¼ th.

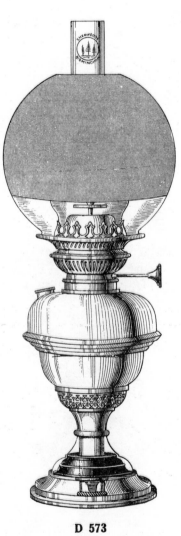

SPECIAL EXPORT LINE.

SPECIAL EXPORT LINE.

Approximate weights and measurements.
Case containing
50 Lamps, Burners and Galleries.

Gross ... **1 3 9**
$33 \times 28 \times 33$
Net ... **1 0 9**

Approximate weights and measurements.
Case containing
100 Lamps, Burners and Galleries.

Gross ... **3 0 18**
$52 \times 33 \times 33$
Net ... **2 0 18**

Approximate weights and measurements.
Case containing
60 ¾ in. Frosted 7½ × 4 in. Globes.
72 Belge Fireproof Chimneys.

Gross ... **1 3 10**
$54 \times 38 \times 40$
Net ... **0 3 10**

Separate weights.
50 lamps ... 77 lbs. brass ... 44 lbs. iron.
100 ,, ... 154 ,, ,, ... 88 ,, ,,

Approximate weights and measurements.
(Original case quantity).
8 doz. ¾ in. Frosted 9¼ × 4 in. Globes.

Gross ... **2 2 4**
$60 \times 39 \times 36$
Net ... **0 3 12**

Approximate weights and measurements.
2 doz. ¾ in. Frosted 7½ × 4 in. Globes.
12 doz. Fireproof Belge Chimneys.

Gross ... **1 2 0**
$36 \times 28 \times 24$
Net ... **0 2 22**

D 573

Florentine Bronze Table Lamp
fitted with
Sherwoods " GRANVILLE BELGE " Burner.
17/- each.
Special price 50 lamps complete,
16/6 each.
Special price 100 lamps complete.
16/- each.
(Drawn, showing detachable iron loading.)

The foot of this lamp is specially constructed with loose detachable iron loading, fitted by means of adjustable screw lock arrangement, so that the iron loadings can be packed separately in accordance with Customs' regulations.

Polished Brass Table Lamps

fitted with

Sherwoods "GRANVILLE BELGE" Burner.

60 c.p. Central Draught Burner.

These Lamps are also supplied Steel Bronze or Florentine Bronze finish to order.

All Lamps are priced without Glass.

Scale ⅕ th.

D 574

Polished Brass Table Lamp
fitted with
Sherwoods "GRANVILLE BELGE" Burner.
4 in. Gallery.
With loose detachable iron loading.
13/- each.

D 575

Polished Brass Table Lamp
fitted with
Sherwoods "GRANVILLE BELGE" Burner.
4 in. gallery.
With loose detachable iron loading.
14/- each.

D 576

Polished Brass Table Lamp
"A" 7 in. Black Base.
Sherwoods "GRANVILLE BELGE" Burner.
4 in. gallery.
13/6 each.

D 577

Polished Brass Table Lamp
fitted with
Sherwoods "GRANVILLE BELGE" Burner.
9¼ in. Shade Holder.
With sand loaded foot.
12/- each.

D 578

Polished Brass Table Lamp
fitted with
Sherwoods "GRANVILLE BELGE" Burner.
4 in. gallery.
15/6 each.

SHERWOODS LAMPS.

Sherwoods "GRANVILLE BELGE" Burner.

60 c.p. Central Draught Burner.

Scale $\frac{1}{5}$ th.

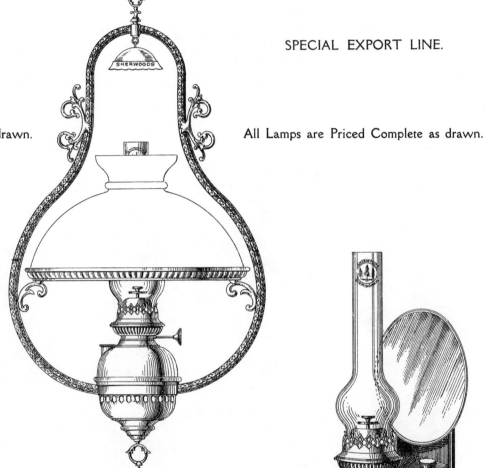

SPECIAL EXPORT LINE.

All Lamps are Priced Complete as drawn.

SPECIAL EXPORT LINE.

All Lamps are Priced Complete as drawn.

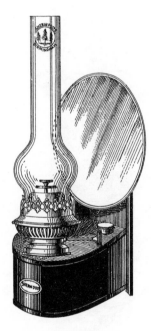

D 580

Florentine Bronze Ornamental Tube Harp,
fitted with
Sherwoods " GRANVILLE BELGE " Burner.
4 in. China Smoke Bell.
14 in. Opal Shade and Chimney.
24/- each.
Special price 50 lamps complete.
22/- each.

Sherwoods " GRANVILLE BELGE " Burner,
60 c.p. C.D. Burner,
Heavy English make.

D 579

Florentine Bronze Fount
fitted with
Sherwoods " GRANVILLE BELGE " Burner.
10/- each.
Special price 50 Lamps.
9/- each.

Approximate weights and measurements,
50 Founts and Burners.

Gross ... 1 3 4
48 × 27 × 27
Net ... 0 3 18

D 581

Strong Bronzed Wall Lamp,
7 in. Silvered Glass Reflector,
fitted with
Sherwoods " GRANVILLE BELGE " Burner,
complete.
11/- each.

Approximate weights and measurements.
50 Harps, Shade Ring and Smoke Burner.

Gross ... 1 2 22
38 × 32 × 28
Net ... 0 3 14

SHERWOODS LAMPS.

Sherwoods "TIGER" Burner.

Heavy 1½in. Single Wick Burner.

Scale ⅕ th.

SPECIAL EXPORT LINE.   SPECIAL EXPORT LINE.

All Lamps are Priced complete as drawn.   All Lamps are Priced complete as drawn.

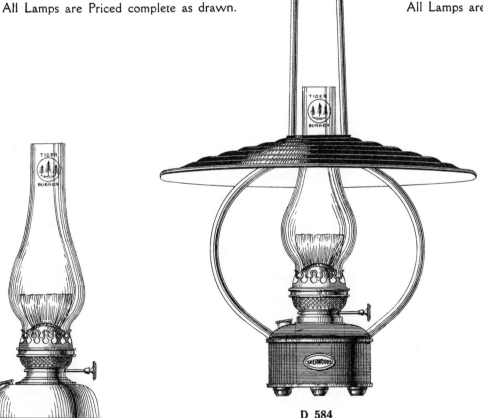

D 582
Polished Brass Fount
fitted with
Sherwoods " TIGER " Burner,
Complete.
9/- each.
Fitting 5¼ in.

D 583
Wire Tripod Stand
required
for use in Street Lamps.
2/6 each.

D 584
Strong Bronzed Hanging Lamp,
16 in. Japanned Reflector,
fitted with
Sherwoods " TIGER " Burner,
Complete.
11/- each.

Sherwoods " TIGER " Burner,
1½ in. Single Wick,
is particularly recommended
for
Street Lamp and Railway Station lighting.

D 585
Strong Bronzed Wall Lamp,
7 in. Silvered Glass Reflector,
fitted with
Sherwoods " TIGER " Burner,
Complete.
10/- each.

Spare Fireproof Chimneys.
12/- doz.
1½ in. wicks per roll 12 yards,
4/6 per roll.

SHERWOODS LAMPS.

Polished Brass Bracket Lamps,

Scale ⅕ th.

All Lamps are Priced Complete as drawn.

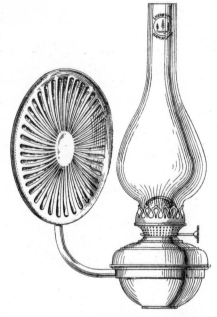

Polished Brass Swing Bracket Lamp.
7 in. Fluted Bright Reflector.

D 586

¾ in. 12ʙ Burner and Chimney.
4/9 each.
Special price 25 doz. lots.
4/3 each.

D 587

L in. 12ʙ Burner and Chimney.
5/- each.
Special price 25 doz. lots.
4/6 each.

Polished Brass Swing Bracket Lamp.
7 in. Plain Bright Reflector.

D 588

¾ in. Eureka Burner and Chimney.
5/- each.
Special Price 25 doz. lots.
4/6 each.

D 589

1 in. Eureka Burner and Chimney.
5/3 each.
Special Price 25 doz. lots.
4/9 each.

D 590
Polished Cast Brass Bracket Lamp
fitted with
No. 133ʙ Extg. Duplex Burner, fixed Gallery.
Assorted Globe and Chimney.
13/- each.

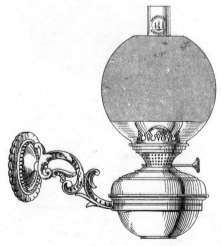

D 591
Polished Cast Brass Bracket Lamp
fitted with
1 in. 12ʙ Burner " F " Mono Globe and Chimney.
8/6 each.

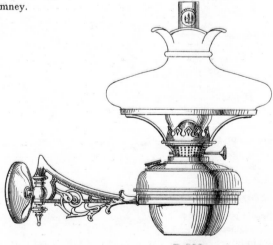

D 592
Polished Cast Brass Bracket Lamp
fitted with
1 in. 12ʙ Burner, 7¼ in. Opal Shade and Chimney.
9/6 each.

Polished Brass Bracket Lamps,

Scale ⅕ th.

D 593
Polished Brass Bracket Lamp
fitted with
Sherwoods 12''' Sun 30 c.p. C.D. Burner.
" F " Mono Globe and Chimney.
13/- each.

D 594
Polished Brass Bracket Lamp
fitted with
Sherwoods 12''' Sun 30 c.p. C.D. Burner.
" F " Mono Globe and Chimney.
15/- each.

All Lamps are Priced

Complete as drawn.

D 595
Polished Brass and Copper Bracket Lamp
fitted with
No. 110B Bijou Duplex Burner.
Assorted Globe and Chimney.
13/6 each.

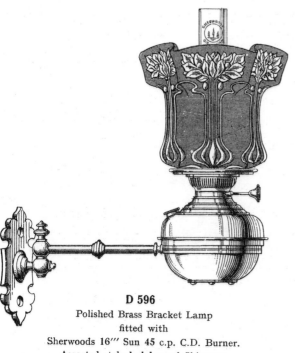

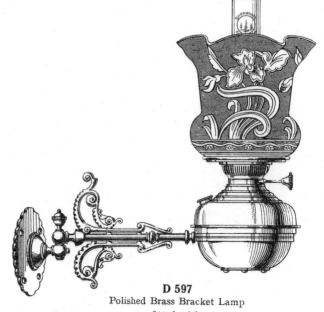

D 596
Polished Brass Bracket Lamp
fitted with
Sherwoods 16''' Sun 45 c.p. C.D. Burner.
Assorted etched globe and Chimney.
21/- each.

D 597
Polished Brass Bracket Lamp
fitted with
Sherwoods 16''' Sun 45 c.p. C.D. Burner.
Assorted Etched Globe and Chimney.
23/- each.

SHERWOODS LAMPS.

Polished Brass Bracket Lamps,

Scale ⅕ th.

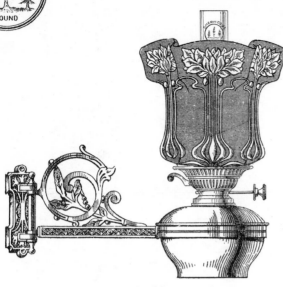

D 598

Polished Cast Brass Bracket Lamp
fitted with
No. 30ᴮ S.W. fixed Gallery, Extg. Duplex Burner.
Assorted Etched Globe and Chimney.
20/- each.

D 599

Polished Cast Brass Bracket Lamp
fitted with
No. 30ᴮ S.W. fixed Gallery, Extg. Duplex Burner
Assorted Etched Globe and Chimney.
22/- each.

All Lamps are Priced

Complete as drawn.

D 600

Polished Brass Bracket Lamp
fitted with
Sherwoods 20‴ Sun Raiser Gallery,
60 c.p. C.D. Burner.
Assorted Etched Globe and Chimney.
28/- each.

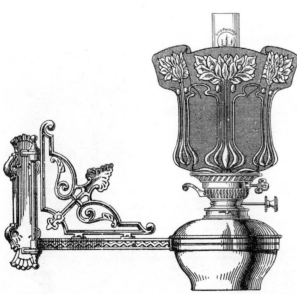

D 601

Polished Cast Brass Bracket Lamp
fitted with
No. 92ᴮ S.W. Raiser gallery, Extg. Duplex Burner.
Assorted Etched Globe and Chimney.
25/- each.

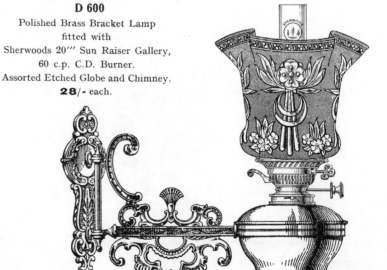

D 602

Polished Cast Brass Bracket Lamp
fitted with
No. 92ᴮ S.W. Raiser gallery Extg. Duplex Burner.
Assorted Etched Globe and Chimney.
27/- each.

Polished Brass Bracket Lamps,

Scale ⅕ th.

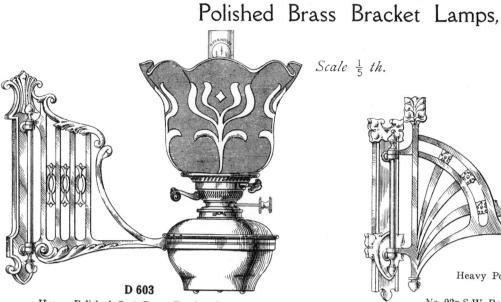

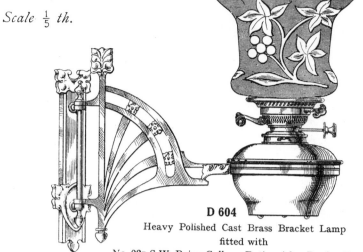

D 603

Heavy Polished Cast Brass Bracket Lamp
fitted with
No. 92B S.W. Raiser Gallery, Extinguisher Duplex Burner.
Assorted English make Globe and Chimney.
36/- each.

D 604

Heavy Polished Cast Brass Bracket Lamp
fitted with
No. 92B S.W. Raiser Gallery, Extinguisher Duplex Burner.
Assorted English make Globe and Chimney.
38/- each.

All Lamps are Priced

Complete as drawn.

D 605

Heavy Polished Brass Bracket Lamp
fitted with
No. 92B S.W. Raiser Gallery, Extinguisher Duplex Burner.
Assorted English make Globe and Chimney.
36/- each.

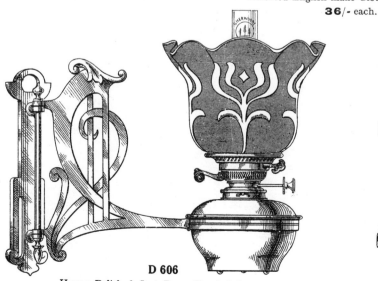

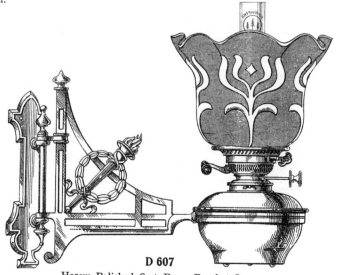

D 606

Heavy Polished Cast Brass Bracket Lamp
fitted with
No. 92B S.W. Raiser Gallery, Extinguisher Duplex Burner.
Assorted English make Globe and Chimney.
40/- each.

D 607

Heavy Polished Cast Brass Bracket Lamp
fitted with
No. 92B S.W. Raiser Gallery, Extinguisher Duplex Burner.
Assorted English make Globe and Chimney.
40/- each.

SHERWOODS LAMPS.

Polished Brass Pull-down Vestibule Lamps.

Fancy Etched Globes.

Scale ⅙ th.

All Lamps are Priced Complete as drawn.

D 608
Polished Brass Pull Down Lamp
fitted with
6''' Cosmos Burner, Crystal Globe and Chimney,
complete.
6/6 each.

Spare Globes 4 × 7½ × 3⅜ in.
1/6 each.

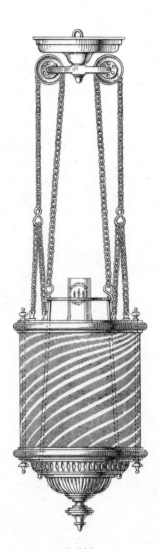

D 609
Extra Strong Polished Brass Pull Down Lamp
fitted with
Duplex Burner, Ruby Cylinder and Chimney,
complete.
30/- each.

Spare Ruby Cylinders 8½ × 8 in.
10/- each.

D 610
Strong Polished Brass Pull Down Lamp
fitted with
10''' Cosmos Burner, Assorted Colours,
Etched Globe and Chimney,
complete.
15/- each.

Spare Globes 4¼ × 9½ × 3⅜ in.
7/- each.

Polished Brass Pull-down Hall Lamps.

Leaded Light Panes.

Scale $\frac{1}{7}$ th.

All Lamps are Priced Complete as drawn.

D 611

6 in. Frame.
Polished Brass Square Hall Lamp
fitted with
No. 29B Extg. Duplex Burner and Chimney,
Leaded Light Panes.
24/- each.

D 612

7 in. Frame.
Polished Brass Round Hall Lamp
fitted with
No. 22B S.W. Extg. Burner and Chimney,
Satin Ruby Flushed Panes.
40/- each.

D 613

8 in. Frame.
Polished Brass Square Hall Lamp
fitted with
No. 29B Extg Duplex Burner and Chimney,
Leaded Light Panes.
36/- each.

SHERWOODS LAMPS.

The "BUNGALOW" Lamp.

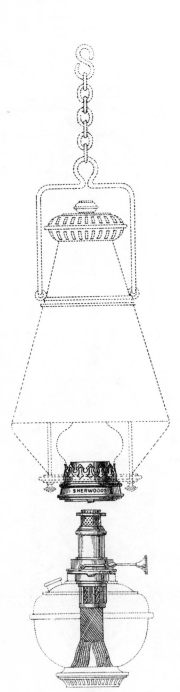

Position for lighting.

SHERWOODS
Wind and Weatherproof
VERANDAH LAMP.

Particularly recommended
for
Bungalow Verandahs
and
Up-country Stores.

Accessories.

Spare Opal Globes,
5/- each.

Spare 20''' Sun Chimney,
8/- per doz.

Spare Brazed Link Chains and Hooks,
5/- each.

Packing.

These Lamps are packed complete per case
with 2 spare globe, 6 chimneys and 12 wicks.

Approximate weight measurements,

Gross ... **0 2 10**
Net ... **0 0 17** ⎱ L26 W21 D25

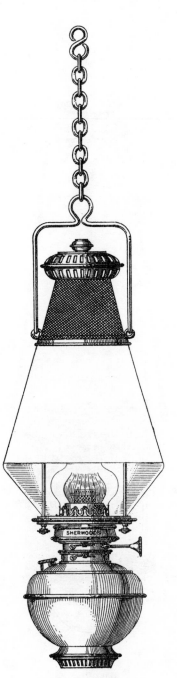

Position when lighted.

No. 1590

THE "BUNGALOW" LAMP.

Sherwoods' Patent Centre Draught Verandah Lamp,
fitted with Patent Windproof 60 C.P. 20''' Sun C.D. Burner,
with bayonet lock fittings, opal and clear globe,
Punkah Top and chimney, with extra strong Jack chain complete as drawn.

45/- each.

Lamp can be lighted without removing any parts.   All parts bayonet lock together.

SHERWOODS LAMPS.

Japanned Hanging Lamps,

fitted with

1 in. Slip and Duplex Burners,

and

Sherwoods 12''' 16''' 20''' 30''' Sun C.D. Burners.

Scale ⅙ th.

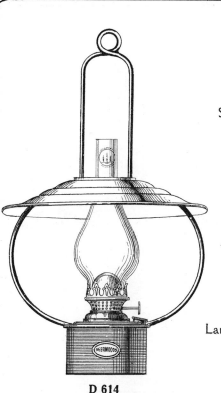

Lamps are Priced

Complete as Drawn.

D 614

Strong Copper Bronzed Hanging Lamp,
fitted with
1 in. 12B Burner and Chimney,
12 in. Bright Tin Reflector.
30/- doz.
Capacity 1½ pints.

D 615

Strong Copper Bronzed Hanging Lamp,
fitted with
Extinguisher Duplex Burner and Chimney,
15 in. Japanned Reflector.
60/- doz.
Capacity 2 pints.

D 616

Extra Strong Black and Gold Hanging Lamp,
fitted with
Sherwoods 20''' Sun 60 c.p. C.D. Burner and Chimney,
18 in. Japanned Reflector.
11/- each.
Capacity 3 pints.

D 617

Extra Strong Black and Gold Hanging Lamp,
fitted with
Sherwoods 30''' Sun 100 c.p. C.D. Burner and Chimney,
22 in. Japanned Reflector.
15/- each.
Capacity 3½ pints.

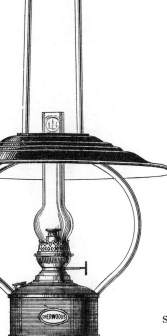

D 618

Strong Copper Bronzed Hanging Lamp,
fitted with
Sherwoods 12''' Sun 30 c.p. C.D. Burner and Chimney,
15 in. Japanned Reflector.
6/- each.
Capacity 1½ pints.

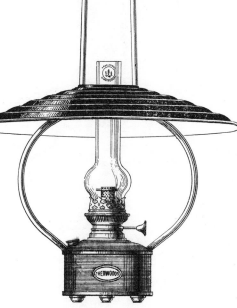

D 619

Strong Copper Bronzed Hanging Lamp,
fitted with
Sherwoods 16''' Sun 45 c.p. C.D. Burner and Chimney,
16 in. Japanned Reflector.
7/- each.
Capacity 2 pints.

REGISTERED
TRADE MARK
SOUND

SHERWOODS LAMPS.

Iron Wire Harps,

fitted with

Sherwoods 12''' 16''' 20''' Sun C.D. Burners.

Scale ⅙ th.

Lamps are Priced   Complete as Drawn.

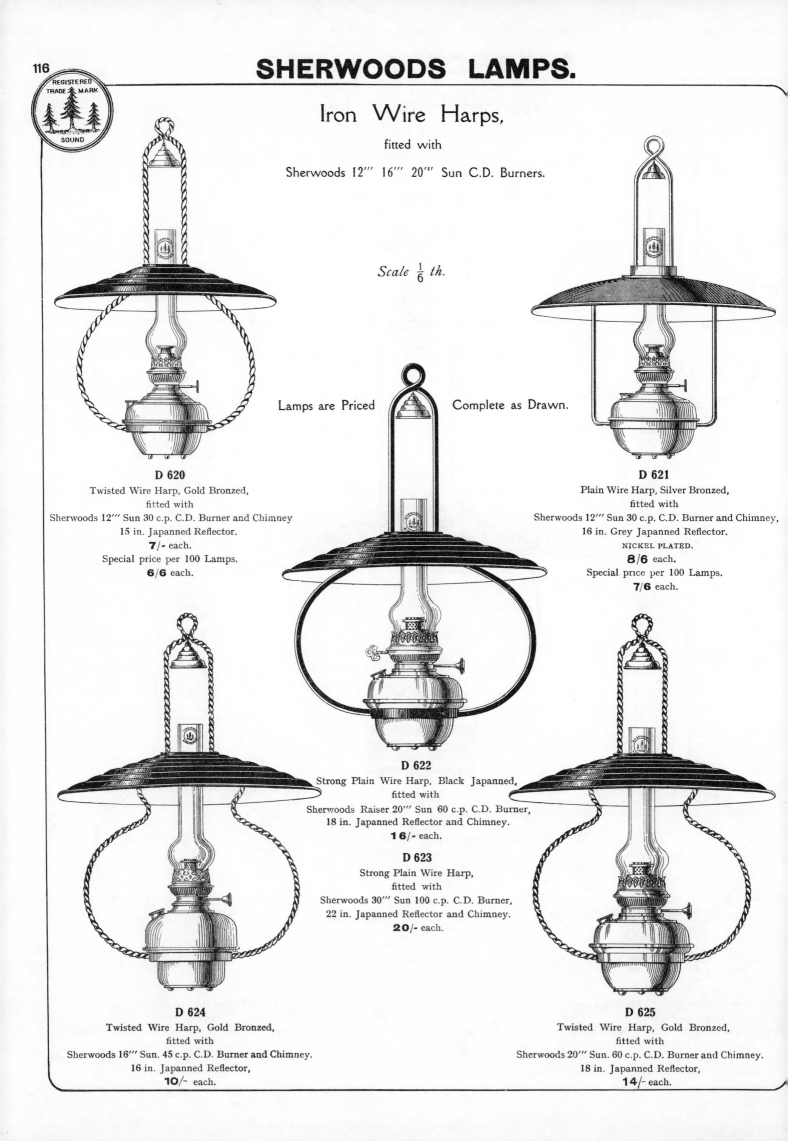

D 620
Twisted Wire Harp, Gold Bronzed,
fitted with
Sherwoods 12''' Sun 30 c.p. C.D. Burner and Chimney
15 in. Japanned Reflector.
7/- each.
Special price per 100 Lamps.
6/6 each.

D 621
Plain Wire Harp, Silver Bronzed,
fitted with
Sherwoods 12''' Sun 30 c.p. C.D. Burner and Chimney,
16 in. Grey Japanned Reflector.
NICKEL PLATED.
8/6 each.
Special price per 100 Lamps.
7/6 each.

D 622
Strong Plain Wire Harp, Black Japanned,
fitted with
Sherwoods Raiser 20''' Sun 60 c.p. C.D. Burner,
18 in. Japanned Reflector and Chimney.
16/- each.

D 623
Strong Plain Wire Harp,
fitted with
Sherwoods 30''' Sun 100 c.p. C.D. Burner,
22 in. Japanned Reflector and Chimney.
20/- each.

D 624
Twisted Wire Harp, Gold Bronzed,
fitted with
Sherwoods 16''' Sun. 45 c.p. C.D. Burner and Chimney.
16 in. Japanned Reflector,
10/- each.

D 625
Twisted Wire Harp, Gold Bronzed,
fitted with
Sherwoods 20''' Sun. 60 c.p. C.D. Burner and Chimney.
18 in. Japanned Reflector,
14/- each.

REGISTERED TRADE MARK
SOUND

SHERWOODS LAMPS.

Polished Brass and Iron Wire Harps,

fitted with

Sherwoods 20''' and 30''' Sun C.D. Burners.

Scale $\frac{1}{6}$ th.

Lamps are Priced Complete as Drawn.

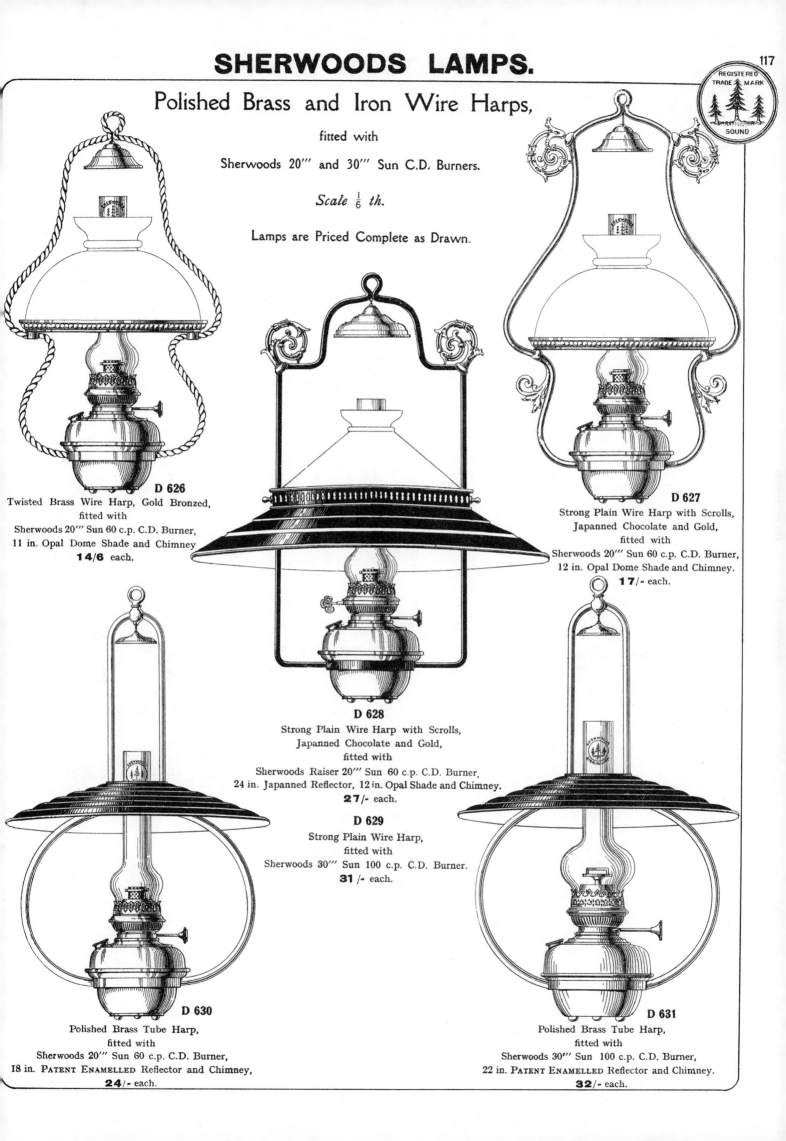

D 626
Twisted Brass Wire Harp, Gold Bronzed,
fitted with
Sherwoods 20''' Sun 60 c.p. C.D. Burner,
11 in. Opal Dome Shade and Chimney
14/6 each.

D 627
Strong Plain Wire Harp with Scrolls,
Japanned Chocolate and Gold,
fitted with
Sherwoods 20''' Sun 60 c.p. C.D. Burner,
12 in. Opal Dome Shade and Chimney.
17/- each.

D 628
Strong Plain Wire Harp with Scrolls,
Japanned Chocolate and Gold,
fitted with
Sherwoods Raiser 20''' Sun 60 c.p. C.D. Burner,
24 in. Japanned Reflector, 12 in. Opal Shade and Chimney.
27/- each.

D 629
Strong Plain Wire Harp,
fitted with
Sherwoods 30''' Sun 100 c.p. C.D. Burner.
31/- each.

D 630
Polished Brass Tube Harp,
fitted with
Sherwoods 20''' Sun 60 c.p. C.D. Burner,
18 in. PATENT ENAMELLED Reflector and Chimney,
24/- each.

D 631
Polished Brass Tube Harp,
fitted with
Sherwoods 30''' Sun 100 c.p. C.D. Burner,
22 in. PATENT ENAMELLED Reflector and Chimney.
32/- each.

SHERWOODS LAMPS.

Polished Brass Tube Harps.

All Lamps are Priced Complete as drawn.

Scale $\frac{1}{6}$ th.

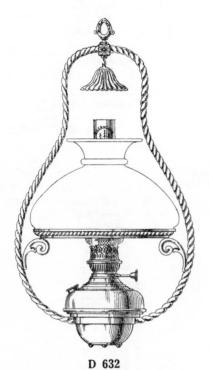

D 632

Polished Brass Tube Harp
fitted with
Sherwoods 12′′′ Sun 30 c.p. C.D. Burner.
9¼ in. Opal Shade and Chimney.
12/- each.

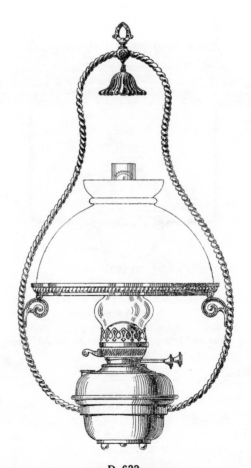

D 633

Polished Brass Tube Harp
fitted with
No. 29B Extg. Duplex Burner.
12 in. Opal Shade and Chimney.
14/- each.

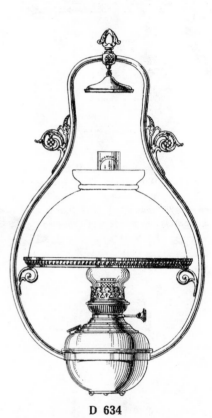

D 634

Polished Brass Tube Harp
fitted with
Sherwoods 16′′′ Sun 45 c.p. C.D. Burner.
11 in. Opal Shade and Chimney.
16/- each.

Polished Brass Tube Harps.

All Lamps are Priced Complete as drawn.

Scale $\frac{1}{6}$ th.

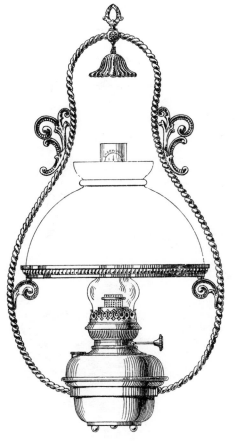

D 635

Polished Brass Tube Harp
fitted with
Sherwoods 20''' Sun 60 c.p. C.D. Burner.
12 in. Opal Shade and Chimney.
19/- each.

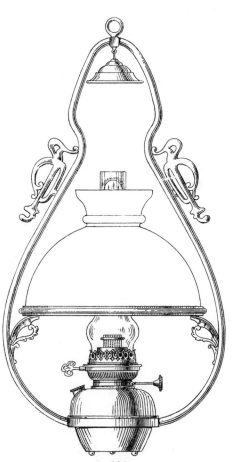

D 636

Polished Brass Tube Harp
fitted with
Sherwoods Raiser 20''' Sun 60 c.p. C.D. Burner.
14 in. Opal Shade and Chimney.
30/- each.

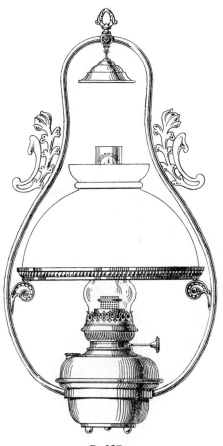

D 637

Polished Brass Tube Harp
fitted with
Sherwoods 20''' Sun 60 c.p. C.D. Burner.
12 in. Opal Shade and Chimney.
21/- each.

SHERWOODS LAMPS.

Polished Brass Tube Harps.

All Lamps are Priced Complete as drawn.

Scale $\frac{1}{6}$ th.

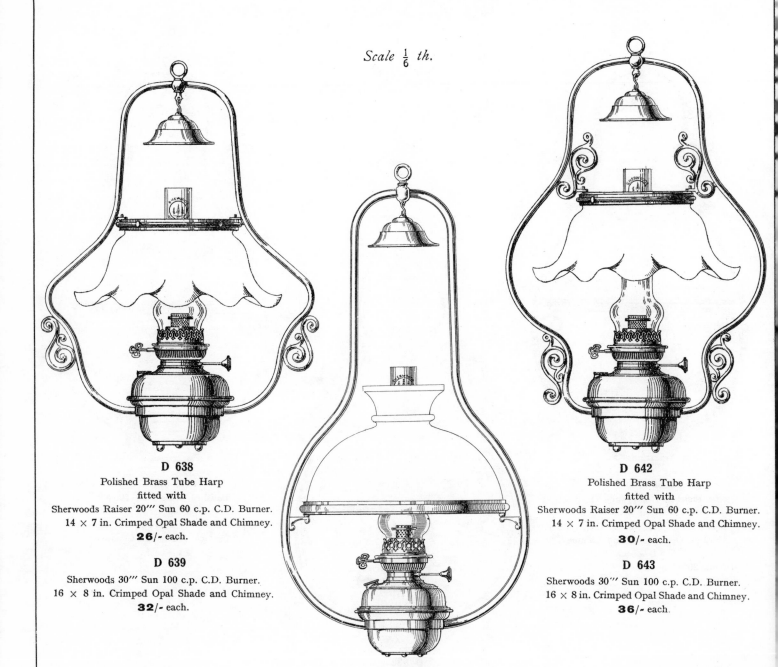

D 638

Polished Brass Tube Harp
fitted with
Sherwoods Raiser 20''' Sun 60 c.p. C.D. Burner.
14 × 7 in. Crimped Opal Shade and Chimney.
26/- each.

D 639

Sherwoods 30''' Sun 100 c.p. C.D. Burner.
16 × 8 in. Crimped Opal Shade and Chimney.
32/- each.

D 640

Polished Brass Tube Harp
fitted with
Sherwoods 20''' Sun 60 c.p. C.D. Burner.
14 in. Opal Shade and Chimney.
28/- each.

D 641

Sherwoods Raiser 20''' Sun 60 c.p. Burner.
complete as shown.
30/- each.

D 642

Polished Brass Tube Harp
fitted with
Sherwoods Raiser 20''' Sun 60 c.p. C.D. Burner.
14 × 7 in. Crimped Opal Shade and Chimney.
30/- each.

D 643

Sherwoods 30''' Sun 100 c.p. C.D. Burner.
16 × 8 in. Crimped Opal Shade and Chimney.
36/- each.

Polished Brass Tube Harps.

All Lamps are Priced Complete as drawn.

Scale $\frac{1}{6}$ *th.*

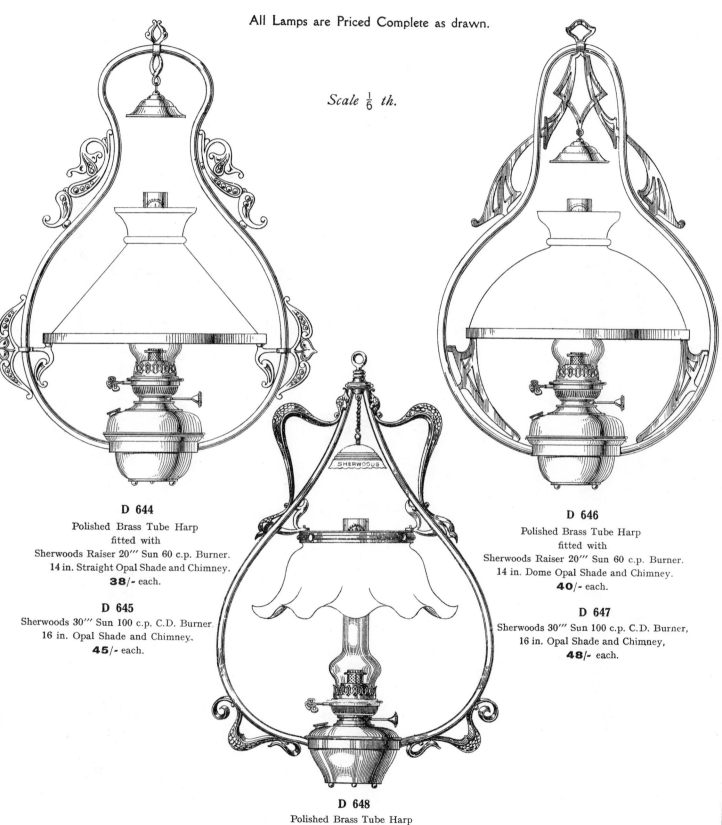

D 644

Polished Brass Tube Harp
fitted with
Sherwoods Raiser 20‴ Sun 60 c.p. Burner.
14 in. Straight Opal Shade and Chimney.
38/- each.

D 645

Sherwoods 30‴ Sun 100 c.p. C.D. Burner.
16 in. Opal Shade and Chimney.
45/- each.

D 646

Polished Brass Tube Harp
fitted with
Sherwoods Raiser 20‴ Sun 60 c.p. Burner.
14 in. Dome Opal Shade and Chimney.
40/- each.

D 647

Sherwoods 30‴ Sun 100 c.p. C.D. Burner,
16 in. Opal Shade and Chimney,
48/- each.

D 648

Polished Brass Tube Harp
fitted with
Sherwoods Raiser 20‴ Sun 60 c.p. Burner.
14 × 7 in. Crimped Opal Shade and Chimney.
45/- each.

SHERWOODS LAMPS.

Polished Brass Hanging Lamps.

Scale $\frac{1}{6}$ th.

All Lamps are Priced   complete as drawn.

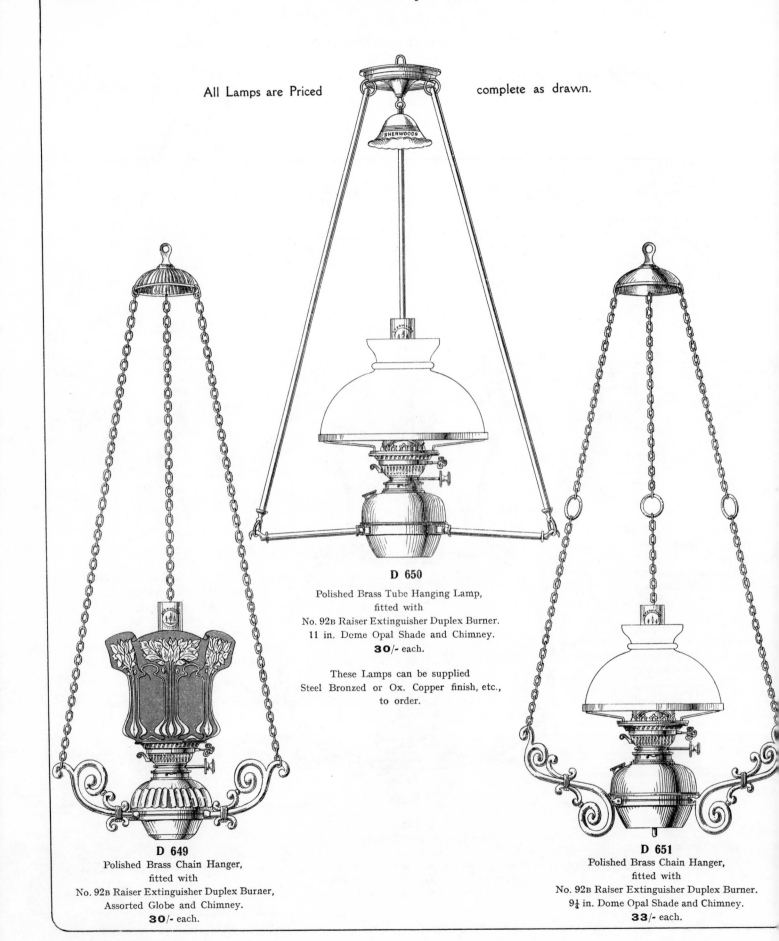

D 650

Polished Brass Tube Hanging Lamp,
fitted with
No. 92B Raiser Extinguisher Duplex Burner.
11 in. Dome Opal Shade and Chimney.
30/- each.

These Lamps can be supplied
Steel Bronzed or Ox. Copper finish, etc.,
to order.

D 649

Polished Brass Chain Hanger,
fitted with
No. 92B Raiser Extinguisher Duplex Burner,
Assorted Globe and Chimney.
30/- each.

D 651

Polished Brass Chain Hanger,
fitted with
No. 92B Raiser Extinguisher Duplex Burner.
9¼ in. Dome Opal Shade and Chimney.
33/- each.

SHERWOODS LAMPS.

Polished Brass Hanging Lamps.

Scale $\frac{1}{6}$ th.

All Lamps are Priced   complete as drawn.

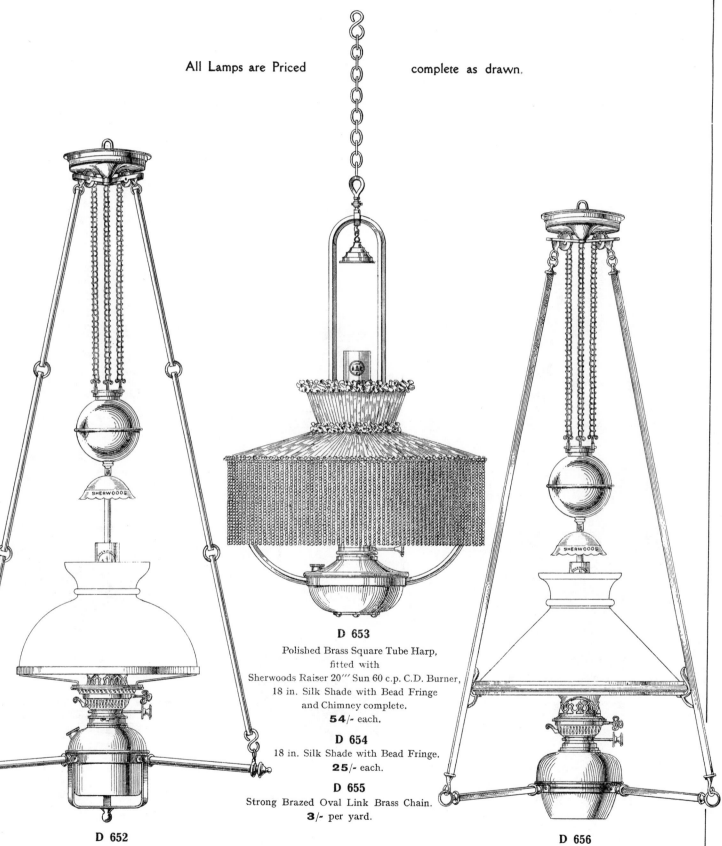

D 653

Polished Brass Square Tube Harp,
fitted with
Sherwoods Raiser 20‴ Sun 60 c.p. C.D. Burner,
18 in. Silk Shade with Bead Fringe
and Chimney complete.
54/- each.

D 654

18 in. Silk Shade with Bead Fringe.
25/- each.

D 655

Strong Brazed Oval Link Brass Chain.
3/- per yard.

D 652

Polished Brass Tube Slide Hanging Lamp,
fitted with
No. 92B S.W. Raiser Extinguisher Duplex Burner
12 in. Dome Opal Shade and Chimney.
44/- each.

D 656

Polished Brass Square Tube Slide Hanging Lamp.
fitted with
No. 92B S.W. Raiser Extinguisher Duplex Burner,
14 in. Straight Opal Shade and Chimney.
50/- each.

SHERWOODS LAMPS.

Polished Brass Suspension Lamps

fitted with

Sherwoods 12''' Sun 30 c p. and 16''' Sun 45 c.p. Central Draught Burners.

Scale $\frac{1}{9}$ th.

All Lamps are Priced without Glass.

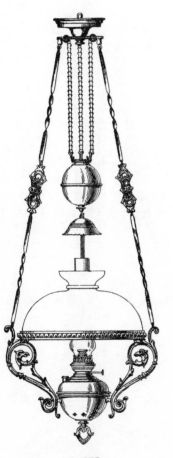

D 657

Polished Brass Suspension Lamp
fitted with
Sherwoods 12''' Sun 30 c.p. C.D. Burner.
12 in. Shade Ring.
28/- each.

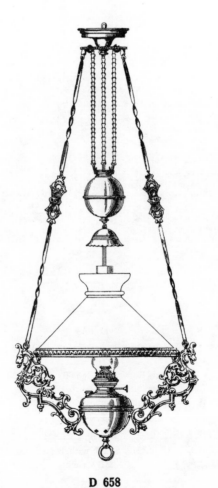

D 658

Polished Brass Suspension Lamp
fitted with
Sherwoods 16''' Sun 45 c.p. C.D. Burner.
14 in. Shade Ring.
45/- each.

D 659

Polished Brass Suspension Lamp
fitted with
Sherwoods 12''' Sun 30 c.p. C.D. Burner.
14 in. Shade Ring.
30/- each.

Polished Brass Suspension Lamps

fitted with

Sherwoods 20''' Sun 60 c.p. Central Draught Burners.

Scale $\frac{1}{9}$ th.

All Lamps are Priced without Glass.

D 660

Polished Brass Suspension Lamp
fitted with
Sherwoods Raiser 20''' Sun 60 c.p. C.D. Burner.
14 in. Shade Ring.
86/- each.

D 661

Polished Brass Suspension Lamp
fitted with
Sherwoods Raiser 20''' Sun 60 c.p. C.D. Burner.
14 in. Shade Ring.
72/- each.

D 662

Polished Brass Suspension Lamp
fitted with
Sherwoods Raiser 20''' Sun 60 c.p. C.D. Burner.
14 in. Shade Ring.
88/- each.

SHERWOODS LAMPS.

Ruby Heating Stoves

fitted with

Sherwoods 16''' Sun 45 c.p., 20''' Sun 60 c.p. and 30''' Sun 100 c.p. Central Draught Burners.

Scale $\frac{1}{5}$ th.

All Lamps are Priced complete.

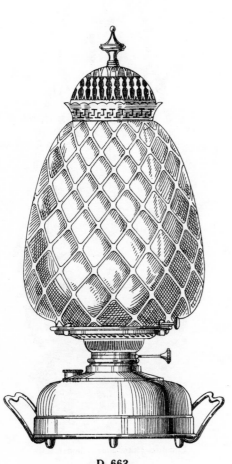

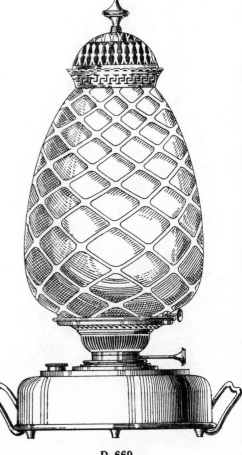

D 665
Polished Brass Heating Stove
fitted with
Sherwoods 16''' Sun 45 c.p. C.D. Burner,
Cast Iron Radiator, Brass Coronet.
Ruby Globe and Chimney.
18/- each.

D 666
16''' Sun Ruby Stove Globes.
5/- each.

D 667
Cast Iron Radiators.
2/- each.

D 668
Brass Stove Coronets.
1/- each.

D 663
Polished Brass Heating Stove
fitted with
Sherwoods 20''' Sun 60 c.p. C.D. Burner,
Cast Iron Radiator, Brass Coronet.
Ruby Globe and Chimney.
25/- each.

D 664
20''' Sun Ruby Stove Globes.
7/- each.

D 669
Polished Brass Heating Stove,
fitted with
Sherwoods 30''' Sun 100 c.p. C.D. Burner,
Cast Iron Radiator, Brass Coronet.
Ruby Globe and Chimney.
36/- each.

D 670
30''' Sun Ruby Stove Globes.
9/- each.

SHERWOODS LAMPS.

Church Fittings

fitted with

Sherwoods 20''' Sun 60 c.p. and 30''' Sun 100 c.p. Central Draught Burners.

Scale $\frac{1}{5}$ th.

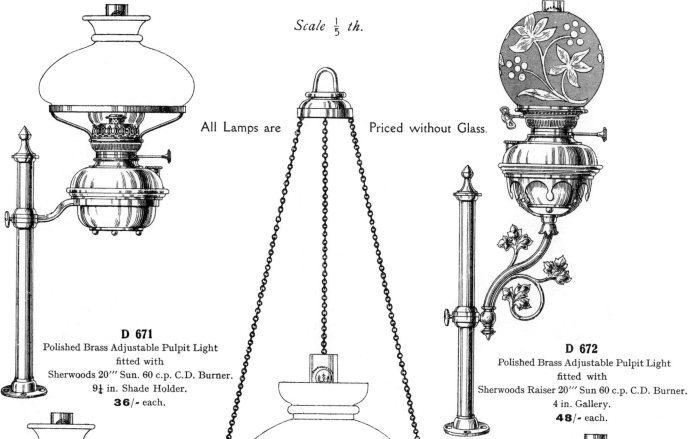

All Lamps are   Priced without Glass.

D 671
Polished Brass Adjustable Pulpit Light
fitted with
Sherwoods 20''' Sun. 60 c.p. C.D. Burner.
9¼ in. Shade Holder.
36/- each.

D 672
Polished Brass Adjustable Pulpit Light
fitted with
Sherwoods Raiser 20''' Sun 60 c.p. C.D. Burner.
4 in. Gallery.
48/- each.

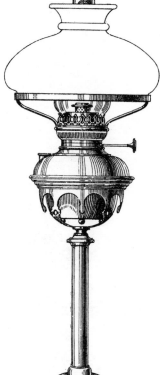

D 673
Polished Brass Pulpit Light
fitted with
Sherwoods 20''' Sun 60 c.p. C.D. Burner.
9¼ in. Shade Holder.

15 in.	18 in.	21 in. high.
27/- each	**28/6** each	**30/-** each.

D 674
Heavy Polished Cast Suspension.
fitted with
Sherwoods Raiser 20''' Sun 60 c.p. C.D. Lurner.
14 in. Shade Ring.
80/- each.

D 675
Sherwoods 30''' Sun 100 c.p. C.D. Burner.
16 in. Shade Ring.
100/- each.

D 676
Polished Brass Pulpit Light
fitted with
Sherwoods 20''' Sun 60 c.p. C.D. Burner.
9¼ in. Shade Holder.
36/- each.

SHERWOODS LAMPS.

Ship Lamps Founts.

Polished Brass and Copper.

Scale ¼ th.

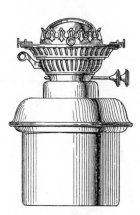

D 677
Small size
Brass and Copper Spun Fount
fitted with
86B ⅝ in. S.W. Dual Burner,
3/- each.
Fitting 3¼ in.

D 678
Large Size
Brass and Copper Spun Fount,
fitted with
No. 44B Extg. Duplex Burner, 3 Screw Gallery.
8/- each.
Fitting 4⅝ in. and 5 in.

D 679
Medium Size.
Brass and Copper Spun Fount
fitted with
86B ⅞ in. S.W. Dual Burner.
4/- each.
Fitting 4⅞ ins.

Polished Gimbal Saloon Bracket Lamps.

Scale. ⅙ th.

All Lamps are Priced   Complete as drawn.

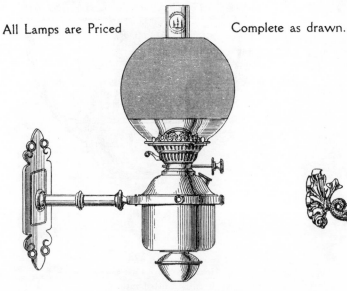

D 680
Cast Dolphin Gimbal Bracket Lamp,
Heavy Glass Fount
fitted with
1 in. Hinge Burner and Chimney.
10/6 each.

D 681
Heavy Cast Polished Gimbal Bracket Lamp,
Iron loaded Foot,
fitted with
No.44B S.W. Extg. Duplex Burner, 3 Screw gallery
¾ in. Frosted Mono Globe and Chimney.
30/- each.

D 682
Cast Dolphin Gimbal Bracket Lamp,
Iron loaded Foot,
fitted with
Sherwoods 12''' Sun 30 c.p. C.D. Burner.
7¼ in. Opal Shade and Chimney.
21/- each.

Ship Lamps.

Polished Gimbal Saloon Bracket Lamps.

Scale ¼ th.

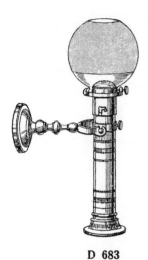

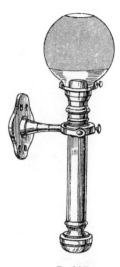

D 683

Polished Brass or Steel Bronzed
Bracket Lamps.
¾ in. Frosted Globe complete.
11/6 each.

D 684

Polished Brass or Steel Bronzed
Bracket Lamp.
¾ in. Frosted Globe complete.
18/- each.

D 685

Polished Brass or Steel Bronzed
Bracket Lamp.
¾ in. Frosted Globe complete.
14/- each.

Polished Gimbal Saloon Hanging Lamps.

Scale ⅙ th.

All Lamps are Priced   complete as drawn.

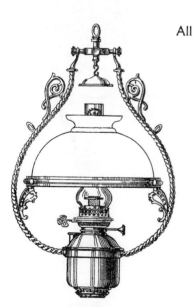

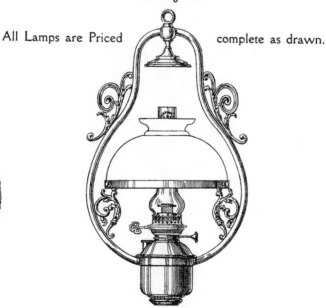

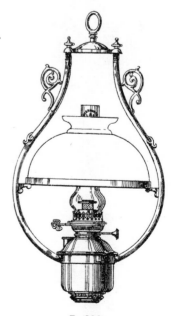

D 686

Polished Brass or Steel Bronzed
Hanging Lamp.
Sherwoods Raiser 20′′′ Sun 60 c.p. C.D. Burner.
11 in. Opal Shade and Chimney.
36/- each.

D 687

Polished Brass or Steel Bronzed
Hanging Lamp.
Sherwoods Raiser 20′′′ Sun 60 c.p. C.D. Burner.
12 in. Opal Shade and Chimney.
42/- each.

D 688

Polished Brass or Steel Bronzed
Hanging Lamp.
Sherwoods Raiser 20′′′ Sun 60 c.p. C.D. Burner.
11 in. Opal Shade and Chimney.
39/- each.

SHERWOODS LAMPS.

Fancy Table and Piano Lamps.

Scale ⅕ th.

D 689
REGENT
Fancy Piano Lamp,
with Clip Sockets.
88B Burner, D 26 Shade Holder and Chimney.
8/6 each.
Silver Plated,
12/6 each.

D 690
PRINCESS
Spun Metal Table Lamp,
Silver Plated.
88B Burner, English Globe and Chimney.
Complete as drawn.
13/- each.

D 691
CONSORT
Fancy Piano Lamp,
with Clip Sockets.
88B Burner, D 26 Shade Holder and Chimney.
9/- each.
Silver Plated,
13/6 each.

Reading Lamp.

Priced with Shades and 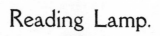 Holders Complete as drawn.

D 692
MARQUISE
Corinthian Pillar Table Lamp.
Silver Plated.
88B Burner, Shade Holder and Chimney.
Complete as drawn.
21/- each.

D 693
PEER
Polished Brass Reading Lamp,
fitted with
10‴ Cosmos Burner, 7¼ in. Opal Shade & Chimney.
Complete as drawn.
9/- each.

D 694
DUCHESS
Square Pillar Table Lamp,
Silver Plated.
88B Burner, Shade Holder and Chimney.
Complete as drawn.
24/- each.

Fancy Table Candle Lamps.

Scale $\frac{1}{5}$ *th.*

D 696

Sliding Shade Holder with Clip Springs, Silver Plated.

1/- each.

D 695

DURHAM

Corinthian Pillow Candle Stand, Silver Plated.

D 26 Shade   D 696 Shade Holder.

Complete as drawn.

15/- each.

D 697

ELY

Square Pillar Candle Stand, Silver Plated.

D 26 Shade, D 696 Shade Holder.

Complete as drawn.

17/- each.

Candelabras.

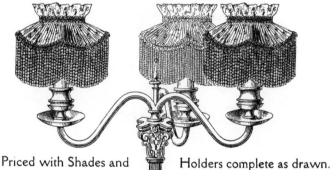

Priced with Shades and   Holders complete as drawn.

D 24

Square Figured Chintz Shade, with Bead Fringe.

6/- each.

D 26

Goffered Gimped Shade with Bead Fringe.

5/- each.

D 698

BEDFORD

Taper Pillar Candle Stand, Silver Plated.

D 24 Shade, D 696 Shade Holder, Complete as drawn.

16/- each.

D 699

YORK

3-arm Corinthian Candelabra Stand, Silver Plated.

D 24 Shades   D 696 Shade Holders.

Complete as drawn.

90/- each.

D 700

CARLISLE

3-arm Branch Candelabra Stand, Silver Plated.

D 24 Shades   D 696 Shade Holders.

Complete as drawn,

60/- each.

Specially prepared hard Sperm No. 6 Candles for above.   See page 139.

SHERWOODS LAMPS.

Electric Fittings.

Priced without Lamps, Shades, Holders or Wires.

Scale $\frac{1}{5}$ *th.*

12 A

Extra Strong Electric Shade Holder
to take Metal Filament Lamp.
18/- doz.

13 A

Brass Shade Carrier.
8/- doz.

11 A

Strong Tripod Shade Holder.
14/- doz.

133

Polished Brass or Steel Bronzed,
with 2½ in. Cast Backs.

$\frac{1}{2}$ × 6 in.	$\frac{1}{2}$ × 9 in.	$\frac{1}{2}$ × 12 in.
13/-	**15/-**	**19/-** per doz.

132

Polished Brass or Steel Bronzed,
with 2½ in. Cast Backs.

$\frac{1}{2}$ × 6 in.	$\frac{1}{2}$ × 9 in.	$\frac{1}{2}$ × 12 in.
13/-	**15/-**	**19/-** per doz.

131

Polished Brass or Steel Bronzed,
with 2½ in. Cast Backs.

$\frac{1}{2}$ × 6 in.	$\frac{1}{2}$ × 9 in.	$\frac{1}{2}$ × 12 in.
13/-	**15/-**	**19/-** per doz.

Ceiling Fittings.

Scale $\frac{1}{6}$ *th.*

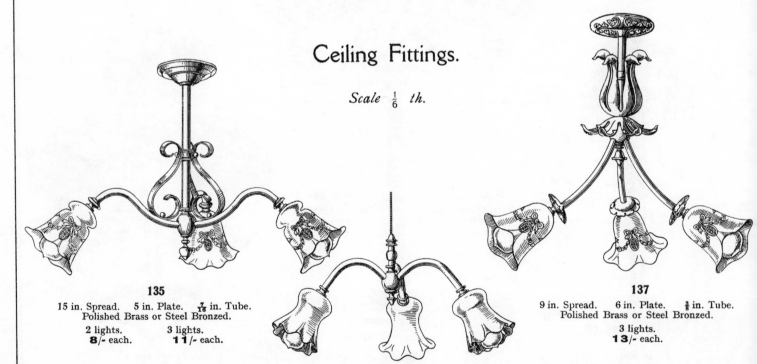

135

15 in. Spread.   5 in. Plate. $\frac{7}{16}$ in. Tube.
Polished Brass or Steel Bronzed.

2 lights.	3 lights.
8/- each.	**11/-** each.

136

12 in. Spread. $\frac{3}{8}$ in. Tube.
Polished Brass or Steel Bronzed

3 lights.
33/- doz.

137

9 in. Spread.   6 in. Plate. $\frac{3}{8}$ in. Tube.
Polished Brass or Steel Bronzed.

3 lights.
13/- each.

Supplied Oxydised Copper and Antique Finish extra to Order.

SHERWOODS LAMPS.

Brackets.

Scale $\frac{1}{5}$ *th.*

Priced without Lamps, Shades, Holders or Wires.

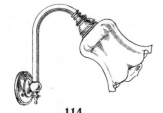

114

5 in. Projection, 4½ in. Rise, 3 in. Back.
Polished Brass or Steel Bronzed,
21/- doz.

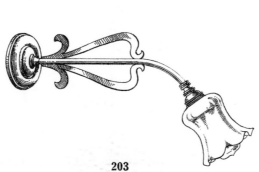

203

11 in. Projection, ⅜ in. Tube, 3½ in. Back.
Polished Brass or Steel Bronzed.
48/- doz.

115

7½ in. Projection, ⁷⁄₁₆ in. Tube, 3¼ in. Back.
Polished Brass or Steel Bronzed.
30/- doz.

206

12 in. Projection, ⁷⁄₁₆ in. Tube, 6 × 3 in. Back.
Polished Brass or Steel Bronzed.
7/6 each.

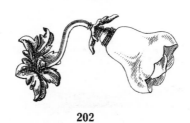

202

4½ in. Projection, ⅜ in. Tube.
Polished Brass or Steel Bronzed.
42/- doz.

207

11 in. Projection, ⁷⁄₁₆ in. Tube, 5 in. Back,
Polished Brass or Steel Bronzed.
8/- each.

209

10 in. Projection, ⁷⁄₁₆ in. Tube, 4½ in. Back.
Polished Brass or Steel Bronzed.
7/- each.

204

7½ in. Projection, ⅜ in. Tube, 4 in. Back.
Polished Brass or Steel Bronzed.
4/6 each.

205

12 in. Projection, ⁷⁄₁₆ in. Tube, 6 × 3 in. Back.
Polished Brass or Steel Bronzed.
7/- each.

Supplied Oxydised Copper and Antique Finish extra to Order.

SHERWOODS LAMPS.

Standards.

Scale $\frac{1}{5}$ th.

2592

Polished or Steel.
4/- each.
Special Price, 6 doz. Lots,
3/8 each.
Height 8½ in.   Base 3¾ in.

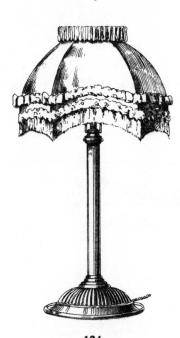

134

Polished or Steel.
2/3 each.
Special Price, 6 doz. Lots,
2/- each.
Height 10 in.   Base 5¾ in.

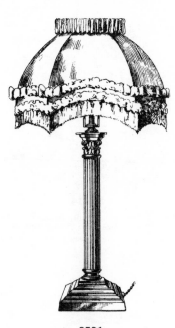

2591

Polished or Steel.
4/6 each.
Special Price, 6 doz. Lots,
4/- each.
Height 10 in.   Base 3¾ in.

All Pillars are Priced without Holders or Shades.

2535/S

Polished or Steel.
5/6 each.
Special Price, 3 doz. Lots,
5/3 each.
Height 9½ in.   Base 4½ in.

2573/E

Polished or Steel.
5/- each.
Special Price, 3 doz. Lots,
4/9 each.
Height 10½ in.   Base 4 in.

2357/E

Polished or Steel.
5/9 each.
6 doz. Lots, **5/6** each.
Height 9½ in.   Base 4¾ in.

Supplied Oxydised Copper and Antique Finish extra to Order.

SHERWOODS LAMPS.

Standards.

Scale $\frac{1}{5}$ th.

2529/E
Polished or Steel.
6/- each.
Special Price. 3 doz. Lots,
5/9 each.
Height 11 in. Base 4½ in.

2411/E
Polished or Steel.
7/- each.
Special Price, 3 doz. Lots,
6/6 each.
Height 12 in. Base 5⅜ in.

2517/E
Polished or Steel.
8/- each.
Special Price, 3 doz. Lots,
7/6 each.
Height 12½ in. Base 5½ in.

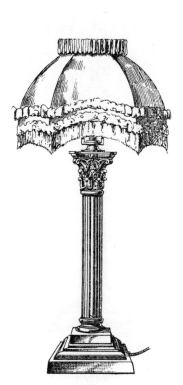

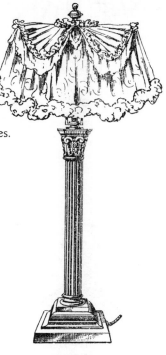

All Pillars are Priced   without Holders or Shades.

2158/E
Cast Foot, Polished or Steel.
14/- each.
Special Price, 3 doz. Lots,
13/- each.
Height 12½ in. Base 4⅞ in.

2223/E
Cast Foot and Corinthian.
25/- each.
Height 16½ in. Base 5¼ in.

2535/E
7/6 each.
Special Price, 3 doz. Lots,
7/- each.
Height 12 in. Base 4½ in.

Supplied Oxydised Copper and Antique Finish extra to Order.

SHERWOODS LAMPS.

Standards.

Scale $\frac{1}{5}$ *th.*

2356/E
Polished or Steel.
7/6 each.
Special Price, 3 doz. Lots,
7/3 each.
Height 9½ in. Base 4¾ in.

121
Polished Cast Brass Tripod.
Adjustable for Table or Bracket,
12/- each.

123
Polished Brass with Plain Tube.
4/- each.
Special Price, 3 doz. Lots,
3/9 each.
Height 12 in. Base 5 in.

Priced without Lamps,   Shades, Holders or Wires.

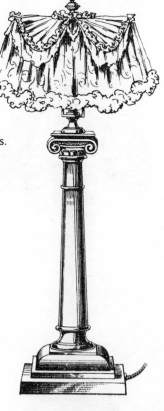

2166/E
Polished Cast Brass.
24/- each.
Height 15 in. Base 5 in.

2156/E
Polished Cast Brass.
48/- each.
Height 19 in. Base 6½ in.

2235/E
Polished Cast Brass.
27/- each.
Height 15½ in. Base 5⅞ in.

Supplied Oxydised Copper and Antique Finish extra to Order.

Portable Standards.

Scale $\frac{1}{6}$ th.

2594
Polished Brass with Plain Taper Tube.
5/6 each.
Height 10½ in. Base 4¾ in.

209
Polished Brass with Black China Base.
4/- each.
Height 12 in. Base 5½ in.

2159
Polished Brass Slide Reading Standard.
12/- each.
Height 24 in. Base 6 in.

GREEN CARDBOARD SHADES.
White inside.
With Brass Collars.
8in. by 3½in. deep, **8/6** doz.

Priced without Lamps, Shades, Holders or Wires.

210
Polished Brass with Three Fancy Cast Scrolls.
10/- each.
Ditto, with Two Fancy Cast Scrolls.
8/- each.
Height 12½ in. Base 6 in.

2593
Polished Brass, with Plain Taper Tube.
6/6 each.
Height 10½ in. Base 3¾ in.

Supplied Oxydised Copper and Antique Finish extra to Order.

SHERWOODS LAMPS.

Polished Telescopic Floor Standards.

Scale $\frac{1}{6}$ th.

SUPERIOR   FINISH.

Full Extension
6 ft.

Full Extension
5 ft. 3 in.

Full Extension
5 ft. 10 in.

Priced without Lamps,   Shades, Holders or Wires.

2212/E	**2364/E**	**2296**
Polished Brass Standard with Cast Foot.	Superior Polished Brass Standard, with Heavy Cast Foot.	Polished Copper and Brass Standard, with Cast Foot.
70/- each.	**95/-** each.	**65/-** each.
D 28	**D 29**	**D 30**
EMPIRE	**THAMES**	**DOMINION**
18in. Silk Gimp Shade, with Bead Fringe,	18in. Silk Pleated Shade, with Bead Fringe,	18in. Silk Vandyke Shade, with Bead Fringe,
18/- each.	**36/-** each.	**24/-** each.

Supplied Oxydised Copper and Antique Finish extra to Order.

Table Candle Lamps.

Scale $\frac{1}{5}$ th.

D 701

Electric Bulb.
5/- each.
Low Voltage 100, 105, 110, 115 and 120 c.p.
High Voltage 200, 210, 220, 230 and 240 c.p.
Required voltage must be specified when ordering.

D 702

THE " VARSITY " LAMP.
Adaptable
for Candle or Electric Light.
Nickel Plated.
D 26 Shade and Shade Holder
for Candle as drawn.
11/- each.

For Electric, D ●●● Adapter is required.
703

D 703 702
Electric Adapter for D ●●● Candle Lamp.
Nickel Plated.
Shade Holder, Bulb, and 2 yards Silk Cord.
11/- each.

Coronation Lamps.

Scale $\frac{1}{3}$ rd.

FANCY NIGHT LIGHT

FOR

NURSERIES, BAZAARS & CONSERVATORIES.

FANCY ILLUMINATION LANTERN

FOR

CARNIVAL AND CHRISTMAS DECORATION.

D 704

Special Candles for D 705, and D 707 Lanterns.
4 hours, **12/-** gross.

SHERWOODS
Specially Prepared
SPERM WAX CANDLES,
Hard Coated for
READING CANDLE LAMPS.

D 705

" STELLITE "
Safety Night Light Lamp.
Nickel Plated.
Assorted Colours, Blue and Red Glasses,
Candle Dish and Candle.
17/- doz.
Special price 6 doz. Lots,
15/- doz.

D 706

Spare Assorted Coloured Glasses.
5/- doz.

SHERWOODS
HARD VEGETABLE WAX
CANDLES

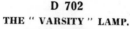

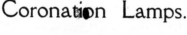

D 707

" DEMON "
Fancy Illumination Lantern,
Octagonal.
Assorted Coloured Cathedral Glass,
Candle Dish and Candle.
48/- gross.
Special Price 12 doz. Lots.
42/- gross.

No. 4	Candle for No. 62 Candle Lamp, ...	$4 \times 1\frac{3}{16}$ in. thick,	**3/6** doz.
No. 6	,, ,, Nos. 24, 51, 61, 71, 72, 109, 111, 114, 115, 116, 197	$4\frac{1}{2} \times \frac{7}{8}$ in. ,,	**2/6** ,,
No. 10	,, ,, Nos. 8, 10, 11, 20, 23, 28, 29, 30, 31, 34, 46, 47, 48, 60, 73	$6\frac{1}{2} \times \frac{7}{8}$ in. ,,	**3/3** ,,

Boxed in dozens.   Subject to Market Fluctuations.

SHERWOODS LAMPS.

Sherwoods "Dreadnought" Lantern.

Central Draught.

Scale ⅓ rd.

NO EQUAL,   **NO RIVAL.**

Approximate weights and measurements, packed 3 doz. per CASK.

Gross ... 1 2 14

38 × 34

Net ... 0 3 20

Approximate weights and measurements, Packed 6 doz. per CASK.

Gross ... 2 2 12

50 × 50

Net ... 1 3 10

Spare Globes.

Clear.   Ruby.

5/- doz.   **15/-** doz.

Spare Burners.
Body and Cone complete.

12/- doz.

1840

DREADNOUGHT
Japanned Windproof Lantern with steel container
with Movable Globe for Lighting,
fitted with
⅝ in. Burner and Globe complete.

ENGLISH MAKE.   **ENGLISH MAKE.**

BRIGHT FINISH.
54/- doz.
Special price 12 doz. lots,
48/- doz.

JAPANNED BRONZE FINISH.
60/- doz,
Special price 12 doz. lots,
54/- doz.

Sherwoods "Squall" Lantern.

Brass Throughout.

Scale $\frac{1}{3}$ rd

THE BEST.

THE BRIGHTEST.

Approximate weights and measurements,
Packed 1 doz. per Case.

Gross ... 0 2 10

33 × 24 × 15

Net ... 0 1 5

Approximate weights and measurements,
packed 3 doz. per CASK.

Gross ... 1 2 14

38 × 34

Net ... 0 3 20

Spare Globes.

Clear.

5/- doz.

Ruby.

15/- doz.

Spare Burners,
Body and Cone complete.

12/- doz.

ENGLISH MAKE.

ENGLISH MAKE.

1841

SQUALL

All Brass Windproof Lantern, double container,
with ~~raised~~ lever for lighting,
fitted with
⅞ in. Burner and Globe complete.

84/- doz.

SHERWOODS LAMPS.

Punkah Tops.

P 46
Nickel Plated Punkah Top,
4/- doz.
For Nos. **7, 8, and 8**A Globes.

P 30
Nickel Plated Punkah Top,
12/- doz.
For Nos. **3, 5, 5**A and 9 Globes.

P 29
Nickel Plated Punkah Top,
3/6 each.
For Nos. **5** and **5**A Globes.

P 196
Nickel Plated Punkah Top,
3/6 each.
For Nos. **5** and **5**A Globes.

Globes.

8
Clear Globe,
Ground Top and Bottom.
4/6 doz.
Per original case 25 doz.
3/6 doz.

8 A
Opal Globe,
Ground Top and Bottom.
6/- doz.

6 A
Best Quality Opal Ship Lamp Globe,
Polished Top and Bottom.
18/- doz.

7
Decorated Globe,
Ground Top and Bottom.
6/- doz.
Per original Case 25 doz.
5/- doz.

5
Best Quality Clear Globe,
Polished Top and Bottom.
12/- doz.

6
Best Quality ¾ Frosted Globe,
Polished Top and Bottom.
18/- doz.
(For No. 25 Candle Lamp)
Steel Bronzed Punkah Top.
24/- doz.

4
Best Quality ¾ Squat Opal Globe.
Polished Top and Bottom.
18/- doz.
(For No. 20 Candle Lamp)
Steel Bronzed Punkah Top.
24/- doz.

5 A
Best Quality ¾ Frosted Globe,
Polished Top and Bottom.
12/- doz.

English Make Globes.

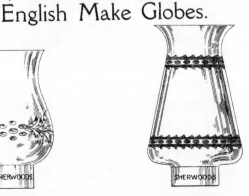

1
Heavy English Make Tulip Globe,
Single etched bands.
30/- doz.

3
Heavy English Make Tulip Globe.
Fancy etched.
16/- doz.

9
New Shape.
Best Quality English Make Globe,
Double etched bands.
26/- doz.

2
Heavy English Make Tulip Globe,
Double etched bands.
33/- doz.

Sherwoods Limited, 44, 46, 48, 50, GRANVILLE STREET, **Birmingham**

Candle Lamps.

ENGLISH MAKE.

"LION BRAND."   *"LION BRAND."*

Scale $\frac{1}{4}$ *th.*

"VICEROY."

197 A
Superior Quality
Nickel Plated Pedestal Candle Lamp
2 light.
No. **3** Globes and **P 30** Punkah Tops,
Complete as drawn.
17/6 each.

197 D
Superior Quality
Nickel Plated Pedestal Candle Lamp,
4 light.
No. **3** Globes and **P 30** Punkah Tops.
27/- each.

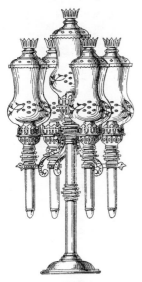

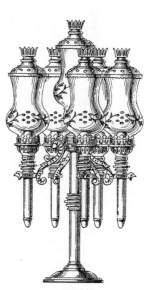

197 C
Superior Quality
Nickel Plated Pedestal Candle Lamp,
5 lights.
No. **3** Globes and **P 30** Punkah Tops.
32/- each.

197 B
Superior Quality
Nickel Plated Pedestal Candle Lamp.
3 light.
No. **3** Globes and **P 30** Punkah Tops,
Complete as drawn.
21/- each.

197 E
Superior Quality
Nickel Plated Pedestal Candle Lamp,
6 lights.
No. **3** Globes and **P 30** Punkah Tops.
40/- each.

All Candle Lamps are priced complete as drawn.

SHERWOODS LAMPS.

Candle Lamps.

INDIAN

CANDLE  LAMPS.

"LION BRAND."

Scale ⅓ rd.

SPECIAL EXPORT LINE.

SPECIAL EXPORT LINE

ACCESSORIES.

	F.E.P	C.I.F.	
Nickel Plated Nozzles ...	2/-	2/6	doz.
,, Punkah Tops	4/-	4/6	,,

ACCESSORIES.

	F.E.P.	C.I.F.	
Strong Brass Springs ...	4/-	5/-	doz.
N. P. Loose Tubes, Springs and Nozzles	14/-	18/-	

CANDLE LAMPS.

Approximate Weight and Measurement.
Packed 100 Lamps per case.

Gross ... 1 3 20

Net ... 1 0 8   39 × 26 × 27

Case at cost, **16/-** each.

CANDLE LAMP GLOBES.

Nos. **7** and **8.**
Approximate Weight and Measurement.
Packed 25 dozen per case.

Gross ... 3 0 0

Net ... 0 3 16   50 × 38 × 38

Original Case Free.

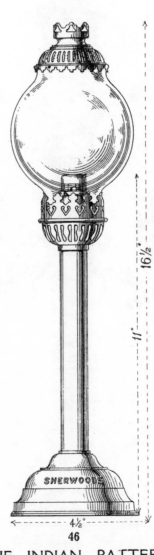

16½″

11″

4½″

46

THE INDIAN PATTERN.

with Loose Inside Candle Tube.

When indenting specify only
SHERWOODS "LION BRAND" CANDLE LAMPS.

When indenting specify only
SHERWOODS "LION BRAND" CANDLE LAMPS.

All Candle Lamps stamped with our name
and Trade Mark we guarantee
ENGLISH MAKE.

All Candle Lamps stamped with our name
and Trade Mark we guarantee
ENGLISH MAKE.

PRICE.

Free Port (London or Liverpool)	**33/-** doz.
Special Price per Shipment, 5 Cases, 500 Lamps	**31/-** ,,
,, ,, ,, 10 ,, 1,000 ,,	**29/-** ,,

PRICE.

C.I.F. Madras, Bombay or Calcutta	**39/-** doz.
Special Price per Shipment, 5 Cases, 500 Lamps	**36/-** ,,
,, ,, ,, 10 ,, 1,000 ,,	**33/-** ,,

Prices are quoted without Globes.

Sherwoods Limited, 44, 46, 48, 50, GRANVILLE STREET, Birmingham

Candle Lamps.

PERSIAN

CANDLE LAMPS.

"LION BRAND."

Scale $\frac{1}{4}$ th.

| SPECIAL EXPORT LINE. | | SPECIAL EZPORT LINE, |

ACCESSORIES.

Nickel Plated Nozzles ... **2/-** doz.

ACCESSORIES.

Brass Springs ... **6/-** doz.

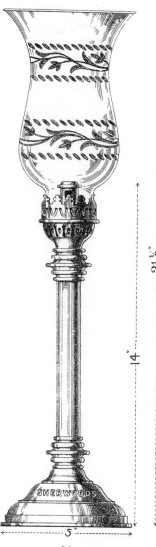

CANDLE LAMPS.

Approximate Weight and Measurements.

Packed 60 per Case.

Gross ... 1 2 0

Net ... 0 3 12   33 × 21 × 31

Case at cost, **14/-** each.

CANDLE LAMP GLOBES.

Nos. **1** and **2**.

Approximate Weight and Measurements.

Packed 70 per Case.

Gross ... 1 1 4

Net ... 0 1 22   35 × 26 × 31

Case at cost **16/-** each.

When indenting specify only

SHERWOODS "LION BRAND" CANDLE LAMPS.

All Candle Lamps stamped with our name
and Trade Mark we guarantee
ENGLISH MAKE.

When indenting specify only

SHERWOODS "LION BRAND" CANDLE LAMPS.

All Candle Lamps stamped with our name
and Trade Mark we guarantee
ENGLISH MAKE.

26

THE PERSIAN PATTERN.

Superior Quality Nickel Plated Table Candle Lamp,
48/- doz.
Special Price per Shipment, 4 Cases, 240 Lamps.
45/- doz.

The above Prices are quoted Free Port England (London or Liverpool).

Prices are quoted without Globes.

SHERWOODS LAMPS.

Candle Lamps.

Scale ¼ th.

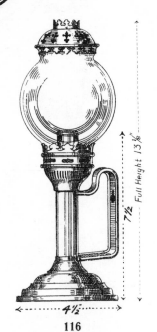

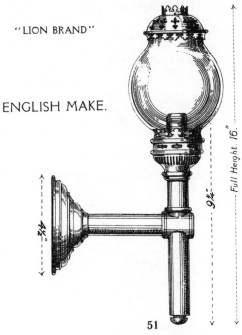

"LION BRAND"

ENGLISH MAKE.

"LION BRAND"

ENGLISH MAKE.

116
Cheap Quality
Nickel Plated Candle Lamp,
Hand and Wall.
24/- doz.
Special price 25 doz. lots.
22/- doz.

51
Cheap Quality
Nickel Plated Candle Lamp,
Bracket and Table.
36/- doz.
Special price 25 doz. lots.
33/- doz.

114
Best Quality
Nickel Plated Candle Lamp,
Hand and Wall.
30/- doz.
Special price 25 doz. lots.
28/- doz.

All Candle Lamps are Priced without Globes.

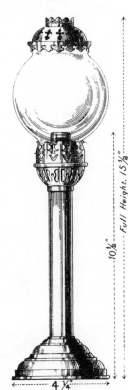

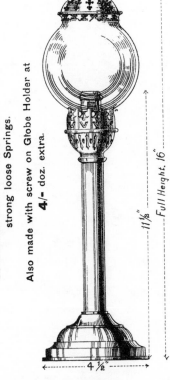

8c and 10c Candle Lamps are fitted with Steel Springs.

Also made with screw on Globe Holder at **4/-** doz. extra.

8b and 10b Candle Lamps are fitted with strong loose Springs.

Also made with screw on Globe Holder at **4/-** doz. extra.

8 C
Cheap Quality
Nickel Plated Candle Lamp.
19/- doz.
Polished Brass.
17/- doz.
Special price 25 doz. lots.
1/- doz. less.

10 C
Cheap Quality
Nickel Plated Candle Lamp.
23/6 doz.
Polished Brass.
21/- doz.
Special price 25 doz. lots.
1/6 doz. less.

8 B
Best Quality
Nickel Plated Candle Lamp.
23/6 doz.
Polished Brass.
21/- doz.
Special price 25 doz. lots.
1/- doz. less.

10 B
Best Quality
Nickel Plated Candle Lamp.
30/6 doz.
Polished Brass.
27/6 doz.
Special price 25 doz. lots.
1/6 doz. less.

Candle Lamps.

Scale ¼ th.

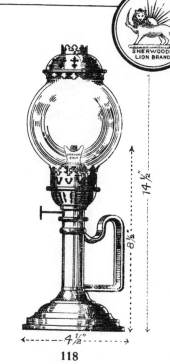

"LION BRAND." ENGLISH MAKE.

"LION BRAND." ENGLISH MAKE.

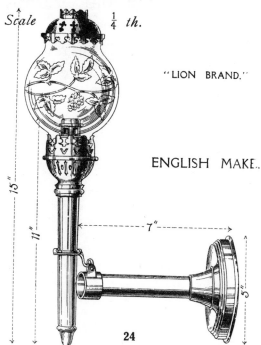

115
Best Quality
Nickel Plated Candle Lamp,
Hand and Wall,
with loose inside candle tube.
35/- doz.

24
Best Quality
Nickel Plated Candle Lamp,
Bracket and Table.
56/- doz.
Polished Brass.
50/- doz.
Special price 25 doz. lots.
2/- doz. less.

118
Best Quality
Nickel Plated Candle Lamp,
Hand and Wall,
with China Burner to burn Kerosine.
36/- doz.

All Candle Lamps are Priced without Globes.

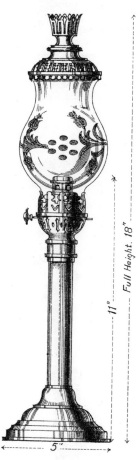

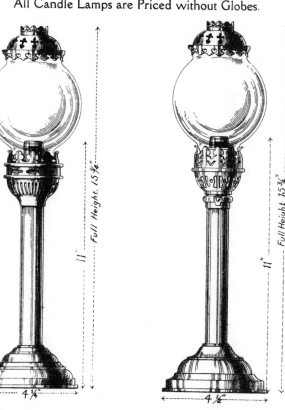

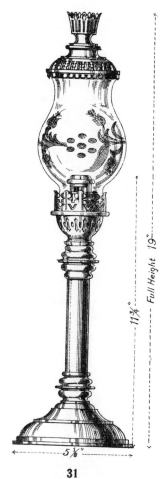

73
Best Quality.
Nickel Plated Candle Lamp,
with Sliding Globe Holder
for lighting without removing Globe.
40/- doz.
With No. 3 Globe and **P 30** Punkah Top,
Complete as drawn.
64/- doz.

11
Cheap Quality
Nickel Plated Candle Lamp
with loose inside candle tube.
28/- doz.

28
Best Quality
Nickel Plated Candle Lamp,
With Lock-fitting Globe Holder.
28/- doz.

31
Best Quality
Nickel Plated Candle Lamp.
42/- doz.
With No. 3 Globe and **P 30** Punkah Top,
Complete as drawn.
66/- doz.

Candle Lamps.

Scale $\frac{1}{4}$ *th.*

"LION BRAND."   "LION BRAND."

ENGLISH MAKE.   ENGLISH MAKE.

All Lamps are Priced   complete as drawn.

47
Superior Quality
Nickel Plated Candle Lamp,
loose inside tube.
No. **5A** Frosted Globe and **P 30** Punkah Top.
6/- each.

23
Superior Quality
Nickel Plated WINDPROOF Candle Lamp,
loose inside tube.
No. **4** Opal Globe and Punkah Top.
10/- each.

30
Superior Quality
Nickel Plated Candle Lamp,
loose inside tube.
No. **5** Clear Globe and **P 30** Punkah Top.
8/- each.

"WINDPROOF."   "WINDPROOF."

All Lamps have loose inside Candle   Tubes with lock catch fitting inside foot.

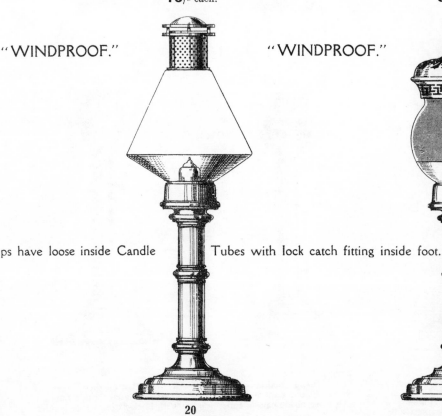

29
Superior Quality
Nickel Plated WINDPROOF Candle Lamp,
loose inside tube.
No. **5** Clear Globe and **P 29** Punkah Top.
11/- each.

20
Superior Quality
Nickel Plated WINDPROOF Candle Lamp,
loose inside tube.
No. **4** Opal Globe and Punkah Top.
11/6 each.

196
Superior Quality
Nickel Plated WINDPROOF Candle Lamp,
loose inside tube.
No. **5A** Frosted Globe and **P 196** Punkah Top
11/- each.

SHERWOODS LAMPS.
Candle Lamps.
Scale ¼ th.

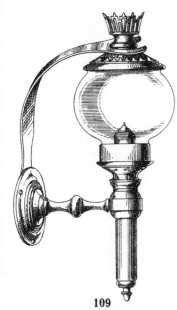

"WINDPROOF."

"LION BRAND."

ENGLISH MAKE.

All Lamps are Priced

109
Superior Quality
Nickel Plated WINDPROOF Candle Lamp,
with cast arm.
No. **5** Clear Globe and **P 29** Punkah Top,
with Steel Spring Clip.
21/- each.

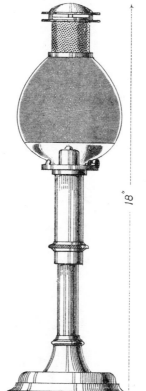

18"

5"

25
Superior Quality.
Nickel Plated WINDPROOF Candle Lamp.
Sliding Globe Holder for lighting without removing Globe,
loose inside tube.
No. **6 A** Frosted Globe and Punkah Top.

12/- each.

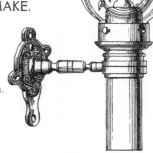

"WINDPROOF."

"LION BRAND."

ENGLISH MAKE.

complete as drawn.

111
Superior Quality
Nickel Plated WINDPROOF Candle Lamp,
with cast arm.
No. **3** Globe and **P 196** Punkah Top,
with 3 set screw in Globe Holder and Top.
30/- each.

Travelling Candle Lamps.

SHERWOODS
Special "SERVICE" Pattern.

Make extra Strong
for
Indian and Colonial Surveys,
and
Tourist, Shooting and Up-country
Expeditions.

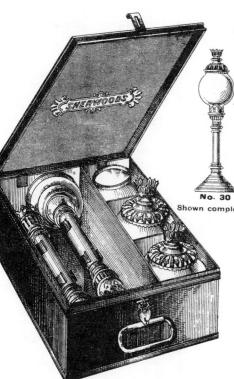

No. 30
Shown complete.

2476
Strong Japanned XXX Tin Candle Lamp Box,
containing two No. **30** Candle Lamps,
complete as drawn.
and one spare Globe, Strong Brass Padlock and Key.
40/- each.
Japanned Chocolate outside.

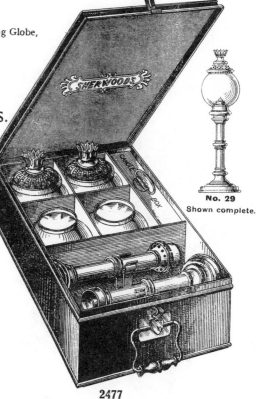

No. 29
Shown complete.

2477
Extra Strong Japanned XXX Tin Candle Lamp Box,
containing two No. **29** Candle Lamps,
complete as drawn,
and two spare Globes, Candle Box, Strong Brass Padlock and Key.
60/- each.
Japanned Chocolate outside and White inside.

Sherwoods Limited, 44, 46, 48, 50, GRANVILLE STREET, Birmingham.

SHERWOODS LAMPS.

Reading Candle Lamps.

Scale ¼ th.

"LION BRAND."   "LION BRAND."

ENGLISH MAKE.

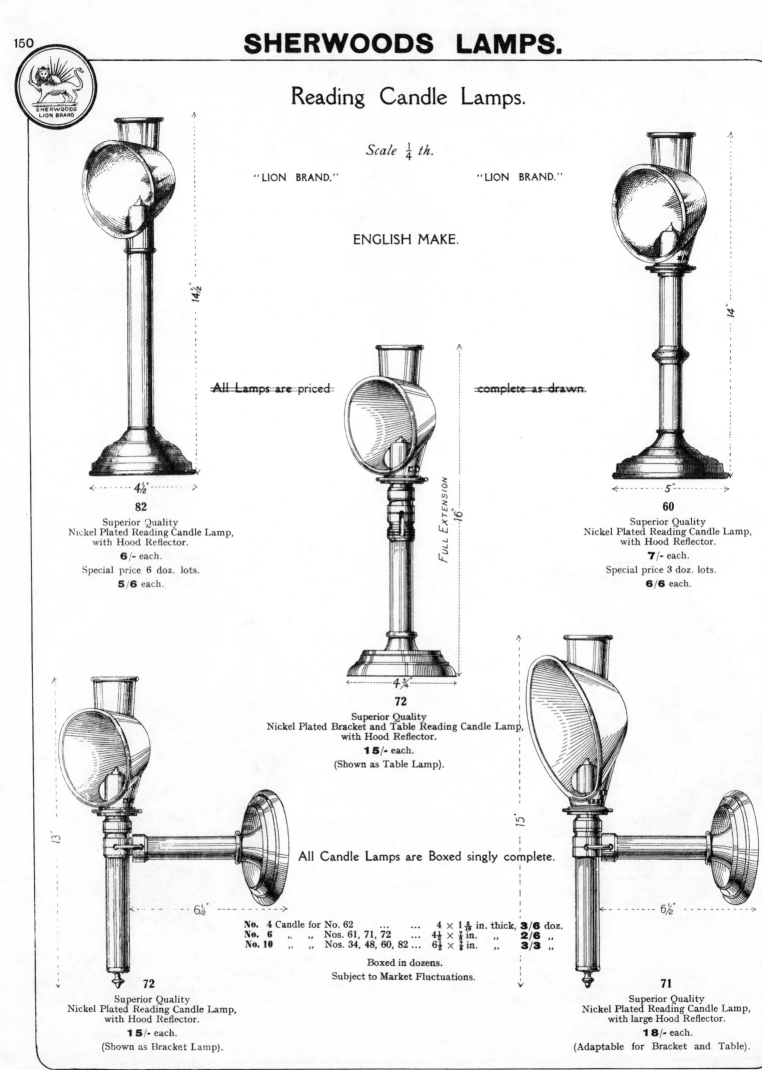

~~All Lamps are priced~~   ~~complete as drawn.~~

82
Superior Quality
Nickel Plated Reading Candle Lamp,
with Hood Reflector.
6/- each.
Special price 6 doz. lots.
5/6 each.

60
Superior Quality
Nickel Plated Reading Candle Lamp,
with Hood Reflector.
7/- each.
Special price 3 doz. lots.
6/6 each.

72
Superior Quality
Nickel Plated Bracket and Table Reading Candle Lamp,
with Hood Reflector.
15/- each.
(Shown as Table Lamp).

All Candle Lamps are Boxed singly complete.

No.	4	Candle for	No. 62	...	...	$4 \times 1\frac{3}{16}$ in. thick,	**3/6**	doz.
No.	6	,,	,, Nos. 61, 71, 72	...	$4\frac{1}{2} \times \frac{7}{8}$ in.	,,	**2/6**	,,
No.	10	,,	,, Nos. 34, 48, 60, 82	...	$6\frac{1}{2} \times \frac{7}{8}$ in.	,,	**3/3**	,,

Boxed in dozens.
Subject to Market Fluctuations.

72
Superior Quality
Nickel Plated Reading Candle Lamp,
with Hood Reflector.
15/- each.
(Shown as Bracket Lamp).

71
Superior Quality
Nickel Plated Reading Candle Lamp,
with large Hood Reflector.
18/- each.
(Adaptable for Bracket and Table).

Sherwoods Limited, 44, 46, 48, 50, GRANVILLE STREET, Birmingham

SHERWOODS LAMPS.

Reading Candle Lamps.

Scale ¼ th.

"LION BRAND."   "LION BRAND."

ENGLISH MAKE.

FULL EXTENSION. 16½"

5"

61
Superior Quality
Nickel Plated Reading Candle Lamp.
Telescopic,
with Hood Reflector.
9/- each.
Special price 3 doz. lots.
8/6 each.

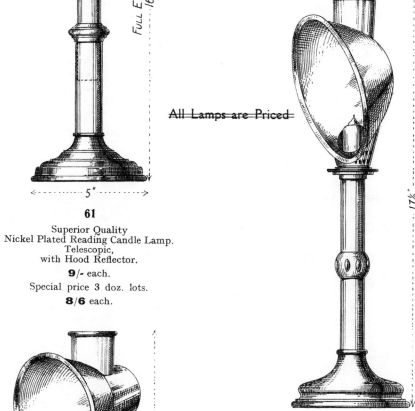

All Lamps are Priced ~~complete as drawn.~~

17½"

4½"

81
Superior Quality
Nickel Plated Reading Candle Lamp,
with large Hood Reflector
11/- each.
Special price 3 doz. lots.
10/6 each.

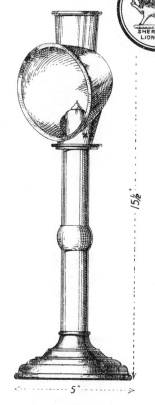

15½"

5"

34
Superior Quality
Nickel Plated Reading Candle Lamp,
loose inside tube,
with Hood Reflector.
9/- each.
Special price 3 doz. lots.
8/6 each.

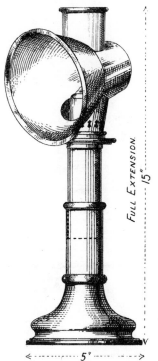

FULL EXTENSION. 15"

5"

62
Superior Quality
Nickel Plated Reading Candle Lamp,
Telescopic,
with deep Hood Reflector.
13/- each.
Special price 3 doz. lots.
12/6 each.

All Candle Lamps are Boxed singly complete.

No. 4	Candle for No. 62	...	...	$4 \times 1\frac{3}{16}$ in. thick,	**3/6** doz.
No. 6	,, ,, Nos. 61, 71, 72	...	$4\frac{1}{2} \times \frac{7}{8}$ in.	,,	**2/6** ,,
No. 10	,, ,, Nos. 34, 48, 60, 82	...	$6\frac{1}{2} \times \frac{7}{8}$ in.	,,	**3/3** ,,

Boxed in dozens.
Subject to Market Fluctuations.

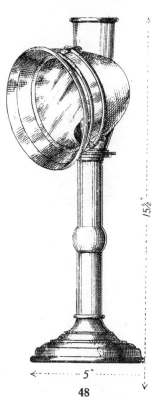

15½"

5"

48
Superior Quality
Nickel Plated Reading Candle Lamp,
loose inside tube,
with detachable glass rim Hood Reflector.
12/- each
Special price 3 doz. lots.
11/6 each.

Sherwoods Limited, 44, 46, 48, 50, GRANVILLE STREET, Birmingham.

SHERWOODS LAMPS.

Accessories.

Scale ⅕ th

KRANZOW CLOCKWORK.
Bottom Key Winder.
11/- each.
KRANZOW PATENT STOP CLOCKWORK.
Bottom Key Winder.
12/- each.

Punkah Top for Nᵒ C. Globe,
Nickel Plated.
4/- each.

WANZER AND PUCCA CLOCKWORK.
Side Key Winder.
9/- each.

82 B
Sherwoods Patent Burner.
Patent (No. 8539).
⅞ in. wick,
with fixed Gallery,
3/- each.
For Nos. **2140, 2589, 2590** Lamps.

82 A
Sherwoods Patent Burner.
Patent (No. 8539).
⅞ in. wick, fixed Gallery,
with Set Screw and Clips,
3/6 each.
For Nos. **2140c, 2560, 2589c, 2590c** Lamps.

Shade Holders.

Nickel Plated 5 in. Gallery,
with Three Set Screws.
12/- doz.

Nickel Plated 10 in. Shade Ring.
18/- doz.

Nickel Plated 10 in. Shade Holder,
with Set Screw.
12/- doz.

Globes.

Kettle Holder and Cooking Ring
for Kranzow and Pucca Lamps.
Painted aluminium finish.
2/- each.

No. C
Squat Opal and Clear Globe.
for 2140 C, 2589 C, 2590 C,
3/- each.

Kettle Holder and Cooking Ring,
for Wanzer Lamp,
Painted aluminium finish,
2/- each.

No. A
5 in. Best Quality Opal Globe,
Polished Top and Bottom.
18/- doz.
By Original Case 6 doz.
15/- doz.

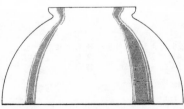

No. B
10 in. Best Quality Dome Opal Shade,
Polished Top and Bottom.
18/- doz.
By Original Case 6 doz.
15/- doz.

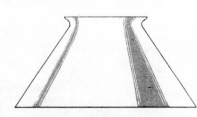

No. E
10 in. Best Quality Straight Opal Shade,
Polished Top and Bottom.
18/- doz.
By Original Case. 6 doz.
15/- doz.
No. G
10 in. Green Cased Opal Shades, **36**/- doz.

No. D
10 in. Spun White Metal Shade.
7/- each.

No. F
10 in. Green Cased Opal Shades, **36**/- doz.

Sherwoods Limited, 44, 46, 48, 50, GRANVILLE STREET, Birmingham

REGISTERED TRADE MARK SOUND

Sherwoods "MECHANICAL" Table Lamps.

The "KRANZOW" Lamp.

Fitted with
SHERWOODS PATENT STOP CLOCKWORK.
(No. 17099).

Scale $\frac{1}{3}$ rd.

SPECIAL EXPORT LINE.

Approximate weight and measurements.
12 Kranzow Mechanical Lamps.

Gross ... **0 2 20**
            28 × 22 × 16
Net ... **0 1 12**

Approximate weight and measurements.
3 doz. **No. A** 5 in. Globes.

Gross ... **1 0 8**
            39 × 27 × 22
Net ... **0 1 5**

Approximate weight and measurements,
3 doz. **No. B, E & F** 10 in. Shades.

Gross ... **1 1 6**
            39 × 27 × 24
Net ... **0 2 4**

These Chimneyless Mechanical Lamps
are recommended for Shooting,
Forest, and Up-Country Expeditions,
and Camp Tent Lighting.

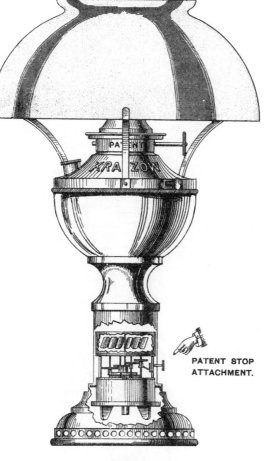

PATENT STOP
ATTACHMENT.

2560 F
THE "KRANZOW" LAMP,
Nickel Plated.
Sherwoods Patent STOP Clockwork,
Side Oil Feeder.
No. F 10 in. Green Cased Opal Shade and Shade Holder.
Complete as drawn.
26/6 each.

Boxed singly with wicks.

SPECIAL EXPORT LINE.

Approximate weights and measurements,
25 Kranzow Mechanical Lamps.

Gross ... **1 0 24**
            28 × 28 × 22
Net ... **0 2 25**

Approximate weight and measurements,
(Original Case Quantity).
6 doz. **No. A** 5 in. Globes.

Gross ... **1 2 20**
            42 × 29 × 33
Net ... **0 2 0**

Approximate weight and measurements,
(Original Case Quantity).
6 doz. **No. B, E & F** 10 in. shades.

Gross ... **2 1 0**
            43 × 34 × 34
Net ... **0 3 0**

These Chimneyless Mechanical Lamps
are recommended for Shooting,
Forest, and Up-Country Expeditions,
and Camp Tent Lighting.

Our Patent Stop Clockwork is the only perfect Stop Clockwork made, which instantly stops or starts the Clockwork when required without injuring the mechanism in any way.

This is effected by means of a lever at the foot of the lamp, and by turning this towards "Stop," or "Start," as required, the action is immediately brought into play.

In addition to this advantage the life of the Clockwork is considerably lengthened by this patent over the old pattern, inasmuch as the mechanism is only working when required.

Sherwoods Limited, 44, 46, 48, 50, GRANVILLE STREET, Birmingham.

SHERWOODS LAMPS.

The "KRANZOW" Lamp.

Fitted with
SHERWOODS PATENT STOP CLOCKWORK.
(No. 17099).

SUITABLE FOR LIGHTING AND COOKING PURPOSES.

Scale ¼ th.

Giving a light equal to 30 candle power
by means of forced draught.
Cost of oil consumption **1 d.** for 12 hours.

Will boil a pint of water in a few minutes.
Can also be used
as a Stove for Frying and Cooking purposes.

"KRANZOW"
Kettle Holder and Cooking Ring,
Painted aluminium finish.
2/- each.

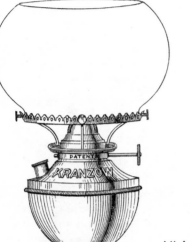

All Lamps are

Priced without Glass.

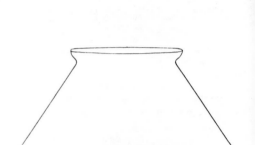

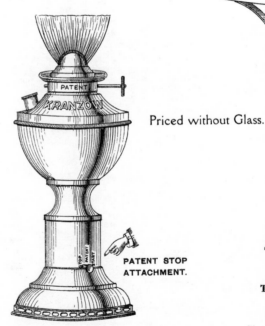

2560/A
THE "KRANZOW" LAMP.
Nickel Plated,
with 5 in. Globe Gallery.
Sherwoods Patent Stop Clockwork
Side Oil Feeder.
23/6 each.
Boxed singly complete with Wick.

These Chimneyless Mechanical Lamps
are recommended for Shooting,
Forest, and Up-Country Expeditions,
and Camp Tent Lighting.

**PATENT STOP
ATTACHMENT.**

2560
THE "KRANZOW" LAMP.
Nickel Plated.
Sherwoods Patent Stop Clockwork.
Side Oil Feeder.
22/6 each.
Boxed singly complete with Wick.
Approximate weight and measurements.
Packed 12 Lamps per Case.

Gross ...	**0 2 20**	28 × 22 × 16
Net ...	**0 1 12**	

2560/E
THE "KRANZOW" LAMP.
Nickel Plated,
with 10 in. Shade Holder.
Sherwoods Patent Stop Clockwork.
Side Oil Feeder.
23/6 each.

Boxed singly complete with Wick.

These Chimneyless Mechanical Lamps
are recommended for Shooting,
Forest, and Up-Country Expeditions,
and Camp Tent Lighting.

**PATENT STOP
ATTACHMENT.**

Our Patent Stop Clockwork is the only perfect Stop Clockwork made, which instantly stops or starts
the Clockwork when required without injuring the mechanism in any way.

This is effected by means of a lever at the foot of the lamp, and by turning this towards "Stop," or "Start,"
as required, the action is immediately brought into play.

In addition to this advantage the life of the Clockwork is considerably lengthened by this patent
over the old pattern, inasmuch as the mechanism is only working when required.

Sherwoods Limited, 44, 46, 48, 50, GRANVILLE STREET, Birmingham

SHERWOODS LAMPS.

The "KRANZOW" Lamp.

These Lamps are fitted with the original superior "Kranzow" Clockwork, with underneath Key Winder.
They are thoroughly tested and adjusted before leaving Works.

SUITABLE FOR LIGHTING AND COOKING PURPOSES.

Scale $\frac{1}{4}$ *th.*

Giving a light equal to 30 candle power
by means of forced draught.
Cost of oil consumption **1 d.** for 12 hours.

Will boil a pint of water in a few minutes.
Can also be used
as a Stove for Frying and Cooking purposes.

"KRANZOW"
Kettle Holder and Cooking Ring,
Painted aluminium finish.
2/- each.

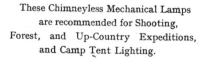

2590 A
THE "KRANZOW" LAMP.
Nickel Plated.
with 5 in. Globe Gallery.
22/- each.
Boxed singly complete with Wick.

All Lamps are

2590
THE "KRANZOW" LAMP.
Nickel Plated.
21/- each.
Boxed singly complete with Wick.

Priced without Glass.

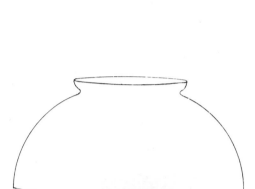

2590 B
THE "KRANZOW" LAMP.
Nickel Plated.
With 10 in. Shade Holder.
22/- each.
Boxed singly complete with Wick.

These Chimneyless Mechanical Lamps
are recommended for Shooting,
Forest, and Up-Country Expeditions,
and Camp Tent Lighting.

Approximate weight and measurements;
Packed 12 Lamps per Case.

Gross ... **0 2 20**
Net ... **0 1 12**   **28 × 22 × 16**

These Chimneyless Mechanical Lamps
are recommended for Shooting,
Forest, and Up-Country Expeditions,
and Camp Tent Lighting.

The above Lamps can be supplied with Oil Feeders at **6d.** each extra.

All Burners are now made with Patent fixed Cones (Pat. No. 8539), and screw into body of Lamp, to ensure a perfectly rigid fitting.

We are the pioneers and largest actual Manufacturers of Mechanical Lamps in England.

Sherwoods Limited, 44, 46, 48, 50, GRANVILLE STREET, Birmingham.

SHERWOODS LAMPS.

The "PUCCA" Lamp.

These Lamps are fitted with original Side Winder Clockworks.   They are thoroughly tested and adjusted before leaving Works.

SUITABLE FOR LIGHTING AND COOKING PURPOSES.

Scale $\frac{1}{4}$ *th.*

Giving a light equal to 30 candle power by means of forced draught.
Cost of oil consumption **1 d.** for 12 hours.

Will boil a pint of water in a few minutes.
Can also be used as a Stove for Frying and Cooking purposes.

"PUCCA"
Kettle Holder and Cooking Ring,
Painted aluminium finish.
2/- each.

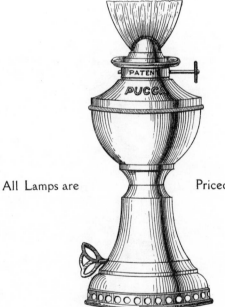

All Lamps are   Priced without Glass.

2589 A
THE " PUCCA " LAMP.
Nickel Plated.
With 5 in. Globe Gallery.
20/- each.
Boxed singly complete with Wick.

2589
THE " PUCCA " LAMP.
Nickel Plated.
19/- each.
Boxed singly complete with Wick.

2589 B
THE " PUCCA " LAMP.
Nickel Plated.
With 10 in. Shade Holder.
20/- each.
Boxed singly complete with Wick.

These Chimneyless Mechanical Lamps are recommended for Shooting, Forest, and Up-Country Expeditions, and Camp Tent Lighting.

Approximate weight and measurements.
Packed 12 Lamps per Case.

Gross ...	0	2	20
Net ...	0	1	12

28 × 22 × 16

These Chimneyless Mechanical Lamps are recommended for Shooting, Forest, and Up-Country Expeditions, and Camp Tent Lighting.

The above Lamps can be supplied with Oil Feeders at **6d.** each extra.

All Burners are now made with Patent fixed Cones (Pat. No. 8539), and screw into body of Lamp, to ensure a perfectly rigid fitting.

We are the pioneers and largest actual Manufacturers of Mechanical Lamps in England.

Sherwoods Limited, 44, 46, 48, 50, GRANVILLE STREET, Birmingham

SHERWOODS LAMPS.

The "WANZER" Lamp,

These Lamps are fitted with the original "Wanzer" Clockwork Side Key Winder.
They are thoroughly tested and adjusted before leaving Works.

SUITABLE FOR LIGHTING AND COOKING PURPOSES.

Scale ¼ th.

Giving a light equal to 30 candle power
by means of forced draught.
Cost of oil consumption **1 d.** for 12 hours.

Will boil a pint of water in a few minutes.
Can also be used
as a Stove for Frying and Cooking purposes.

"WANZER"
Kettle Holder and Cooking Ring,
Painted aluminium finish.
2/- each.

All Lamps are   Priced without Glass.

2140 A
THE " WANZER " LAMP.
Nickel Plated.
With 5 in. Globe Gallery.
21/- each.
Boxed singly complete with Wick.

2140
THE " WANZER " LAMP.
Nickel Plated.
20/- each.
Boxed singly complete with Wick.

2140 B
THE " WANZER " LAMP.
Nickel Plated.
With 10 in. Shade Holder.
21/6 each.
Boxed singly complete with Wicks.

These Chimneyless Mechanical Lamps
are recommended for Shooting,
Forest, and Up-Country Expeditions,
and Camp Tent Lighting.

Approximate weight and measurements.
Packed 12 Lamps per Case.

Gross ...	0	2	20	
Net ...	0	1	12	28 × 22 × 16

These Chimneyless Mechanical Lamps
are recommended for Shooting,
Forest, and Up-Country Expeditions,
and Camp Tent Lighting.

The above Lamps can be supplied with Oil Feeders at **6d.** each extra.

All Burners are now made with Patent fixed Cones (Pat. No. 8539), and screw into body of Lamp, to ensure a perfectly rigid fitting.

We are the pioneers and largest actual Manufacturers of Mechanical Lamps in England.

Sherwoods Limited, 44, 46, 48, 50, GRANVILLE STREET, Birmingham.

SHERWOODS LAMPS.

Windproof "MECHANICAL" Lamps.

EXTRAS.
Nickel Plated Punkah Tops.
4/- each.
Burner and Cone with Screws, and Clips on Gallery.
3/6 each.

Scale $\frac{1}{4}$ th.

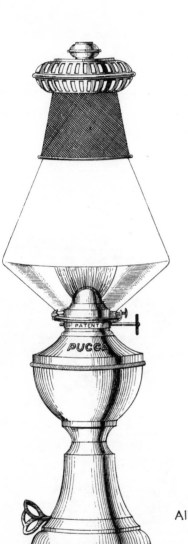

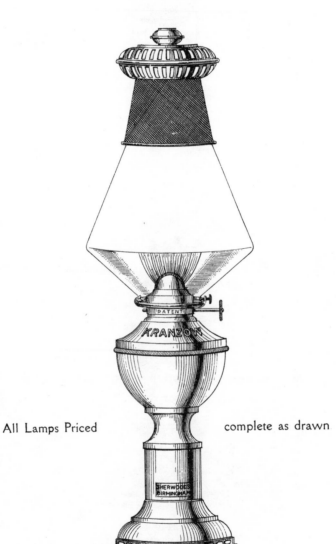

All Lamps Priced   complete as drawn

2589 C
WINDPROOF " PUCCA " LAMP.
Nickel Plated.
With Opal Globe and Punkah Top.
26/- each.
Complete as drawn.

These Chimneyless Mechanical Lamps
are recommended for Shooting,
Forest, and Up-Country Expeditions,
and Camp Tent Lighting.

2590C
WINDPROOF " KRANZOW " LAMP.
Nickel Plated.
With Opal Globe and Punkah Top.
28/- each.
Complete as drawn.

2140 C
WINDPROOF " WANZER " LAMP.
Nickel Plated.
With Opal Globe and Punkah Top.
27/- each.
Complete as drawn

These Chimneyless Mechanical Lamps
are recommended for Shooting,
Forest, and Up-Country Expeditions,
and Camp Tent Lighting.

The above Lamps can be supplied with Oil Feeders at **6d.** each extra.

All Burners are now made with Patent fixed Cones (Pat. No. 8539), and screw into body of Lamp, to ensure a perfectly rigid fitting.

We are the pioneers and largest actual Manufacturers of Mechanical Lamps in England.

Sherwoods Limited, 44, 46, 48, 50, GRANVILLE STREET, Birmingham

SHERWOODS LAMPS.

The "KRANZOW" Lamp.

Fitted up as

BRACKET LAMPS AND HANGING LAMP.

Scale $\frac{1}{5}$ *th.*

All Lamps Priced   complete as drawn.

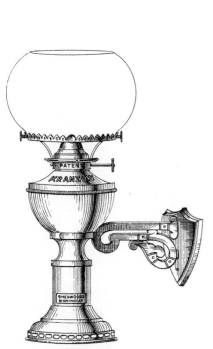

2590A/2604
THE " KRANZOW " LAMP.
Nickel Plated
with Heavy Cast Bracket.
5 in. Gallery and Opal Globe,
Complete as drawn.
29/- each.

2604
Heavy Cast Bracket,
Nickel Plated.
5/6 each.

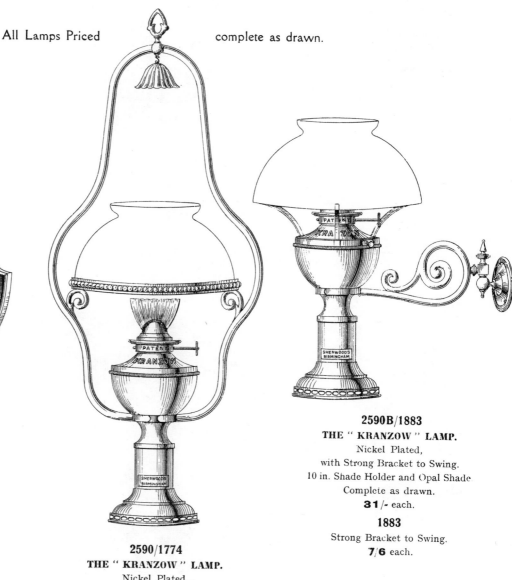

2590/1774
THE " KRANZOW " LAMP.
Nickel Plated,
with Tube Harp 10 in. Opal Shade.
Complete as drawn.
28/- each.

1774
Tube Harp with 10 in. Shade Ring.
Nickel Plated.
5/6 each.

2590B/1883
THE " KRANZOW " LAMP.
Nickel Plated,
with Strong Bracket to Swing.
10 in. Shade Holder and Opal Shade
Complete as drawn.
31/- each.

1883
Strong Bracket to Swing.
7/6 each.

The above Lamps can be supplied with Oil Feeders at **6d.** each extra.

All Burners are now made with Patent fixed Cones (Pat. No. 8539), and screw into body of Lamp, to ensure a perfectly rigid fitting.

We are the pioneers and largest actual Manufacturers of Mechanical Lamps in England.

Sherwoods Limited, 44, 46, 48, 50, GRANVILLE STREET, Birmingham.

Sherwoods Special Service Outfit.

Sherwoods Special Service Outfit.

TIN OIL CAN.

THE "KRANZOW" LAMP.

2472

Extra Strong XX Japanned Box
containing
" Kranzow " Lamp, 1 doz. Wicks and Oil Can," with Strong Brass Padlock and Key,
Complete as drawn.
40/- each.

Travelling Mechanical Lamps.

Travelling Boxes specially constructed for Jungle, Camp, and Up-country use.

SHADE HOLDER.

WHITE METAL SHADE.

KETTLE HOLDER.

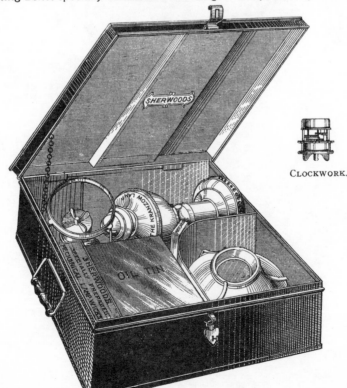

CLOCKWORK.

TIN OIL CAN.

THE " KRANZOW " LAMP.

THE " KRANZOW " LAMP.

2475

Extra Strong XXX Japanned Box,
containing
" Kranzow " Lamp, 10 in. Metal Shade, Shade Holder, Kettle Holder, Oil Can,
1 doz. Wicks and spare Clockwork, with Strong Brass Padlock and Key,
Complete as drawn.
80/- each.

Travelling Camp Lantern.

Sherwoods Special Service Outfit.

2572

" GRANVILLE "

Camp and Jungle Lantern.

26/- each.
Special price quantities 1 doz. lots.
24/- each.

2572 A

" GRANVILLE "

Camp and Jungle Lantern,
with Japanned Strong XX Tin Travelling Box,
containing
oil can, trimming scissors, 1 roll wick,
with strong brass padlock and key,
complete as drawn.
46/- each.
Special price quantities 1 doz. lots.
44/- each.

(drawn ready for use).

(drawn complete in Travelling Box).

Travelling Spirit Stove.

Travelling Boxes specially constructed for Jungle, Camp, and Up-country use.

JAPANNED WIND SHIELD.

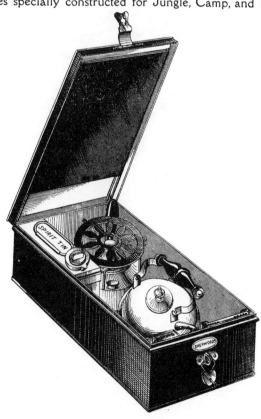

TIN SPIRIT CAN.

BRASS SPIRIT STOVE.

POLISHED COPPER KETTLE.

2474

" ELITE "

Japanned Strong XX Tin Travelling Spirit Stove Outfit,
containing
No. 20 Brass Spirit Stove, 1½-pint Copper Kettle, and 1 doz. Wicks,
with Strong Brass Padlock and Key,
Complete as drawn.
33/- each.

Sherwoods Limited, 44, 46, 48, 50, GRANVILLE STREET, Birmingham.

SHERWOODS LAMPS.

Sherwoods Chimneyless Lamps.

The "SYNTAX" Lamp.

Scale $\frac{1}{4}$ th.

SPECIAL EXPORT LINE.

Approximate Case Weight and Measurements.
6 doz. Lamps with Burner.

Gross ... **1 3 0**
39 × 28 × 30
Net ... **0 3 2**

Approximate Case Weight and Measurements.
8 doz. Frosted Globes.

Gross ... **2 0 10**
40 × 39 × 34
Net ... **0 2 8**

Pine Moon Frosted Globes,
(Packed 12 doz. per Case).
10/- doz.

SPECIAL EXPORT LINE.

Approximate Case Weight and Measurements.
12 doz. Lamps with Burner.

Gross ... **3 0 6**
47 × 35 × 36
Net ... **1 2 4**

Approximate Case Weight and Measurements.
12 doz. Frosted Globes.
(Original Case Quantity).

Gross ... **3 0 6**
58 × 40 × 35
Net ... **0 3 12**

Specially prepared " Syntax " Wicks.
(Boxed in dozens).
1/- per box.

D 708

Sherwoods "SYNTAX" Lamp.

fitted with

Sherwoods 1″ Extinguisher Burner. Pine Moon Frosted Globe.

Complete as drawn

Polished Brass.	Steel Bronzed Relieved.
60/- doz.	**64/-** doz.
Special price 12 doz. lots,	Special price 12 doz. lots.
58/- doz.	**62/-** doz.
Special price 24 doz. lots,	Special price 24 doz. lots.
56/- doz.	**60/-** doz.

All Lamps are tested by machinery
before leaving our Works
and are
guaranteed not to leak.

All Lamps are tested by machinery
before leaving our Works
and are
guaranteed not to leak.

SHERWOODS LAMPS.

Sherwoods Chimneyless Lamps.

Scale $\frac{1}{5}$ *th.*

D709
Black and Gold Wall Lamp
7 in. Bright Tin Reflector,
fitted with
Sherwoods 1 in. Extinguisher Burner.
Pine Moon Frosted Globe.
4/- each.

D 710
Polished Brass Table Lamp
fitted with
Sherwoods 1 in. Extinguisher Burner.
Pine Moon Frosted Globe.
7/6 each.

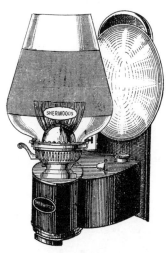

D 711
Copper Bronzed Wall Lamp,
6 in. Silvered Glass Reflector,
fitted with
Sherwoods 1 in. Extinguisher Burner.
Pine Moon Frosted Globe.
6/- each.

All Lamps are priced complete as drawn.

D 712
Polished Brass or Steel Bronzed Table Lamp.
" B " 6¼ in. Black Base,
fitted with
Sherwoods 1 in. Extinguisher Burner.
Pine Moon Frosted Globe.
6/6 each.

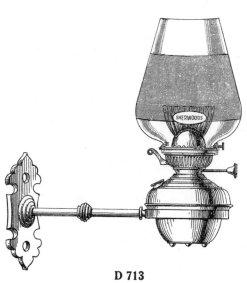

D 713
Polished Brass Bracket Lamp,
fitted with
Sherwoods 1 in. Extinguisher Burner.
Pine Moon Frosted Globe.
11/- each.

D 714
Polished Brass or Steel Bronzed Table Lamp,
" B " 6¼ in. Black Base,
fitted with
Sherwoods 1 in. Extinguisher Burner.
Pine Moon Frosted Globe.
7/- each.

Sherwoods Limited, 44, 46, 48, 50, GRANVILLE STREET, Birmingham.

SHERWOODS LAMPS.

Sherwoods Chimneyless Windproof Lamps.
The "EMPRESS" Lamp.

Scale $\frac{1}{3}$ th.

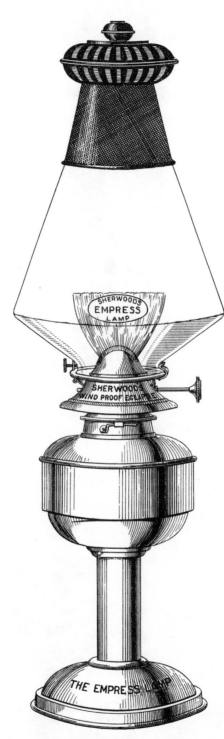

SPECIAL EXPORT LINE.

Approximate weights and measurements.
3 doz. Lamps, Burners and Punkah Tops.

Gross	...	**1**	**3**	**20**	
					30 × 24 × 30
Net	...	**1**	**0**	**20**	

Approximate weights and measurements.
3 doz. No. **10** Opal Globes.

Gross	...	**1**	**1**	**0**	
					52 × 27 × 19
Net	...	**0**	**2**	**0**	

Spare Windproof Burners
(Bayonet Duplex fitting).
3/- each.

Spare Punkah Tops.
2/6 each.

This Burner is specially constructed with
Hinged Gallery for Lighting,
and is made
to Suit any Bayonet Fitting Table Lamp.

SPECIAL EXPORT LINE.

Approximate weights and measurements.
6 doz. Lamps, Burners and Punkah Tops.

Gross	...	**3**	**1**	**12**	
					48 × 30 × 30
Net	...	**2**	**1**	**12**	

Approximate weights and measurements.
6 doz. No. **10** Opal Globes.

Gross	...	**1**	**3**	**20**	
					52 × 36 × 27
Net	...	**1**	**0**	**0**	

Spare 1 in. Wicks
(Boxed in dozens).
1/- doz.

Spare No. **10** Opal Globes.
3/- each.

This Burner is specially constructed with
Hinged Gallery for Lighting,
and is made
to Suit any Bayonet Fitting Table Lamp.

D 715
Polished or Steel Bronzed Table Lamp
fitted with
Sherwoods 1 in. Chimneyless Windproof Burner
No. **10** Opal Globe and Punkah Top,
Complete as drawn.
14/- each.
Special price 3 doz. Lamps complete.
13/6 each.
Special price 6 doz. Lamps complete.
13/- each.

Sherwoods Limited, 44, 46, 48, 50, GRANVILLE STREET, Birmingham.

SHERWOODS LAMPS.

Sherwoods Chimneyless Windproof Lamps.

With Hinge Gallery for Lighting.

Scale $\frac{1}{5}$ th.

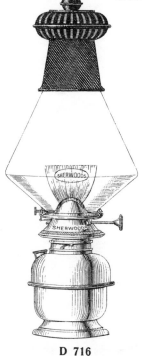

D 716

Polished Brass Safety Lamp,
loaded foot.
Sherwoods 1 in. Chimneyless Windproof Burner.
No. **10** Opal Globe and Punkah Top.

12/- each.

All Lamps are priced   complete as drawn.

D 717

Polished Brass Table Lamp.
Sherwoods 1 in. Chimneyless Windproof Burner.
No. **10** Opal Globe and Punkah Top.

11/- each.

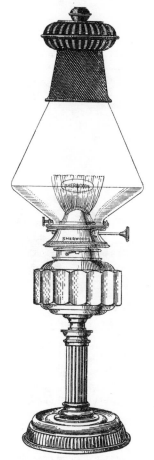

D 718

Copper Bronzed Wall Lamp,
Fitted with
Sherwoods 1 in. Chimneyless Windproof Burner.
6 in. Silvered Glass Reflector.
No. **10** Opal Globe and Punkah Top.

13/- each.

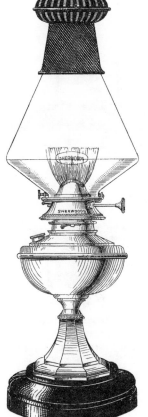

D 719

Polished Brass Table Lamp.
H **7** in. Black Base.
Sherwoods 1 in. Chimneyless Windproof Burner.
No. **10** Opal Globe and Punkah Top.

15/- each.

D 720

Polished Cast Bracket Lamp.
F10 Cut Glass Fount.
Sherwoods 1 in. Chimneyless Windproof Burner.
No. **10** Opal Globe and Punkah Top.

22/- each.

D 721

Polished Brass Table Lamp.
F11 Cut Glass Fount.
Sherwoods 1 in. Chimneyless Windproof Burner.
No. **10** Opal Globe and Punkah Top.

16/- each.

Sherwoods Limited, 44, 46, 48, 50, GRANVILLE STREET, **Birmingham.**

SHERWOODS LAMPS.

Sherwoods' "SIMPLEX" Burner.

Heavy 1" Single Wick Extinguisher Burner.

Inside Bayonet Lock Fitting.

Scale $\frac{1}{5}$ th.

144 B

" SIMPLEX "

Heavy 1 in. single wick Extinguisher Burner,
with Collar.

Inside Bayonet Lock Fitting.

4/- each.

144 B

Spare Bayonet Lock Collars.

5/6 doz.

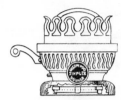

144 B

" SIMPLEX "

Drawn showing Inside Bayonet Lock Fitting
arrangement.

Outside fitting of Collar 2⅜ in.

All Lamps are priced complete as drawn.

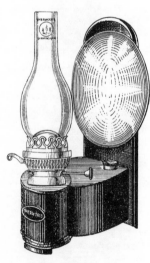

D 722

Copper Bronzed Wall Lamp
fitted with
Sherwoods " SIMPLEX " Burner.
6 in. Silvered Glass Reflector.
Short Straight Fireproof Chimney.

7/6 each.

Sherwoods " SIMPLEX " Burner.
Strong well-made 1 in. single wick Burner
Bayonet Lock Fitting,
with Self-acting Automatic Extinguisher.
Giving a light equal to 25 Candle Power,
at minimum consumption of Oil.

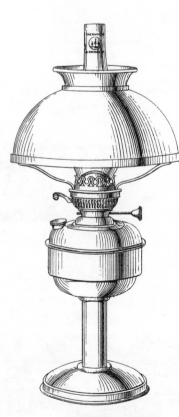

D 723

Polished Brass Table Lamp
fitted with
Sherwoods " SIMPLEX " Burner.
9¼ in. White Metal Shade and Chimney.

15/6 each.

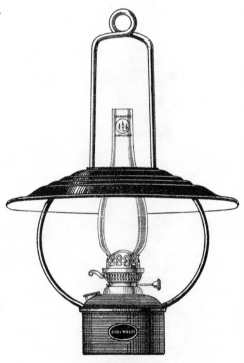

D 724

Strong Copper Bronzed Hanging Lamp
fitted with
Sherwoods " SIMPLEX " Burner.
15 in. Japanned Reflector,
Long Straight Fireproof Chimney.

7/- each.

Sherwoods " SIMPLEX " Burner.
Strong well-made 1 in. single wick Burner,
Bayonet Lock Fitting,
with Self-acting Automatic Extinguisher.
Giving a light equal to 25 Candle Power
at minimum consumption of Oil.

Sherwoods Limited, 44, 46, 48, 50, GRANVILLE STREET, Birmingham

Accessories.

for

Sherwood's 1″ Single Wick Extinguisher Punkah Burners.

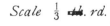

Scale $\frac{1}{3}$ *rd.*

No. 1

Sherwoods 1 in. single wick Extg. Punkah Burner.
Bayonet Catch Collar
Wick and Feeder Wicked.

5/- each.

No. 1

Steel Bronzed Punkah Top
(inside fitting).

2/6 each.

1 in. Short Straight Chimney.
$2\frac{1}{16}$ in. fitting.
5/- doz.
Best Fireproof Quality.

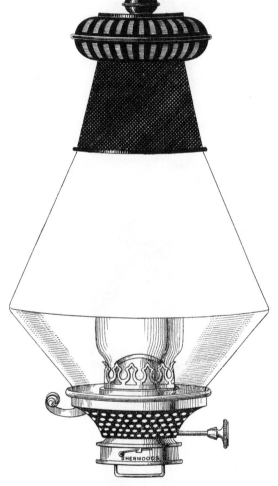

No. 1

Sherwoods 1 in. single wick Extg. Punkah Burner.
No. 12 Globe, Chimney and Punkah Top,
Wick and Feeder Wicked.
Complete as drawn.

12/- each.

Specially prepared 1 in. wicks for Punkah Burners
Purified by Chemical Process.

1/- doz.
Boxed in dozens.

1 in. Long Straight Chimney.
$2\frac{1}{16}$ in. fitting.
5/- doz.
Best Fireproof Quality.

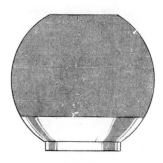

No. 11

$\frac{3}{4}$ in. Frosted Punkah Globe.

2/- each.
$4 \times 3\frac{3}{8}$ in. fitting.

No. 12

$\frac{3}{4}$ in. Opal Punkah Globe.

4/- each.
$4 \times 3\frac{3}{8}$ in. fitting.

SHERWOODS LAMPS.

Punkah Table Lamp.

Fitted with

Sherwood's 1″ Single Wick Extinguisher Punkah Burner.

The "RAJAH" Lamp.

Scale ¼ th.

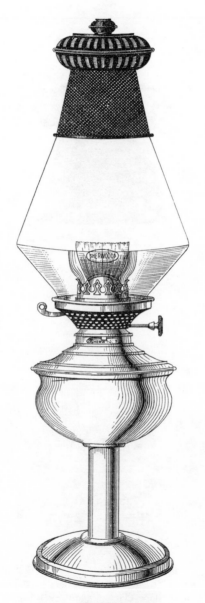

SPECIAL EXPORT LINE.

Approximate weight and measurements.
3 doz. Lamps, Burners and Punkah Tops

Gross ... **1 3 20**

              30 × 24 × 30

Net ... **1 0 20**

Approximate weights and measurements.
3 doz. No. **12** Opal Globes.
6 doz. 1 in. Fireproof Straight Chimneys.

Gross ... **1 1 20**

              50 × 30 × 26

Net ... **0 2 24**

All Lamps are tested by machinery
before leaving our Works
and are
guaranteed not to leak.

SPECIAL EXPORT LINE.

Approximate weights and measurements.
6 doz. Lamps, Burners and Punkah Tops.

Gross ... **3 1 12**

              48 × 30 × 30

Net ... **2 1 12**

Approximate weights and measurements.
6 doz. No. **12** Opal Globes.
9 doz. 1 in. Fireproof Straight Chimneys.

Gross ... **2 0 0**

              50 × 30 × 44

Net ... **1 0 20**

All Lamps are tested by machinery
before leaving our Works
and are
guaranteed not to leak.

D 725

Polished or Steel Bronzed Table Lamp.
fitted with
Sherwoods 1 in. single wick Punkah Burner.
No. **12** Opal Globe, Chimney and Punkah Top.
complete as drawn.

16/6 each.

Special price 3 doz. Lamps complete.

16/- each.

Special price 6 doz. Lamps complete.

~~17/6 each.~~
15/6 each.

Sherwoods Limited, 44, 46, 48, 50, GRANVILLE STREET, Birmingham.

SHERWOODS LAMPS.

Punkah Table Lamps.

Fitted with

Sherwoods 1″ Single Wick Extinguisher Punkah Burner.

All Lamps are priced complete as drawn.

Scale $\frac{1}{5}$ th.

D 726

Polished or Steel Bronzed Lamp.
" B " 6¼ in. Black Base.
Sherwoods 1 in. single wick Extg. Punkah Burner.
No. **11** Frosted Globe and Punkah Top.
14/- each.

D 727

Polished or Steel Bronzed Lamp.
" H " 7 in. Black Base.
Sherwoods 1 in. single wick Extg. Punkah Burner.
No. **11** Frosted Globe and Punkah Top.
15/- each.

D 728

Polished or Steel Bronzed Lamp
fitted with
Sherwoods 1 in. single wick Extg. Punkah Burner.
No. **12** Opal Globe and Punkah Top.
16/- each.

D 729

Polished or Steel Bronzed Lamp.
" A " 7 in. Black Base
fitted with
Sherwoods 1 in. single wick Extg. Punkah Burner.
No. **12** Opal Globe and Punkah Top.
18/6 each.

D 730

Polished or Steel Bronzed Lamp
fitted with
Sherwoods 1 in. single wick Extg. Punkah Burner.
No. **12** Opal Globe and Punkah Top.
18/- each.

Sherwoods Limited, 44, 46, 48, 50, GRANVILLE STREET, Birmingham.

SHERWOODS LAMPS.

Punkah Lamps,

Fitted with

Sherwoods 1″ Single Wick Extinguisher Punkah Burner.

Scale $\frac{1}{5}$ th.

D 731

Polished Brass or Steel Bronzed Lamp
with loaded foot.
Sherwoods 1 in. single wick Extg. Punkah Burner.
No. **11** Frosted Globe and Punkah Top.
13/- each.

D 732

Copper Bronzed Wall Lamp
fitted with
Sherwoods 1 in. single wick Extg. Punkah Burner.
6 in. Silvered Glass Reflector.
No. **11** Frosted Globe and Punkah Top.
12/6 each.

All Lamps are priced   complete as drawn.

D 733

Polished Brass or Steel Bronzed Lamps,
fitted with
Sherwoods 1 in. single wick Extg. Punkah Burner
No. **12** Opal Globe and Punkah Top.

15/6 each.

D 735

Polished Brass or Steel Bronzed Lamp
fitted with
Sherwoods 1 in. single wick Extg. Punkah Burner.
No. **12** Opal Globe and Punkah Top.
20/- each.

D 734

Polished Cast Brass Bracket Lamp
F **10** cut Crystal Fount.
Sherwoods 1 in. single wick Extg. Punkah Burner.
No. **11** Frosted Globe and Punkah Top.

23/- each.

D 736

Polished Brass or Steel Bronzed Lamp
fitted with
Sherwoods 1 in. single wick Extg. Punkah Burner.
No. **12** Opal Globe and Punkah Top.

21/- each.

Punkah Hanging Lamps.

Fitted with

Sherwoods 1″ Single Wick Extinguisher Punkah Burner.

Scale $\frac{1}{6}$ th.

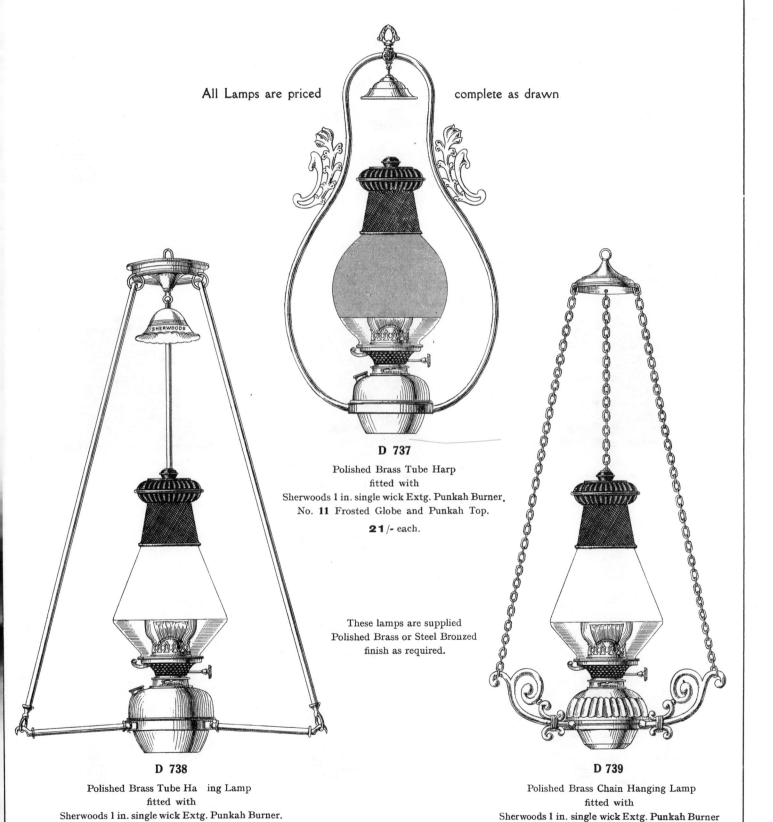

All Lamps are priced   complete as drawn.

D 737

Polished Brass Tube Harp
fitted with
Sherwoods 1 in. single wick Extg. Punkah Burner.
No. **11** Frosted Globe and Punkah Top.

21/- each.

These lamps are supplied
Polished Brass or Steel Bronzed
finish as required.

D 738

Polished Brass Tube Ha ing Lamp
fitted with
Sherwoods 1 in. single wick Extg. Punkah Burner.
No. **12** Opal Globe and Punkah Top.

27/- each.

D 739

Polished Brass Chain Hanging Lamp
fitted with
Sherwoods 1 in. single wick Extg. Punkah Burner
No. **12** Opal Globe and Punkah Top.

30/- each.

Sherwoods Limited, 44, 46, 48, 50, GRANVILLE STREET, Birmingham.

SHERWOODS LAMPS.

Punkah Fittings,
Globes, Punkah Tops and Accessories.

Scale $\frac{1}{5}$ th.

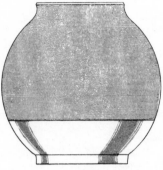

No. 14
¾ in. Frosted Punkah Globe.
2/6 each.
4⅞ in. bottom fitting.

No. 5
Steel Bronzed Punkah Bands,
Small size 8 in.   **18/-** doz.
Special price gross lots.
15/- doz.
Large size, 10 in.   **30/-** doz.
Special price gross lots.
27/- dozen.

No. 15
¾ in. Opal Punkah Globe.
4/- each.
4⅞ in. bottom fitting.

No. 2
Steel Bronzed Punkah Top.
36/- doz.
Special price 12 doz. lots.
30/- doz.
(Outside fitting for No. 14 Globes).

No. 3
Steel Bronzed Punkah Top.
36/- doz.
Special price 12 doz. lots.
30/- doz.
(Inside fitting for Nos. 15 and 17 Globes).

No. 4
Steel Bronzed Punkah Top.
42/- doz.
Special price 12 doz. lots.
36/- doz.
(Outside fitting for No. 16 Globe).

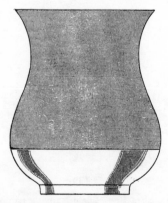

No. 16
¾ in. Frosted Punkah Globe.
3/- each.
4⅞ in. bottom fitting.

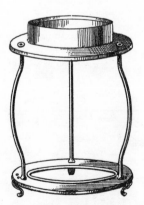

No. 14 A
Punkah Shade Holder,
three Steel Clips.
30/- doz.
5 in. fitting for Punkah Duplex Burner.

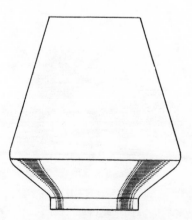

No. 17
¾ in. Opal Punkah Globe.
5/- each.
4⅞ in. bottom fitting.

Sherwoods Limited, 44, 46, 48, 50, GRANVILLE STREET, **Birmingham.**

Duplex Punkah Burners.

Scale $\frac{1}{3}$ rd.

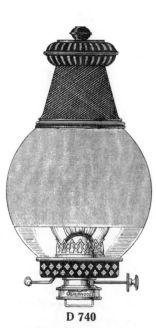

D 740

Sherwoods No. **2** Punkah Duplex Burner,
No. **2** Punkah Top.
No. **14** Frosted Globe and Chimney.
14/- each.

D 742

Sherwoods Improved No. **2** Duplex Punkah Burner,
No. **3** Punkah Top.
No. **17** Opal Globe and Chimney.
16/6 each.

D 743

Sherwoods Raiser Gallery No. **3** Duplex Punkah Burner.
No. **3** Punkah Top.
No. **17** Opal Globe and Chimney.
18/6 each.

D 741

Sherwoods No. **2** Duplex Punkah Burner.
No. **4** Punkah Top.
No. **16** Frosted Globe and Chimney.
15/- each.

No. 2

Sherwoods Duplex Punkah Burner.
Improved Deep Gallery.
Single Bar Winder and Safety self-acting Extinguisher.
Bayonet Cork Lined Collar.
8/- each.

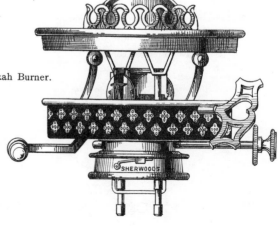

No. 3

Sherwoods Duplex Punkah Burner
with Raiser Gallery.
Single Bar Winder and Safety Self-acting Extinguisher,
Bayonet Cork Lined Collar.
10/- each.

SHERWOODS LAMPS.

Punkah Table Lamps,

fitted with

Duplex Punkah Burner,

The "FORRESTER" Lamp.

Scale $\frac{1}{4}$ th.

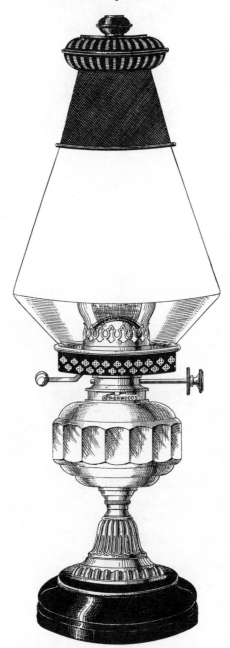

SPECIAL EXPORT LINE.

Approximate weights and measurements,
Packed in No. **3** CASK.

3 doz. Marble Base Stands.

Gross ... 1 3 20

28 × 28

Net ... 1 1 4

Approximate weights and measurements.
3 doz. Cut Glass Founts, Punkah Burners & Tops.

Gross ... 2 0 5

40 × 24 × 28

Net ... 1 0 19

Approximate weights and measurements
(original Case quantity).

3 doz. No. 12 Opal Globes.

Gross ... 2 1 6

50 × 33 × 37

Net ... 0 3 24

SPECIAL EXPORT LINE.

Approximate weights and measurements,
Packed in No. **1** CASK.

6 doz. Marble Base Stands.

Gross ... 3 1 12

40 × 31

Net ... 2 1 0

Approximate weights and measurements.
6 doz. Punkah Burners and Tops.

Gross ... 1 3 20

46 × 24 × 20

Net ... 1 1 4

Approximate weights and measurements
(original Case quantity).

6 doz. Cut Glass Founts.

Gross ... 1 3 2

38 × 27 × 27

Net ... 1 0 14

D 744

Polished or Steel Bronzed Lamp
fitted with
No. 2 S.W. Safety Punkah Duplex Burner.
5 in. Punkah Top No. 17 Opal Globe and Chimney.
Complete as drawn.
21/- each.
Special price 3 doz. Lamps complete.
20/6 each.
Special price 6 doz. Lamps complete.
20/- each.

SPECIAL EXPORT LINE.

SPECIAL EXPORT LINE.

Sherwoods Limited, 44, 46, 48, 50, GRANVILLE STREET, Birmingham

Punkah Table Lamps,

fitted with

Duplex Punkah Burners.

Globes extra.   Chimneys extra.   Punkah Tops extra.

Scale $\frac{1}{5}$ th.

D 745

Polished or Steel Bronzed Lamp.
"A" 7 in. Black Base.
No. **2** S.W. Extinguisher
Duplex Punkah Burner.
D137 5½ in. Cut Crystal Fount.
12/9 each.

D 746

No. **3** S.W. Raiser Extinguisher
Punkah Duplex Burner.
14/9 each.

D 747

Polished or Steel Bronzed Lamp.
"A" 7 in. Black Base.
No. **2** S.W. Extinguisher
Duplex Punkah Burner.
D137 5½ in. Cut Crystal Fount.
12/9 each.

D 748

No. **3** S.W. Raiser Extinguisher
Punkah Duplex Burner.
14/9 each.

D 749

Polished or Steel Bronzed Lamp.
"A" 7 in. Black Base.
No. 2 S.W. Extinguisher Duplex Punkah Burner.
D 137 5½ in. Cut Crystal Fount.
12/7 each.

D 750

No. 3 S.W. Raiser Extg. Punkah Duplex Burner.
14/7 each

D 751

Polished Brass or Steel Bronzed Lamp.
with loaded foot.
No. 2 S.W. Extinguisher Duplex Punkah Burner.
11/6 each.

D 752

No. 3 S.W. Extinguisher Duplex Punkah Burner.
13/6 each.

D 753

Polished or Steel Bronzed Lamp.
"A" 7 in. Black Base.
No. 2 S.W. Extinguisher Duplex Punkah Burner.
D 137 5½ in. Cut Crystal Fount.
12/7 each.

D 754

No. 3 S.W. Raiser Extinguisher Punkah Burner.
14/7 each.

SHERWOODS LAMPS.

Punkah Table Lamps,

fitted with

Duplex Punkah Burners.

Globes extra. Chimneys extra. Punkah Tops extra.

Scale $\frac{1}{5}$ th.

D 755
Polished or Steel Bronzed Lamp
No. **2** S.W. Extinguisher
Duplex Punkah Burner.
15/- each.

D 756
No. **3** S.W. Extinguisher Raiser
Duplex Punkah Burner.
17/- each.

D 757
Polished or Steel Bronzed Lamp.
No. **2** S.W. Extinguisher
Duplex Punkah Burner.
16/- each.

D 758
No. **3** S.W. Extinguisher Raiser
Duplex Punkah Burner.
18/- each.

D 759
Polished or Steel Bronzed Lamp.
" D " 7½ in. Black Base.
No. **2** S.W. Extinguisher PunkahDuplex Burner.
16/- each.

D 760
No. **3** S.W. Extg. Raiser Duplex Punkah Burner.
18/- each.

D 761
Polished or Steel Bronzed Lamp,
F **10** Cut Crystal Fount
No. **2** S.W. Extinguisher Duplex Punkah Burner.
22/- each.

D 762
No. **3** S.W. Extg. Raiser Duplex Punkah Burner.
(as drawn).
24/- each.

D 763
Polished or Steel Bronzed Lamp.
" E " 8¼ in. Black Base.
No. **2** S.W. Extinguisher Duplex Punkah Burner
18/- each

D 764
No. **3** S.W. Extg. Raiser Duplex Punkah Burner
20/- each.

Sherwoods Limited, 44, 46, 48, 50, GRANVILLE STREET, **Birmingham**

Punkah Table Lamps,

fitted with

Duplex Punkah Burners.

Globes extra.

Chimneys extra.

Punkah Tops extra.

Scale $\frac{1}{5}$ *th.*

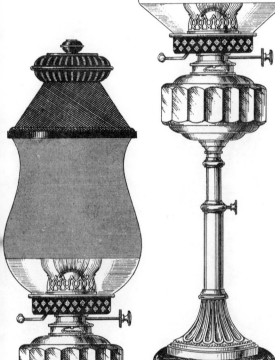

D 765

Polished or Steel Bronzed Lamp,
Telescopic.
" D " 7½ in. Black Base.
No. **2** S.W. Extinguisher
Duplex Punkah Burner.
20/- each.

D 766

No. **3** S.W. Extinguisher Raiser
Duplex Punkah Burner.
22/- each.

D 767

Polished or Steel Bronzed Lamp,
Telescopic.
No. **2** S.W. Extinguisher
Duplex Punkah Burner.
21/- each.

D 768

No. **3** S.W. Extinguisher Raiser
Duplex Punkah Burner.
23/- each.

D 769

Polished or Steel Bronzed Lamp.
" A " 7 in. Black Base.
No. **2** S.W. Extinguisher Duplex Punkah Burner
15/- each.

D 770

No. **3** S.W. Extg. Raiser Duplex Punkah Burner.
17/- each.

D 771

Polished or Steel Bronzed Lamp.
" E " 8¼in. Black Base.
No. **2** S.W. Extinguisher Duplex Punkah Burner.
18/6 each.

D 772

No. **3** S.W. Extg. Raiser Duplex Punkah Burner.
(as drawn).
20/6 each.

D 773

Polished or Steel Bronzed Lamp.
" A " 7 in. Black Base.
No. **2** S.W. Extinguisher Duplex Punkah Burner.
15/6 each.

D 774

No. **3** S.W. Extg. Raiser Duplex Punkah Burner.
17/6 each.

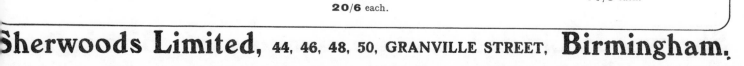

Sherwoods Limited, 44, 46, 48, 50, GRANVILLE STREET, Birmingham.

REGISTERED TRADE MARK
SOUND

SHERWOODS LAMPS.

Punkah Table Lamps,

fitted with

Duplex Punkah Burners.

Globes extra.　　　　　Chimneys extra.　　　　　Punkah Tops extra.

Scale $\frac{1}{5}$ *th.*

D 775
Polished or Steel Bronzed Lamp
fitted with
No. **2** S.W. Extinguisher
Duplex Punkah Burner.
18/- each.

D 776
No. **3** S.W. Extinguisher Raiser
Duplex Punkah Burner.
20/- each.

D 777
Polished or Steel Bronzed Lamp
fitted with
No. **2** S.W. Extinguisher
Duplex Punkah Burner.
20/- each.

D 778
No. **3** S.W. Extinguisher Raiser
Duplex Punkah Burner.
22/- each.

D 779
Polished or Steel Bronzed Lamp
fitted with
No. **2** S.W. Extinguisher Duplex Punkah Burner.
15/6 each.

D 780
No. **3** S.W. Extg. Raiser Duplex Punkah Burner.
17/6 each.

D 781
Polished or Steel Bronzed Lamp
fitted with
No. **2** S.W. Extinguisher Duplex Punkah Burner.
21/- each.

D 782
No. **3** S.W. Extg. Raiser Duplex Punkah Burner.
(as drawn).
23/- each.

D 783
Polished or Steel Bronzed Lamp
fitted with
No. **2** S.W. Extinguisher Duplex Punkah Burner.
17/- each.

D 784
No. **3** S.W. Extg. Raiser Duplex Punkah Burner.
19/- each.

Sherwoods Limited, 44, 46, 48, 50, GRANVILLE STREET, Birmingham

Punkah Table Lamps,

fitted with

Duplex Punkah Burners.

Globes extra.   Chimneys extra.   Punkah Tops extra.

Scale $\frac{1}{5}$ th.

D 785

Polished or Steel Bronzed Lamp
fitted with
No. **2** S.W. Extinguisher
Duplex Punkah Burner
21/- each.

D 786

No. **3** S.W. Extinguisher Raiser
Duplex Punkah Burner.
23/- each.

D 787

Polished or Steel Bronzed Lamp
fitted with
No. **2** S.W. Extinguisher
Duplex Punkah Burner
23/- each.

D 788

No. **3** S.W. Extinguisher Raiser
Duplex Punkah Burner.
25/- each.

D 789

Polished or Steel Bronzed Lamp
fitted with
No. **2** S.W. Extinguisher Duplex Punkah Burner.
25/- each.

D 790

No: **3** S.W. Extg. Raiser Duplex Punkah Burner.
27/- each.

D 791

Polished or Steel Bronzed Lamp
fitted with
No. **2** S.W. Extinguisher Duplex Punkah Burner.
30/- each.

D 792

No. **3** S.W. Extg. Raiser Duplex Punkah Burner.
(as drawn).
32/- each.

D 793

Polished or Steel Bronzed Lamp
fitted with
No. **2** S.W. Extinguisher Duplex Punkah Burner.
27/- each.

D 794

No. **3** S.W. Extg. Raiser Duplex Punkah Burner.
29/- each.

SHERWOODS LAMPS.

Punkah Table Lamps

fitted with

Raiser Duplex Punkah Burners.

Scale $\frac{1}{5}$ th.

All Lamps are priced   complete as drawn.

D 795
Polished Brass Lamp
fitted with
No. **3** S.W. Extg. Raiser Duplex Punkah Burner.
D 28 15 in. " EMPIRE " Shade.
5 in. Punkah Top, Clear Globe and Chimney.
Complete as drawn.
60/- each.

D 796
Polished Brass Lamp
fitted with
No. **3** S.W. Extg. Raiser Duplex Punkah Burner.
D 29 15 in. " THAMES " Shade.
5 in. Punkah Top, Clear Globe and Chimney,
Complete as drawn.
76/- each.

D 797
Silver Plated.
100/- each.

D 798
Polished Brass Lamp
fitted with
No. **3** S.W. Extg. Raiser Duplex Punkah Burner.
D 30 15 in. " DOMINION " Shade.
5 in. Punkah Top, Clear Globe and Chimney,
Complete as drawn.
68/- each.

Sherwoods Limited, 44, 46, 48, 50, GRANVILLE STREET, Birmingham

SHERWOODS LAMPS.

Punkah Table and Floor Lamps

fitted with

Raiser Duplex Punkah Burners.

Scale $\frac{1}{5}$ th.

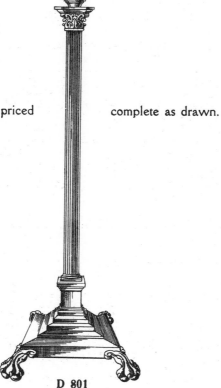

All Lamps are priced   complete as drawn.

D 799
Polished Cast Brass Lamp
fitted with
No. 3 S.W. Extg. Raiser Duplex Punkah Burner.
D 28 15 in. " EMPIRE " Shade.
5 in. Punkah Top, Clear Globe and Chimney,
Complete as drawn.
72/- each.

D 800
Silver Plated.
102/- each.

D 801
Polished Brass Cast Floor Lamp
fitted with
No. 3 S.W. Extg. Raiser Duplex Punkah Burner.
D 29 18 in. " THAMES " Shade.
D 74 Basket and 5 in. Punkah Top,
Clear Globe and Chimney.
Complete as drawn.
170/- each.

D 802
Spare 6½ × 4⅞ in. Clear cylinder Globes.
2/6 each.

D 803
Polished Cast Brass Lamp
fitted with
No. 3 S.W. Extg. Raiser Duplex Punkah Burner.
D 30 15 in. DOMINION Shade.
5 in. Punkah Top, Clear Globe and Chimney.
Complete as drawn.
82/- each.

D 804
Silver Plated.
106/- each.

Sherwoods Limited, 44, 46, 48, 50, GRANVILLE STREET, Birmingham.

SHERWOODS LAMPS.

Polished Brass Punkah Bracket Lamps.

Polished Brass or Steel Bronzed.

Scale ⅕ th.

All Lamps are priced

complete as drawn.

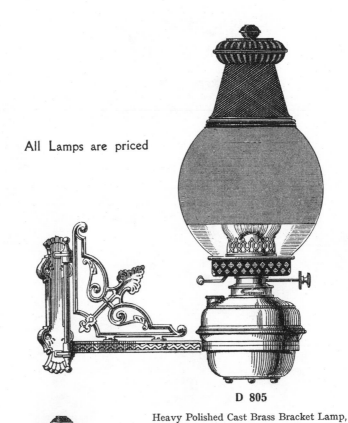

D 805

Heavy Polished Cast Brass Bracket Lamp,
fitted with
No. **2** S.W. Extg. Duplex Punkah Burner.
No. **2** Punkah Top.
No. **14** Frosted Globe and Chimney.
29/- each.

D 806

No. **3** S.W. Extg. Raiser Duplex Punkah Burner, etc.
31/- each.

D 807

Heavy Polished Cast Brass Bracket Lamp,
fitted with
No. **3** S.W. Extg. Raiser Duplex Punkah Burner.
No. **3** Punkah Top.
No. **15** Opal Globe and Chimney.
40/- each.

D 808

Heavy Polished Cast Brass Bracket Lamp,
fitted with
No. **3** S.W. Extg. Raiser Duplex Punkah Burner.
No. **3** Punkah Top.
No. **17** Opal Globe and Chimney.
42/- each.

SHERWOODS LAMPS.

Polished Brass Punkah Bracket Lamps.

Polished Brass or Steel Bronzed.

Scale $\frac{1}{5}$ th.

All Lamps are priced   complete as drawn.

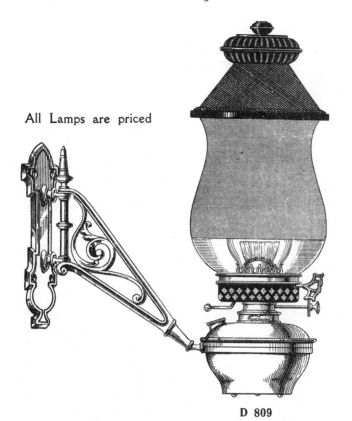

D 809

Heavy Polished Cast Brass Bracket Lamp,
fitted with
No. **3** S.W. Extg. Raiser Duplex Punkah Burner.
No. **4** Punkah Top.
No. **16** Frosted Globe and Chimney.
37/- each.

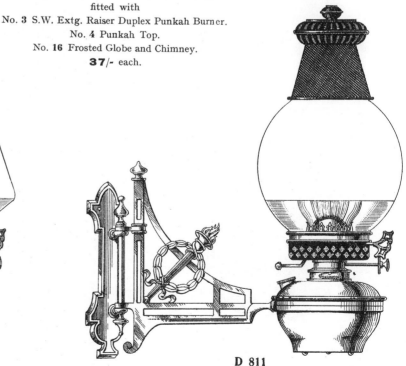

D 810

Heavy Polished Cast Brass Bracket Lamp,
fitted with
No. **3** S.W. Extg. Raiser Duplex Punkah Burner.
No. **3** Punkah Top.
No. **17** Opal Globe and Chimney.
42/- each.

D 811

Heavy Polished Cast Brass Bracket Lamp,
fitted with
No. **3** S.W. Extg. Raiser Duplex Punkah Burner.
No. **3** Punkah Top.
No. **15** Opal Globe and Chimney.
43/- each.

SHERWOODS LAMPS.

Copper Bronzed Punkah Wall Lamps,

fitted with

Duplex Punkah Burners.

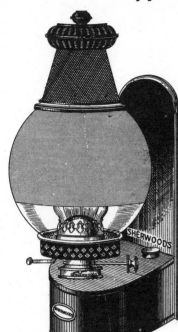

Scale ⅕ th.

All Lamps are priced complete as drawn.

D 312

Copper Bronzed Wall Lamp,
fitted with
No. 2 S.W. Extg. Duplex Punkah Burner.
No. 2 Punkah Top.
No. 14 Frosted Globe and Chimney.
16/- each.

D 813 No. 3 S.W. Extg. Raiser Duplex Punkah Burner, etc.
18/- each.

D 814

Strong hand-made Copper Bronzed Wall Lamp,
fitted with
No. 2 S.W. Extg. Duplex Punkah Burner.
No. 3 Punkah Top.
No. 15 Opal Globe and Chimney.
19/- each.

D 815 No. 3 S.W. Extg. Raiser Duplex Punkah Burner, etc.
21/- each.

Polished Brass Punkah Wall Lamps.

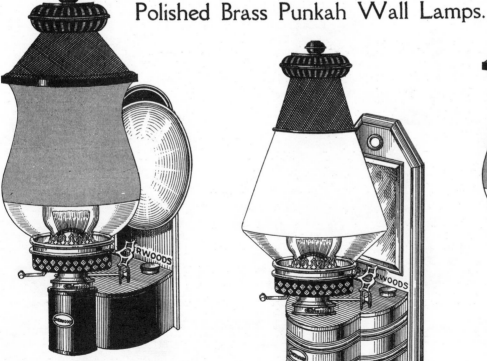

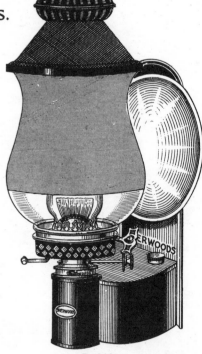

D 816

Strong hand-made Copper Bronzed Wall Lamp,
fitted with
No. 2 S.W. Extg. Duplex Punkah Burner.
7 in. Silvered Glass Reflector.
No. 4 Punkah Top.
No. 16 Frosted Globe and chimney.
19/6 each.

D 817

No. 3 S.W. Extg. Raiser Duplex Punkah Burner, etc.
21/6 each.

D 818

Polished Brass Wall Lamp,
fitted with
No. 3 S.W. Extg. Raiser Duplex Punkah Burner,
bevelled glass mirror reflector.
No. 3 Punkah Top.
No. 17 Opal Globe and Chimney.
28/6 each.

D 819

Extra large
Strong hand-made Copper Bronzed Wall Lamp,
fitted with
No. 2 S.W. Extg. Duplex Punkah Burner,
8 in. silvered glass reflector.
No. 4 Punkah Top.
No. 16 Frosted Globe and Chimney.
22/- each.

D 820

No. 3 S.W. Extg. Raiser Duplex Punkah Burner, etc.
24/- each.

Sherwoods Limited, 44, 46, 48, 50, GRANVILLE STREET, Birmingham.

SHERWOODS LAMPS.

Polished Brass Tube Harps,

fitted with

Duplex Punkah Burners.

Scale ⅙ th

All Lamps are priced complete as drawn.

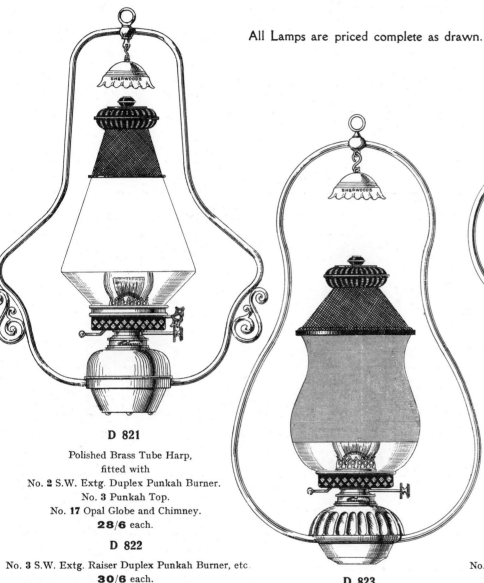

D 821

Polished Brass Tube Harp,
fitted with
No. **2** S.W. Extg. Duplex Punkah Burner.
No. **3** Punkah Top.
No. **17** Opal Globe and Chimney.
28/6 each.

D 822

No. **3** S.W. Extg. Raiser Duplex Punkah Burner, etc.
30/6 each.

D 823

Polished Brass Tube Harp,
fitted with
No. **2** S.W. Extg. Duplex Punkah Burner.
No. **4** Punkah Top.
No. **16** Frosted Globe and Chimney.
24/6 each.

D 824

No. **3** S.W. Extg. Raiser Duplex Punkah Burner, etc.
26/6 each.

D 825

Brass Harp only.
5/6 each.
Special price 3 dozen lots **5/3** each.
,,   ,,   6 ,,   ,,   **5/-**   ,,
,,   ,,   12 ,,   ,,   **4/9**   ,,

D 826

Polished Brass Tube Harp,
fitted with
No. **2** S.W. Extg. Duplex Punkah Burner.
No. **2** Punkah Top.
No. **14** Frosted Globe and Chimney.
30/- each.

D 827

No. **3** S.W. Extg. Raiser Duplex Punkah Burner, etc.
32/- each.

These lamps are supplied polished brass or steel bronzed finish as required.

Sherwoods Limited, 44, 46, 48, 50, GRANVILLE STREET, Birmingham.

SHERWOODS LAMPS.

Polished Brass Hanging Lamps,

fitted with

Duplex Punkah Burners.

Scale $\frac{1}{6}$ *th*

All Lamps are priced complete as drawn.

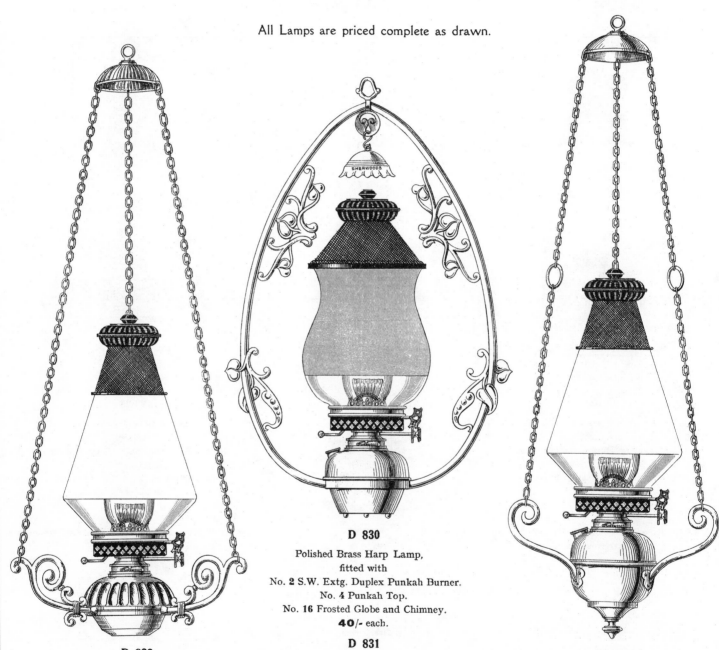

D 830

Polished Brass Harp Lamp,
fitted with
No. **2** S.W. Extg. Duplex Punkah Burner.
No. **4** Punkah Top.
No. **16** Frosted Globe and Chimney.
40/- each.

D 831

No. **3** S.W. Extg. Raiser Duplex Punkah Burner, etc.
42/- each.

These lamps are supplied
Polished Brass or Steel Bronzed
finish as required.

D 828

Polished Brass Chain Hanger,
fitted with
No. **2** S.W. Extg. Duplex Punkah Burner.
No. **3** Punkah Top.
No. **17** Opal Globe and Chimney.
36/- each.

D 829

No. **3** S.W. Extg. Raiser Duplex Punkah Burner, etc.
38/- each.

D 832

Polished Brass Chain Hanger,
fitted with
No. **2** S.W. Extg. Duplex Punkah Burner.
No. **3** Punkah Top.
No. **17** Opal Globe and Chimney.
38/- each.

D 833

No. **3** S.W. Extg. Raiser Duplex Punkah Burner.
40/- each.

Sherwoods Limited, 44, 46, 48, 50, GRANVILLE STREET, **Birmingham**

Polished Brass Hanging Lamps,

fitted with

Duplex Punkah Burners.

Scale ⅙ th

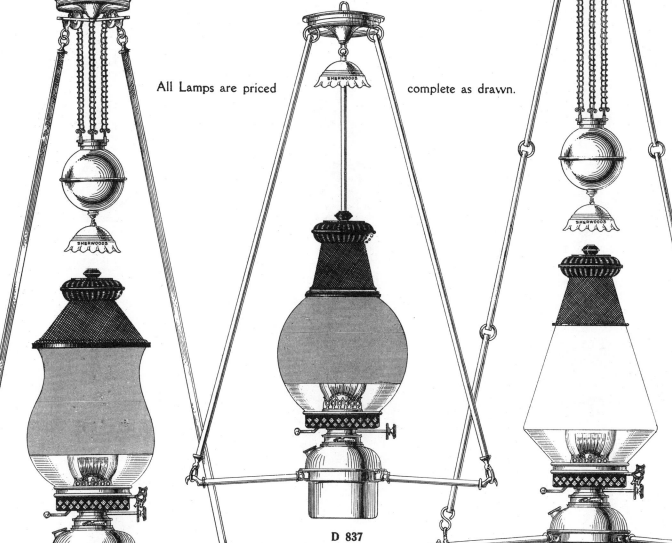

All Lamps are priced   complete as drawn.

D 834

Pollshed Brass Square Tube Slide Hanging Lamp,
fitted with
No. **2** S.W. Extg. Duplex Punkah Burner.
No. **4** Punkah Top.
No. **16** Frosted Globe and chimney.
48/- each.

D 835

No. **3** S.W. Extg. Raiser Duplex Punkah Burner, etc.
50/- each.

D 836

Slide Hanging Lamp only.
27/- each.

D 837

Polished Brass Tube Hanging Lamp,
fitted with
No. **2** S.W. Extg. Duplex Punkah Burner.
No. **2** Punkah Top.
No. **14** Frosted Globe and chimney.
30/- each.

D 838

No. **3** S.W. Extg. Raiser Duplex Punkah Burner, etc.
32/- each.

D 839

Hanging Lamp only,
13/- each.

These lamps are supplied
Polished Brass or Steel Bronzed
finish as required.

D 840

Polished Brass Tube Slide Hanging Lamp,
fitted with
No. **2** S.W. Extg. Duplex Punkah Burner.
No. **3** Punkah Top.
No. **17** Opal Globe and chimney.
43/- each.

D 841

No. **3** S.W. Extg. Raiser Duplex Punkah Burner, etc.
45/- each.

D 842

Slide Hanging Lamp only.
23/- each.

Sherwoods Limited, 44, 46, 48, 50, GRANVILLE STREET, Birmingham.

SHERWOODS LAMPS.

SHERWOODS
Chimney Punkah Tops.

Steel Bronzed Finish.

Scale $\frac{1}{5}$ *th.*

D 843

12''' Sun Chimney, Punkah Top,
Steel Bronzed.
2/- each.
1½ in. fitting.

D 845

Duplex Chimney, Punkah Top,
Steel Bronzed.
2/- each.
1⅝ in. fitting.

D 844

16''' Sun Chimney, Punkah Top,
Steel Bronzed.
2/- each.
1¼ in. fitting.

D 846

Belge Chimney, Punkah Top,
Steel Bronzed.
2/- each.
1⅞ in. fitting.

Prices quoted for Punkah Tops only.

See page 6
for prices of chimneys.

D 847

20''' Sun Chimney, Punkah Top,
Steel Bronzed.
2/- each.
1⅞ in. fitting.

When fitting Chimney Punkah Tops, it is most important they fit easily.
Chimneys when heated expand, and if the tops fit tightly, they are liable to crack.
The tops can be eased by opening the bottom pierced perforations.

Sherwoods Limited, 44, 46, 48, 50, GRANVILLE STREET, **Birmingham**

SHERWOODS
Patent Windproof 20‴ Sun 60 c.p. c.d. Burner.

(Pat. No. 14367)

The only perfect central draught Windproof Burner made.

Scale ⅓ rd.

D 848

Air Diffuser.
10/- dozen.

D 850

Central Tube Air Baffle.
1/- each.

D 851

Chimney, Punkah Top,
2/- each.

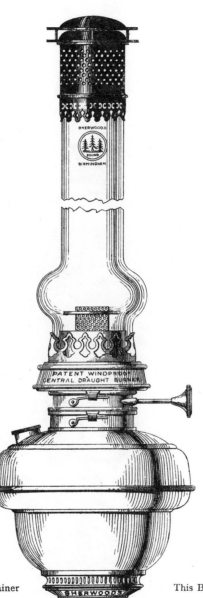

200

SHERWOODS
Patent Windproof Central Draught Burner,
Chimney and Chimney Punkah,
complete as drawn.
18/- each.
fitting 5¼ inch.

D 849

Patent Windproof Burner CONE,
Bayonet Catch fitting.
5/- each.

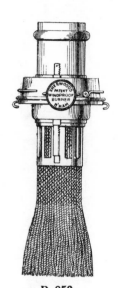

D 852

Patent Windproof Burner Body,
Bayonet Catch fitting.
4/- each.

This Burner locks together and is fitted to Oil Container
by means of Bayonet Catches
constructed to overcome the usual method of screwing together.

This Burner locks together and is fitted to Oil Container
by means of Bayonet Catches
constructed to overcome the usual method of screwing together.

This Lamp is recommended for lighting where a sudden draught is liable to occur,
and is particularly suitable for lighting STORES, SCHOOLS, CHURCHES, and places subject to draughts.

SHERWOODS LAMPS.

Polished Brass Table Lamps
fitted with
Heavy Single Winder Extinguisher Duplex Burners
and
Chimney Punkah Tops.

Scale $\frac{1}{5}$ *th.*

All Lamps are priced complete as drawn.

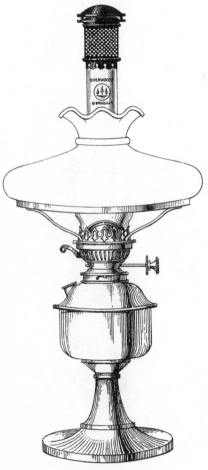

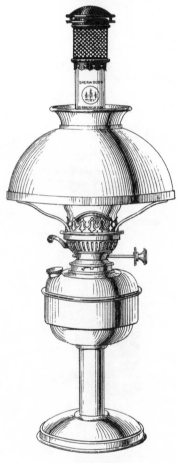

D 853

Polished Brass Table Lamp,
fitted with
No. **22B** S.W. Extinguisher Duplex Burner,
9¼ in. Opal Shade, Chimney,
and
Chimney Punkah Top.
16/- each.

D 854

With 9¼ in. Green Cased Opal Shade etc.
18/- each.

D 855

Polished Brass Table Lamp,
Cut Crystal Fount.
No. **122B** S.W. Extinguisher Duplex Burner.
7½ in. × 4 in. Mono. Frosted Globe,
and
Chimney Punkah Top.
15/- each.

D 856

Polished Brass Table **Lamp,**
fitted with
No. **22** S.W. Extinguisher Duplex Burner.
10 in. White Metal Shade, Chimney,
and
Chimney Punkah Top.
20/- each.

D 857

With 9¼ in. Green Cased Opal Shade etc.
16/6 each.

These Lamps are recommended for Railway Waiting Rooms, Dining Rooms and Office Lighting.

Polished Brass Table Lamps

fitted with

Sherwoods 12′′′ 30 c.p. and 16′′′ 45 c.p. c.d. Sun Burners

and

Chimney Punkah Tops.

Scale $\frac{1}{5}$ *th.*

All Lamps are priced complete as drawn.

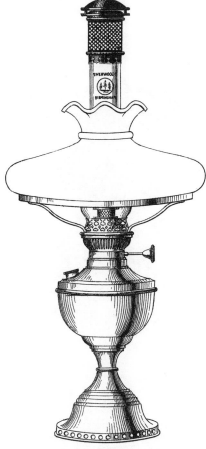

D 858

Polished Brass Table Lamp,
fitted with
Sherwoods 16′′′ Sun 45 c.p. C.D. Burner,
9¼ in. Opal Shade, Chimney,
and
Chimney Punkah Top.
13/- each.

D 859

With 9¼ in. Green Cased Opal Shade etc.
15/- each.

D 860

Polished Brass Table Lamp,
fitted with
Sherwoods 12′′′ Sun 30 c.p. C.D. Burner,
7¼ in. Green Cased Opal Shade, Chimney,
and
Chimney Punkah Top.
11/- each.

D 861

Polished Brass Table Lamp,
fitted with
Sherwoods 16′′′ Sun 45 c.p. C.D. Burner,
10 in. White Metal Shade, Chimney,
and
Chimney Punkah Top.
22/6 each.

D 862

With 9¼ in. Green Cased Opal Shade etc.
19/- each.

These Lamps are recommended for Railway Waiting Rooms, Dining Rooms, and Office Lighting.

Sherwoods Limited, 44, 46, 48, 50, GRANVILLE STREET, Birmingham,

SHERWOODS LAMPS.

Polished Brass Table Lamps

fitted with

Sherwoods patent WINDPROOF 60 c.p. C.D. Burner.

(Pat. No. 14367.)

and

Chimney Punkah Tops.

Scale $\frac{1}{5}$ th.

All lamps are priced   complete as drawn.

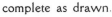

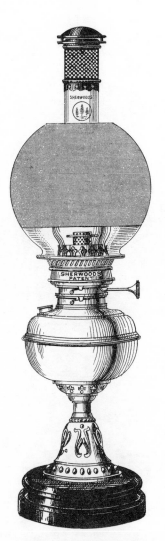

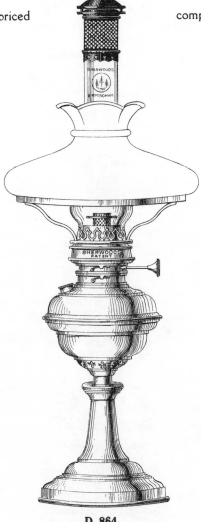

D 863

Polished Brass Table Lamp.
"A" 7 in. Black Base.
Sherwoods Patent Windproof 60 c.p. C.D. Burner.
7½ × 4 in. Frosted Globe, Chimney
and
Chimney Punkah Top.
24/- each.

D 864

Polished Brass Table Lamp,
fitted with
Sherwoods Patent Windproof 60 c.p. C.D. Burner.
9¼ in. Opal Shade Chimney
and
Chimney Punkah Top.
27/- each.

D 865

With 9¼ in. Green Cased Opal Shades, etc.
29/- each.

D 866

With 10 in. White Metal Shade, etc.
33/- each.

D 867

Polished Brass Table Lamp.
" E " 8¼ in. Black Base.
Sherwoods Patent Windproof 60 c.p. C.D. Burner.
Assorted Etched Globe, Chimney
and
Chimney Punkah Top.
28/- each.

SHERWOODS LAMPS.

Polished Brass Table Lamps

fitted with

Sherwoods patent WINDPROOF 60 c.p. C.D. Burner.

(Pat. No. 14367.)

and

Chimney Punkah Tops.

Scale $\frac{1}{5}$ th.

All lamps are priced complete as drawn.

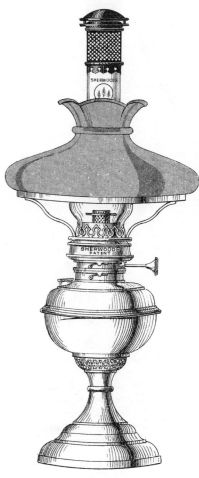

D 868
Polished Brass Table Lamp,
fitted with
Sherwoods Patent Windproof 60 c.p. C.D. Burner.
9¼ in. Opal Shade, Chimney
and
Chimney Punkah Top.
23/6 each.

D 869
Polished Brass Table Lamp,
" D " 7½ in. Black Base.
Sherwoods Patent Windproof 60 c.p. C.D. Burner.
9¼ in. Opal Shade, Chimney
and
Chimney Punkah Top.
27/- each.

D 870
With 9¼ in. Green Cased Opal Shade, etc.
29/- each.

D 871
With 10 in. White Metal Shade, etc.
33/- each.

D 872
Polished Brass Table Lamp,
fitted with
Sherwoods Patent Windproof 60 c.p. C.D. Burner.
9¼ in. Green Cased Opal Shade, Chimney
and
Chimney Punkah Top.
25/6 each.

SHERWOODS LAMPS.

Polished Brass Tube Harps

fitted with

Sherwoods patent WINDPROOF 60 c.p. C.D. Burner.

(Pat. No. 14367.)

Scale $\frac{1}{6}$ th.

All lamps are priced complete as drawn.

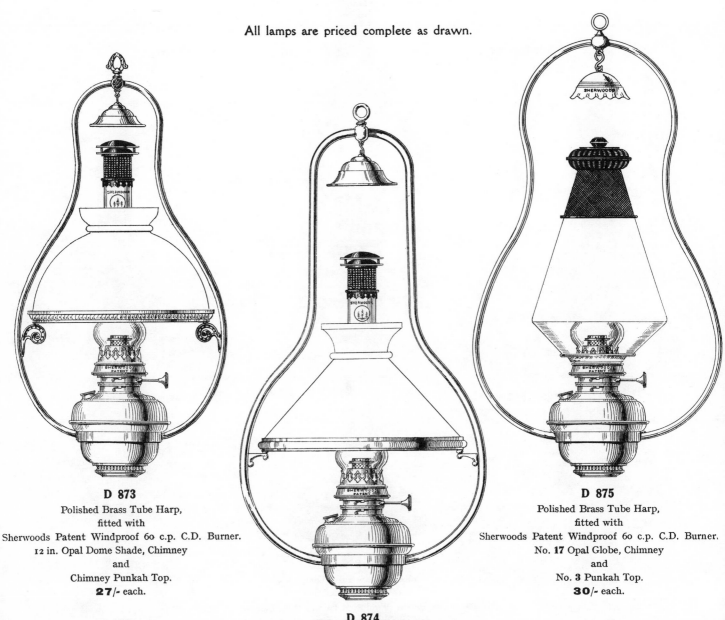

D 873
Polished Brass Tube Harp,
fitted with
Sherwoods Patent Windproof 60 c.p. C.D. Burner.
12 in. Opal Dome Shade, Chimney
and
Chimney Punkah Top.
27/- each.

D 874
Polished Brass Tube Harp,
fitted with
Sherwoods Patent Windproof 60 c.p. C.D. Burner.
14 in. Opal Straight Shade, Chimney
and
Chimney Punkah Top.
34/- each.

D 875
Polished Brass Tube Harp,
fitted with
Sherwoods Patent Windproof 60 c.p. C.D. Burner.
No. **17** Opal Globe, Chimney
and
No. **3** Punkah Top.
30/- each.

Sherwoods Limited, 44, 46, 48, 50, GRANVILLE STREET, **Birmingham.**

SHERWOODS LAMPS.

Polished Brass Tube Harps

fitted with

Sherwoods patent WINDPROOF 60 c.p. C.D. Burner.

(Pat. No. 14367.)

Scale $\frac{1}{6}$ *th.*

All lamps are priced complete as drawn.

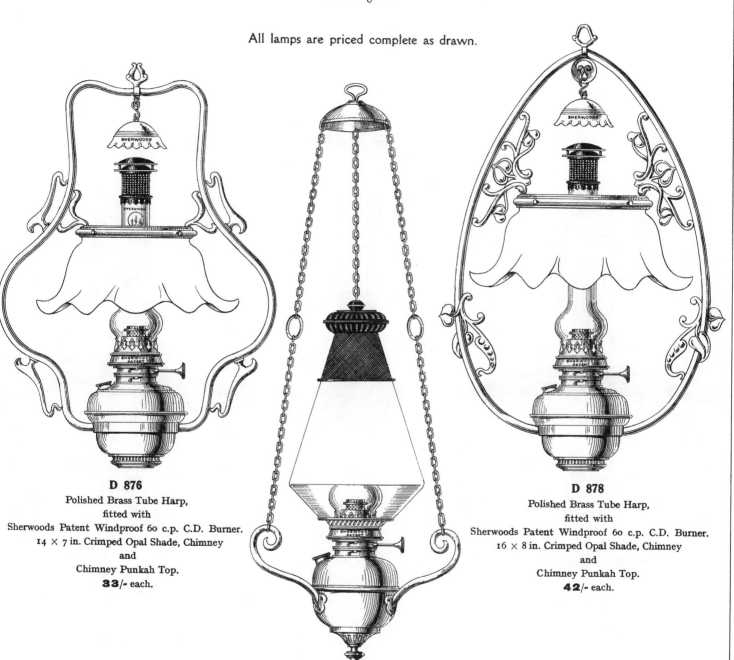

D 876
Polished Brass Tube Harp,
fitted with
Sherwoods Patent Windproof 60 c.p. C.D. Burner.
14 × 7 in. Crimped Opal Shade, Chimney
and
Chimney Punkah Top.
33/- each.

D 877
Polished Brass Chain Hanger,
fitted with
Sherwoods Patent Windproof 60 c.p. C.D. Burner.
No. **17** Opal Globe, Chimney
and
No. **3** Punkah Top.
40/- each.

D 878
Polished Brass Tube Harp,
fitted with
Sherwoods Patent Windproof 60 c.p. C.D. Burner.
16 × 8 in. Crimped Opal Shade, Chimney
and
Chimney Punkah Top.
42/- each.

Sherwoods Limited, 44, 46, 48, 50, GRANVILLE STREET, **Birmingham.**

SHERWOODS LAMPS.

Polished Brass and Wire Harps

fitted with

Sherwoods patent WINDPROOF 60 c.p. C.D. Burner.

(Pat. No. 14367.)

Scale $\frac{1}{6}$ th.

All lamps are priced   complete as drawn.

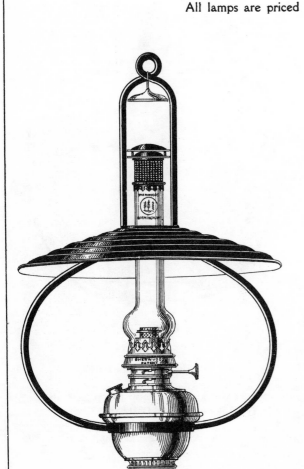

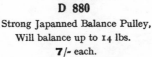

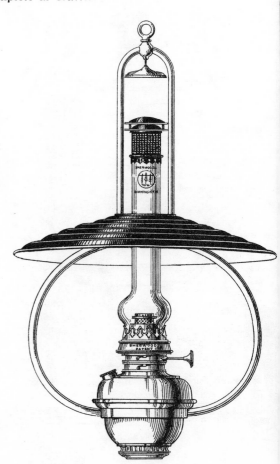

D 879

Strong Black Japanned Wire Harp,
fitted with
Sherwoods Patent Windproof 60 c.p. C.D. Burner.
18 in. Japanned Reflector, Chimney
and
Chimney Punkah Top.
21/- each.

D 880

Strong Japanned Balance Pulley,
Will balance up to 14 lbs.
7/- each.

This Pulley is supplied empty with hole at top
for shot loading. Can be adjusted to required weight.

D 881

Polished Brass Tube Harp,
fitted with
Sherwoods Patent Windproof 60 c.p. C.D. Burner.
18 in. Patent Enamelled Reflector Chimney
and
Chimney Punkah Top.
32/- each.

Sherwoods Limited, 44, 46, 48, 50, GRANVILLE STREET, **Birmingham.**

SHERWOODS LAMPS.

Polished Brass Bracket Lamps

fitted with

Sherwoods patent WINDPROOF 60 c.p. C.D. Burner.

(Pat. No. 14367.)

Scale $\frac{1}{5}$ th.

All lamps are priced

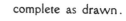

complete as drawn.

D 883

Strong Bronzed Wall Lamp,
fitted with
Sherwoods Patent Windproof
60 c.p. C.D. Burner.
7 in. Silvered Glass Reflector.
$7\frac{1}{2} \times 4$ in. Mono-Frosted Globe Chimney
and
Chimney Punkah Top.
20/- each.

D 882

Polished Cast Brass Bracket Lamp,
fitted with
Sherwoods Patent Windproof 60 c.p. C.D. Burner,
Assorted Etched Globe Chimney
and
Chimney Punkah Top.
33/- each.

D 884

Polished Cast Brass Bracket Lamp,
fitted with
Sherwoods Patent Windproof 60 c.p. C.D. Burner.
Assorted English Make Globe Chimney
and
Chimney Punkah Top.
42/- each.

Index

Price Guide

Page	Item No.	U.S. Dollars	Page	Item No.	U.S. Dollars	Page	Item No.	U.S. Dollars
6		10-25	65		175-275	80	#D476	225
7		25-45	66		175	80	#D477	225
8		35-75	67		175-250	80	#D478	230
9		not	68		175	80	#D479	250
		available	69		175-350	80	#D480	250
16		15-35	70	#D420	175	81	#D481	250
17		15-35	70	#D421	200	81	#D482	250
18		15-35	70	#D422	175	81	#D483	275
19		15-35	70	#D423	225	81	#D484	300
20		25-45	70	#D424	225	81	#D485	275
21		25-45	70	#D425	225	82		100-150
22		20-35	71	#D426	250	83	#D493	350
23		20-35	71	#D427	225	83	#D494	300
24		20-35	71	#D428	250	83	#D496	375
25		35-60	71	#D429	250	84		250-375
26		35-60	71	#D430	225	85		250-375
27		35-60	71	#D431	250	86	#D507	300
28		30-55	72	#D432	175	86	#D508	400
29		30-55	72	#D433	200	86	#D509	300
30		30-60	72	#D434	200	87	#D510	300
32		35-55	72	#D435	250	87	#D511	400
33		35-55	72	#D436	250	86	#D512	325
34		20-35	72	#D437	275	88	#D513	325
35		20-35	73	#D438	250	88	#D514	350
36		15-75	73	#D439	300	88	#D515	325
36	#D202	75	73	#D440	250	89	#D516	375
37		15-75	73	#D441	250	89	#D517	350
38		25-60	73	#D442	275	89	#D518	375
38	#D223	60	73	#D443	275	90	#D519	125
38	#D224	60	74		175	90	#D520	150
39		25-60	75	#D446	200	90	#D521	125
40		10-85	75	#D447	175	91	#D522	145
41		10-85	75	#D448	200	91	#D523	165
42		65-125	75	#D449	200	91	#D524	150
43		65-125	75	#D450	175	92		200
44		75-125	75	#D451	225	93		255
45		75-125	76	#D452	150	94	#D529	200
46		30-95	76	#D453	150	94	#D530	200
47		30-95	76	#D454	175	94	#D531	175
48		60-140	76	#D455	175	94	#D532	175
49		60-140	76	#D456	175	94	#D533	175
50		15-35	77	#D457	185	95	#D534	175
51		15-80	77	#D459	185	95	#D535	185
52		30 85	77	#D461	185	95	#D536	225
53		65-150	77	#D462	175	95	#D537	175
54		150-250	77	#D463	175	95	#D538	225
55		150-250	78	#D464	200	96		190
56		45-130	78	#D465	200	97		200
57		45-130	78	#D466	200	98	#D542	150
58		50-150	78	#D467	225	98	#D543	150
59		50-150	78	#D468	210	98	#D544	175
60		150-275	79	#D469	175	98	#D545	200
61		150-275	79	#D471	175	98	#D546	175
62		175	79	#D473	225	99	#D547	200
63		175-275	79	#D474	200	99	#D548	200
64		175	79	#D475	225	99	#D549	195

Page	Item No.	U.S. Dollars	Page	Item No.	U.S. Dollars	Page	Item No.	U.S. Dollars
149	#109	40	169	#D729	200	184	#D818	180
149	#25	150	169	#D730	175	184	#D819	150
149	#111	175	170	#D731	100	185	#D821	150
149	#2476	200	170	#D733	150	185	#D823	175
149	#2477	200	170	#D732	135	185	#D826	150
150		125-200	170	#D735	175	186	#D828	150
151		125-200	170	#D734	150	186	#D830	175
152		5-35	170	#D736	150	186	#D832	150
153	#2560F	150	171	#D737	250	187	#D834	200
154	#2560/A	125	171	#D738	225	187	#D837	250
154	#2560	125	171	#D739	240	187	#D840	225
154	#2560/E	125	172		10-45	188		25-35
155	#2590A	125	173	#D740	45	189	#200	75
155	#2590	125	173	#D741	75	190	#D853	200
155	#2590B	125	173	#D742	55	190	#D855	225
156		125-150	173	#No.2	20	190	#D856	210
157		125-150	173	#No.3	30	191	#D858	200
158		100	174		200	191	#D860	200
159	2590A/ 2604	125	175	#D745	225	191	#D861	200
159	2590/ 1774	150	175	#D747	250	192	#D863	200
			175	#D749	225	192	#D864	250
159	2590B /1883	125	175	#D751	150	192	#D867	275
160	#2472	175	175	#D753	275	193	#D868	200
160	#2475	200	176	#D755	150	193	#D869	225
161	#2572	100	176	#D757	175	193	#D872	250
161	#2572A	175	176	#D759	175	194	#D873	150
161	#2474	150	176	#D761	225	194	#D874	175
162		140	176	#D763	175	194	#D875	150
163	#D709	125	177	#D765	250	195	#D876	200
163	#D710	140	177	#D767	250	195	#D877	150
163	#D711	125	177	#D769	250	195	#D878	225
163	#D712	175	177	#D771	275	196	#D879	100
163	#D713	125	177	#D773	250	196	#D880	60
163	#D714	175	178	#D775	225	196	#D881	100
164		150	178	#D777	225	197	#D882	225
165	#D716	100	178	#D779	250	197	#D883	150
165	#D717	150	178	#D781	275	197	#D884	250
165	#D718	125	178	#D783	290			
165	#D719	175	179	#D785	225			
165	#D720	150	179	#D787	250			
165	#D721	200	179	#D789	300			
166	#144B	15	179	#D791	300			
166	#144B	3	179	#D793	225			
166	#144B	15	180	#D795	275			
166	#D722	150	180	#D796	325			
166	#D723	175	180	#D798	300			
166	#D724	125	181	#D799	275			
167	#No.1	15	181	#D801	250			
167	#No.1	20	181	#D803	325			
167		5	182	#D805	250			
167	#No.11	15	182	#D807	225			
167	#No.12	20	182	#D808	250			
168		150	183	#D809	225			
169	#D726	175	183	#D810	250			
169	#D727	225	183	#D811	275			
169	#D728	150	184	#D312	150			
			184	#D814	150			
			184	#D816	175			

The values of the lighting devices in this price guide will vary tremendously depending on the location and condition of the pieces. The prices here are based on examples in excellent condition. As condition deteriorates the value may decrease by as much as 75%. Dealers' margins of approximately 50% must be considered when trying to seel them an item.